BLACK AMERICA SERIES

THE VILLE
ST. LOUIS

MAP OF THE VILLE

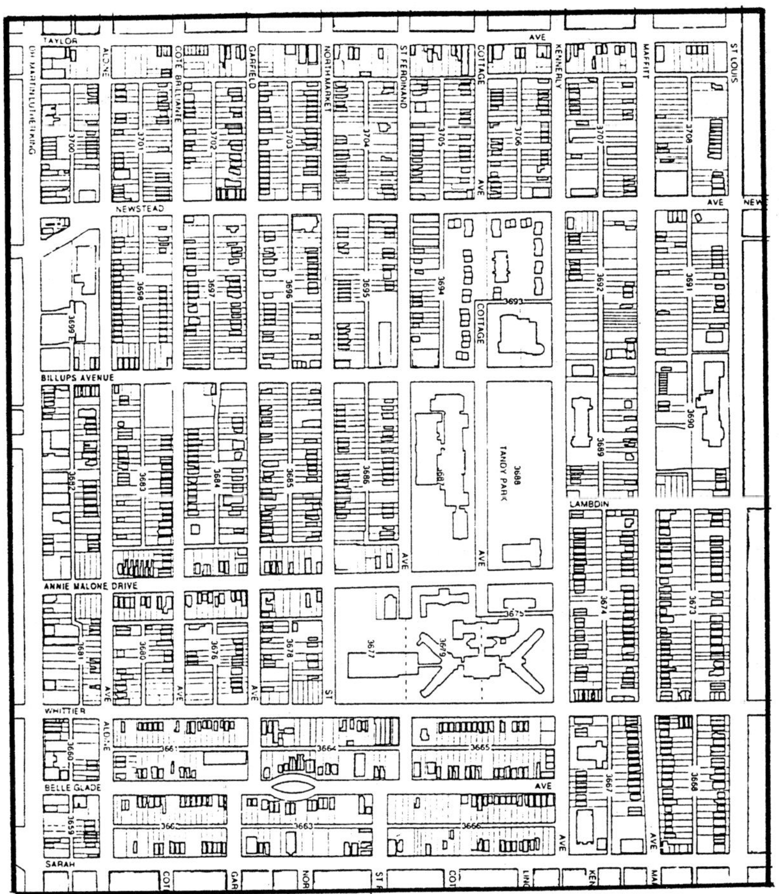

Map courtesy of the St. Louis Landmark Association

BLACK AMERICA SERIES

THE VILLE
ST. LOUIS

John A. Wright Sr.

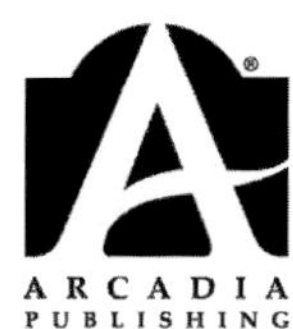

ISBN 978-0-7385-0815-3

Published by Arcadia Publishing
Charleston, South Carolina

Printed in the United States of America

Library of Congress Catalog Card Number: 2001091281

For all general information contact Arcadia Publishing at:
Telephone 843-853-2070
Fax 843-853-0044
E-Mail sales@arcadiapublishing.com
For customer service and orders:
Toll-Free 1-888-313-2665

Visit us on the Internet at www.arcadiapublishing.com

This book is dedicated to my mother and all those who made it possible for individuals like myself to be able to experience a special place in time called "The Ville."

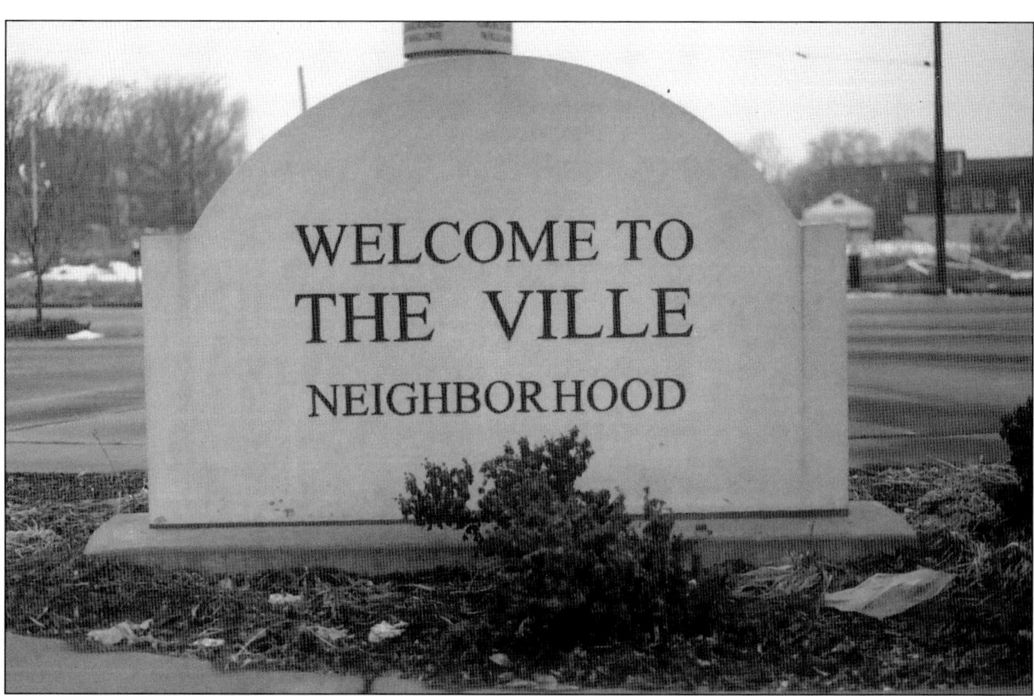

Contents

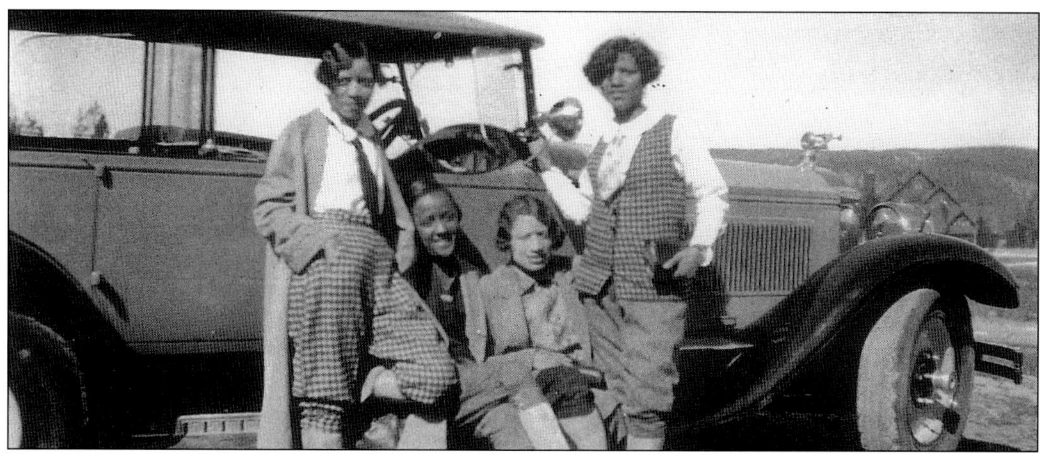

(Photo courtesy of Berenice Colbert.)

ACKNOWLEDGMENTS

I would like to give a special thanks to Patricia Whitener for assistance in editing this book, and to my wife Sylvia who gave of her time also to provide editing assistance and photo reviews. Special words of appreciation go to Vivian Dreer, Odessa Farrell, and John and Odester Saunders for their assistance and their efforts in keeping our history alive.

Thanks also goes to the individuals and institutions for their help and support in making this book possible. The individuals are: Carolyn Toft, Janet Bosley, Ida Woolfolk, James Vincent, Christopher Heffern, Charles Elleard Whitney, Thomas Webster, Hazel Lee, Sandra Lois Wallace, Rosetta Chinn, Claude Wilson, Robert Tabscott, Geraldine Johnson, Sister Patricia Hottinger, Monsignor Patrick Malloy, Mary Seematter, Sister Charline Sullivan, Carolyn Smith, Ken Sowell, Savannah Young, Eugene Slaughter, Demosthenes DuBose, Frank Richards, Bernie Hayes, Leslie F. Bond, Frederick Hill, Edward Tripp, Johnetta Haley, Garola S. Ward, Joyce and Andrew Pruitt, Dianne White, Richard Anderson, Doris Wesley, Yvette Ford, Rev. David A. Foote, Jackie Dace, Betty Jean Johnson, Sharon Huffman, Alice Herndon, Jacquelyn Creighton, Ella Brown, Mary Heady, Etoil Pearson, Claramarie Cannon, Berenice Colbert, John Brooks, Odessa Owens, Dorothy and Edmond Squires, Rudy Dyer, Beatrice Harris, Margaret Bush Wilson, Olivia Blackmore, Phillip Brown, Helen Baily, Evelyn Rice-Peebles, Elaine Snyder, Charles Brown, Jean Neal, John Bernard, Dorothy Brown, Jamie Graham, Mable George, Arzella Abernathy, Lois Moore, and Sister Teresa Eagan, CSJ. The institutions are: St. Louis Public Library (Main and Julia Davis Branch), Mercantile Library, Midwest Jesuit Archives, Kingdom of Callaway County Historical Society, Lincoln University, St. James AME Church, St. Phillips Lutheran Church, Newstead Avenue Baptist Church, St. Matthews Church, Pleasant Grove Baptist Church, Missouri Historical Society, Annie Malone Children's Home, State of Missouri Archives, St. Louis Public Schools Archives, The City of St. Louis Park and Recreation Department, Archdiocese of St. Louis Archives, Sisters of St. Joseph of Carondelet, NBC Lounge, the St. Louis Landmark Association, and the University of Missouri-St. Louis, Western Manuscript Collection. If anyone's name was omitted, please accept my apology. You know who you are and what your contribution has added to this publication.

Introduction

For decades, The Ville was St. Louis' premier African-American community and the center of black culture. This area of less than one square mile is bounded by Dr. Martin Luther King Drive on the south and St. Louis Avenue on the north, by Sarah Avenue on the east and Taylor Avenue on the west. To many of St. Louis' African Americans, The Ville still holds a symbolic meaning and represents a special place in time.

The Ville's development began after 1860, when Charles M. Elleard purchased the tract of land from George W. Goode, an attorney from Virginia. Elleard was an entrepreneur with many interests which included horse racing, farming, and horticulture. After a period of time, a small town known as Elleardsville (later shortened to "The Ville") developed around a nursery maintained by Elleard. It was annexed to the City of St. Louis in 1876. In the beginning, the area attracted mostly German and Irish immigrants, along with a few African Americans. The neighborhood's first black institution, Elleardsville Colored School No. 8 (later renamed Simmons School), opened in 1873. Further African-American presence was established when Antioch Baptist Church organized in 1884 in The Ville, and St. James African Methodist Episcopal Church organized the following year.

Sumner High School, the first secondary school for African Americans west of the Mississippi River, was moved to The Ville in 1910 after a group of concerned citizens petitioned the Board of Education for the relocation of the school from the central business district. The Board of Education acknowledged the citizens' request in spite of strong protest from white residents. The movement of Sumner and its Normal School for teachers, and the opening of John Marshall Elementary School in 1918 and Charles Henry Turner School for the disabled in 1925, recognized The Ville as the center of the black community. These institutions gave The Ville the distinction of being one of the few St. Louis communities in which black children could attend school from kindergarten through professional training.

While these institutions served as a magnet to draw African Americans, other community factors also played a role in the development of the community. During The Ville's developmental years most of the city's institutions and facilities were segregated, and much of its residential property had deed restrictions that prohibited African Americans from renting or owning. Although many of the streets that surrounded The Ville had restrictive covenants, blacks were allowed to purchase homes in The Ville. Between 1920 and 1950, the number of black residents in The Ville increased from 8 to 95 percent of the total population. These residents shopped in the black owned businesses located in the neighborhood, and over time The Ville became a self-contained community.

Despite segregation in the city, Ville residents were able to find employment in the community's institutions. In 1917, Annie Turnbo Pope Malone established Poro College, a manufacturing plant and training school for agents selling her line of beauty products. The College provided nearly 200 jobs for residents and served as a social center for the neighborhood. Homer G. Phillips Hospital, the largest institution in The Ville, from its opening in 1937 until its closing in 1979, employed more than 800 at its peak time. The hospital served as a major training facility for black health care professionals from all over the world.

After the United States Supreme Court ruled in 1948 in *Shelley v. Kramer* that restrictive covenants could not be enforced by the courts, housing opportunities opened up for blacks outside The Ville. Additional options also became available after the 1954 Supreme Court decision in *Brown v. the Board of Education of Topeka, Kansas*, that segregation in schools was unlawful. After these decisions, the population of The Ville community dropped nearly 38 percent between 1950 and 1970.

Today the residents are committed to recapturing the spirit of the community's famous past. Many institutions have chosen to remain, home construction is beginning to take place, businesses are starting to open, and plans are in place for the recycling of Homer G. Phillips Hospital.

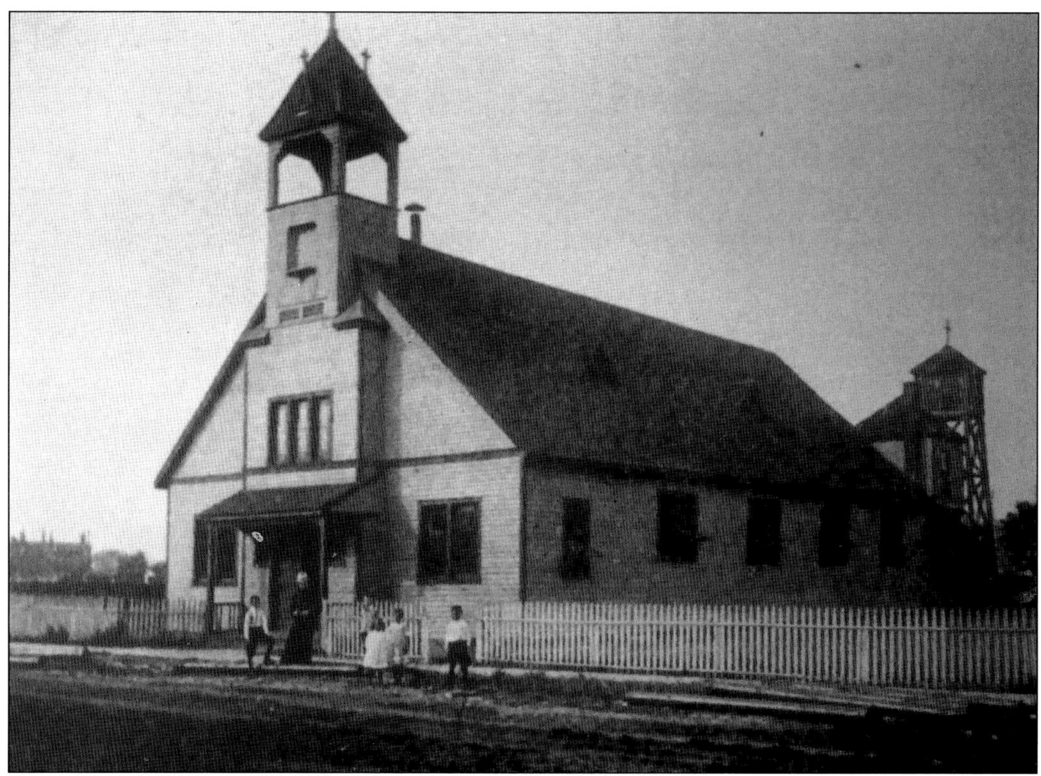

St. Matthew's Catholic Church is seen here in the late 1890s. (Photo courtesy of the St. Louis Archdiocese Archives.)

One

The Ville
A Place in Time

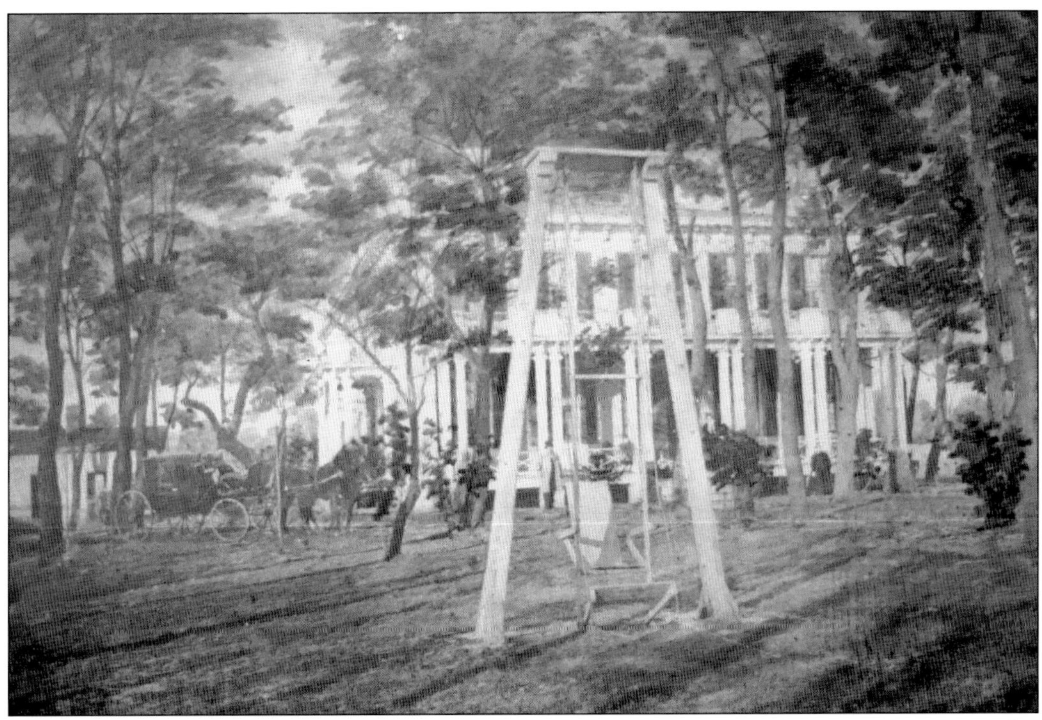

Charles Elleard built this home on Goode Avenue (now Annie Malone Drive) at the northwest corner of St. Charles Rock Road (now Dr. Martin Luther King Drive). The 1860 Census Agricultural Schedule listed Elleard as the owner of 200 acres of improved land with a cash value of $300. Elleard grew corn, oats, peas, beans, potatoes, and orchard produce. It is from this location that the community we now know as "The Ville" developed. (Photo courtesy of Christopher Heffern.)

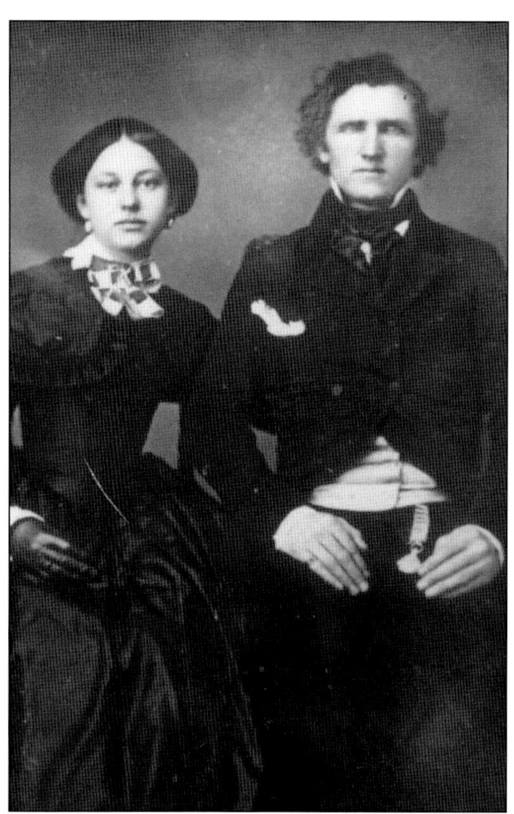

Charles Elleard, pictured here with his wife Lucinda, was born in New York around 1820, and came to St. Louis in the 1860s. The couple had one daughter, Virginia. Both his wife and daughter were born in Missouri—Lucinda in 1839, and Virginia in 1858. Prior to coming to St. Louis, Elleard panned for gold and served as a constable under the Whig party in San Francisco, California. (Photo courtesy of Christopher Heffern.)

The estate of Charles Elleard stretched from Goode Avenue (now Annie Malone Drive) to Newstead Avenue and from Old St. Charles Rock Road (later Dr. Martin Luther King Drive) to Cote Brilliante Avenue. A small town grew up around the nursery, pictured here, and in 1876 it was annexed to the city. Over time, Elleardsville (shortened to "the Ville") attracted German and Irish immigrants, along with some African-American citizens. This winter scene of the Elleards Floral Company provides a glimpse of the nucleus of Elleardsville as it existed in the 1880s. (Photo courtesy of Christopher Heffern.)

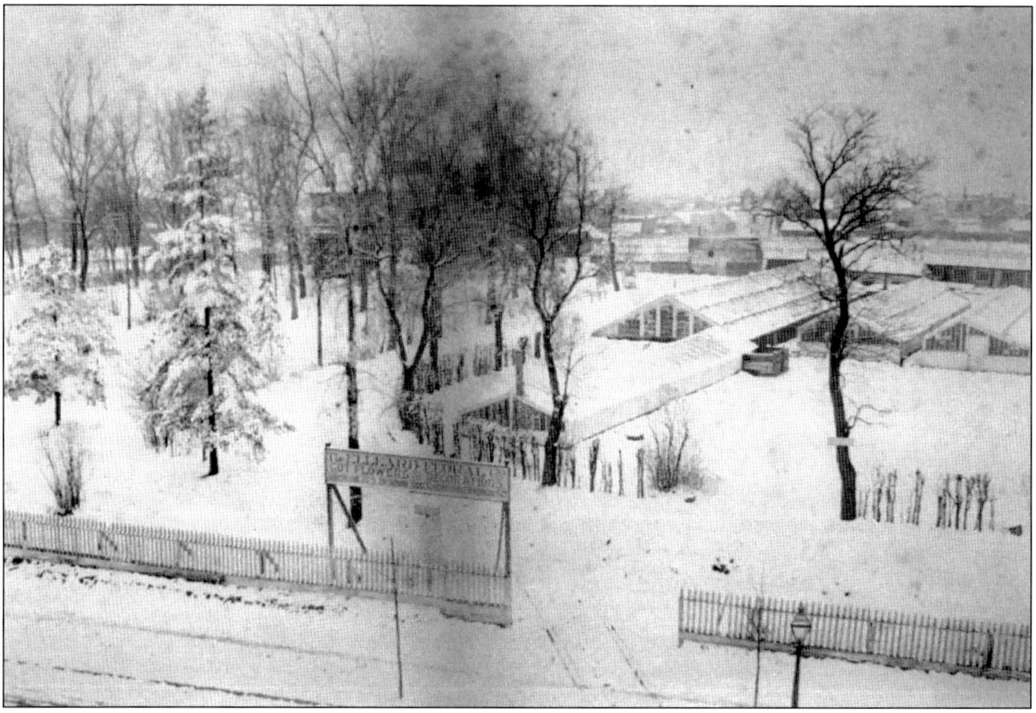

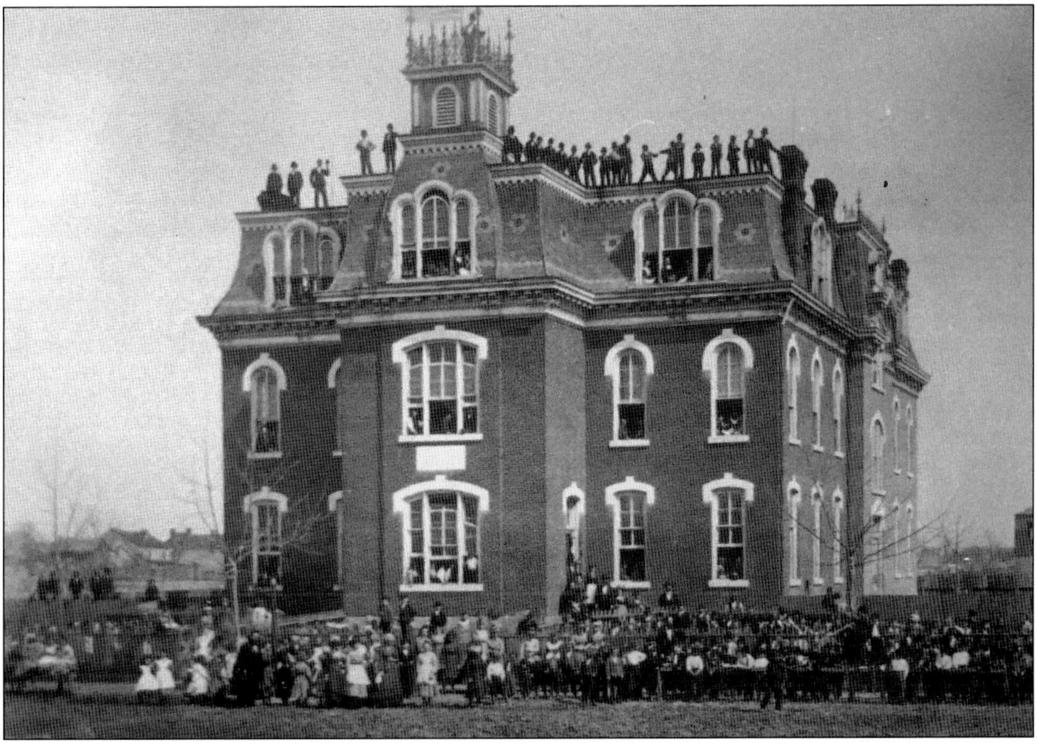

This three story mansard style building on Belle Glade and North Market avenues was known as Elleardsville School. It served the white students of the community from 1870 until 1906 when it closed. (Photo courtesy of the St. Louis Public Schoo Archives.)

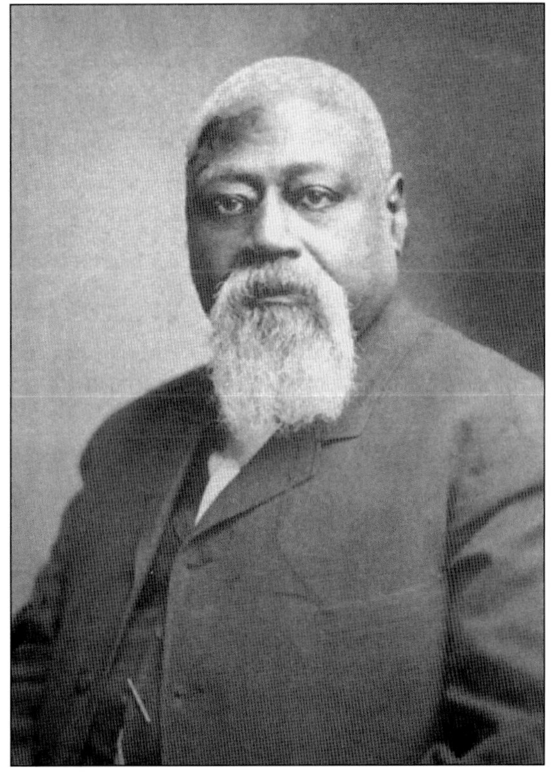

The distinguished gentleman in this photograph is James Milton Turner, who lived at 1516 Goode Avenue (now Annie Malone Drive). Turner was instrumental in establishing schools for African Americans in Missouri. He was born a slave in St. Louis county and freed at age four. At 14, he attended Oberlin College and went on to be appointed the Second Assistant State Superintendent of Colored Schools in Missouri. Between 1871 and 1878, he became the first powerful black in the Diplomatic Corps when he was appointed Ambassador to Liberia. (Photo courtesy of the Kingdom of Callaway Historical Society.)

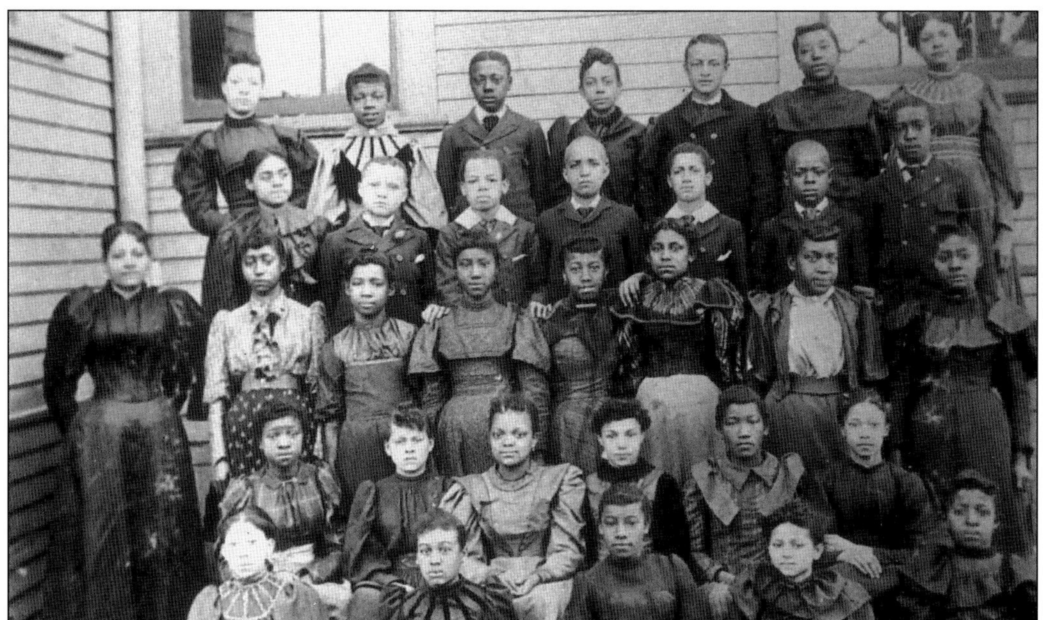

The first African-American institution in The Ville was Elleardsville Colored School No. 8, which opened in 1873 with an enrollment of 53 students. In 1891 the school was renamed for Dr. William J. Simmons, a Baptist clergyman, educator, and author. This photograph of the school's students was taken in 1891 outside of their four-room frame school building on Claggart Street (now St. Louis Avenue). (Photo courtesy of the St. Louis Public Schools Archives.)

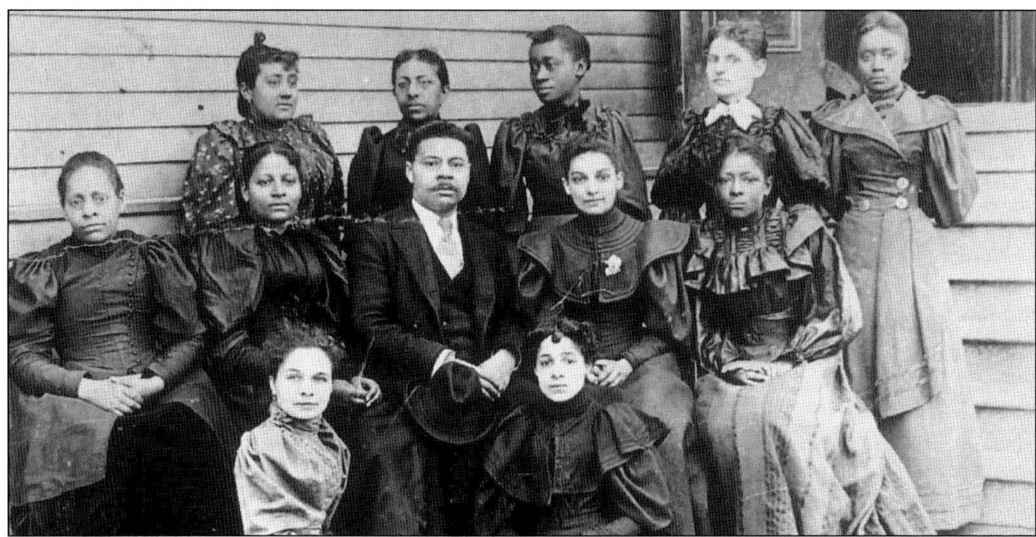

Pictured here are some of the early faculty members of Elleardsville Colored School No. 8. The school opened with an all white staff. By 1877, black teachers had replaced the white staff and had begun serving in administrative positions. Richard Cole, the only male in this picture, was one of the first African-American teachers in the St. Louis public school system. He served as principal of Simmons Elementary School for 50 years. Cole Elementary School in St. Louis is named in his honor. (Photo courtesy of the St. Louis Public Schools Archives.)

The Ville attracted many middle class and professional African-Americans such as Dr. William P.T. Jones, pictured here. Jones, who lived at 2417 Goode Avenue (now Annie Malone Drive), was the first known African-American physician in Missouri. A neighbor, Philip H. Murray, who lived on the same street near Cottage, was the publisher of the *St. Louis Advance,* the first African-American newspaper in St. Louis. (Photo courtesy of the University of Missouri-Western Manuscript Collection.)

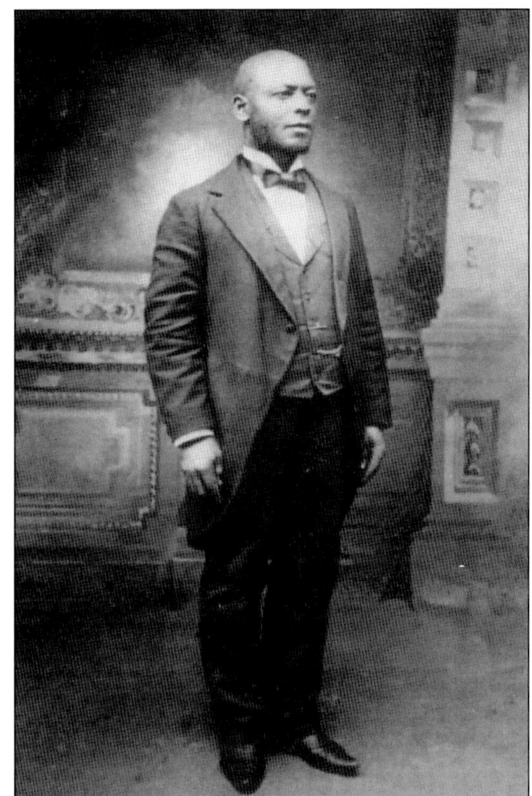

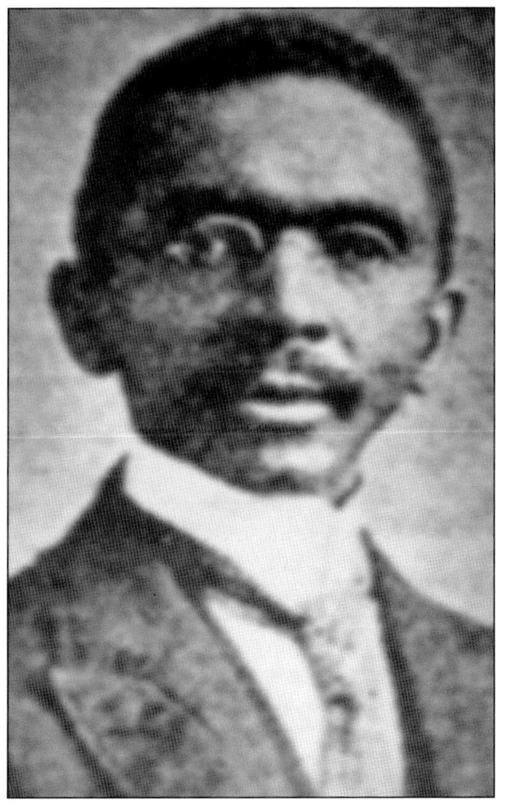

Pictured here is Walter M. Farmer, who lived in the 2400 block of Goode Avenue (now Annie Malone Drive). He was the first African-American graduate of Washington University's Law School. Farmer was also one of the founding members of the Anniversary Club, St. Louis' oldest African-American men's social club. The club was founded in 1892. (Photo courtesy of the University of Missouri-Western Manuscript Collection.)

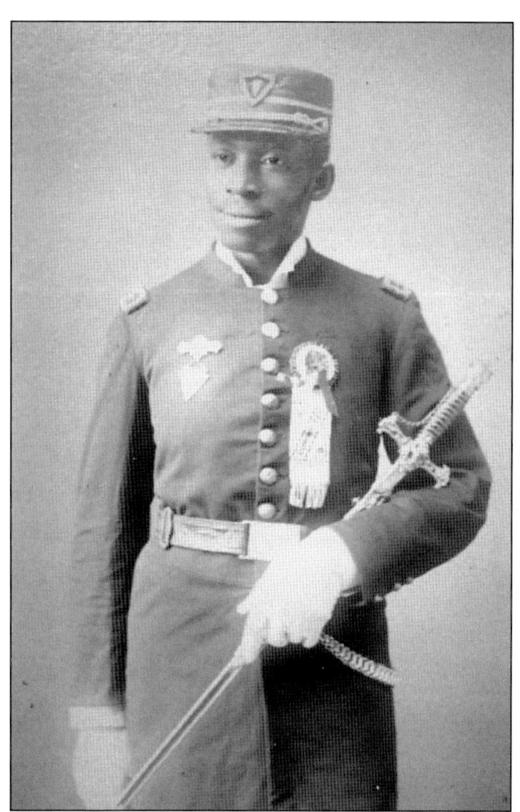

Besides professionals, The Ville also attracted many hard working non-professionals such as Charles Robert Owsley, a receiving clerk at a millinery factory, who moved to 4335 North Market with his family in 1908. The Owsleys were the parents of seven children: two boys, and five girls. Charles is shown here in his Knights of Pythian Uniform. The Pythians were a secret fraternal organization founded in 1868. It became active in St. Louis in 1870. (Photo courtesy of Berenice Colbert.)

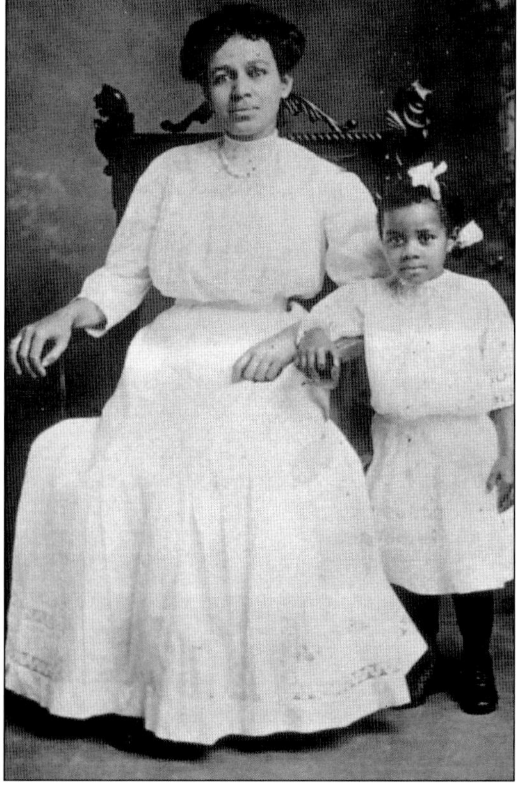

Emma Clara Davis Owsley, the wife of Charles Robert Owsley and home maker, is pictured here with her daughter Berenice. Berenice became a St. Louis City and public school social worker and a teacher at Sumner High School and at Curtis Elementary School in the St. Louis Public School system. At the time of her retirement, she was teacher-in-charge at Curtis Elementary School. Her sister Clarabelle became principal of Dessaline Elementary School in St. Louis. (Photo courtesy of Berenice Colbert.)

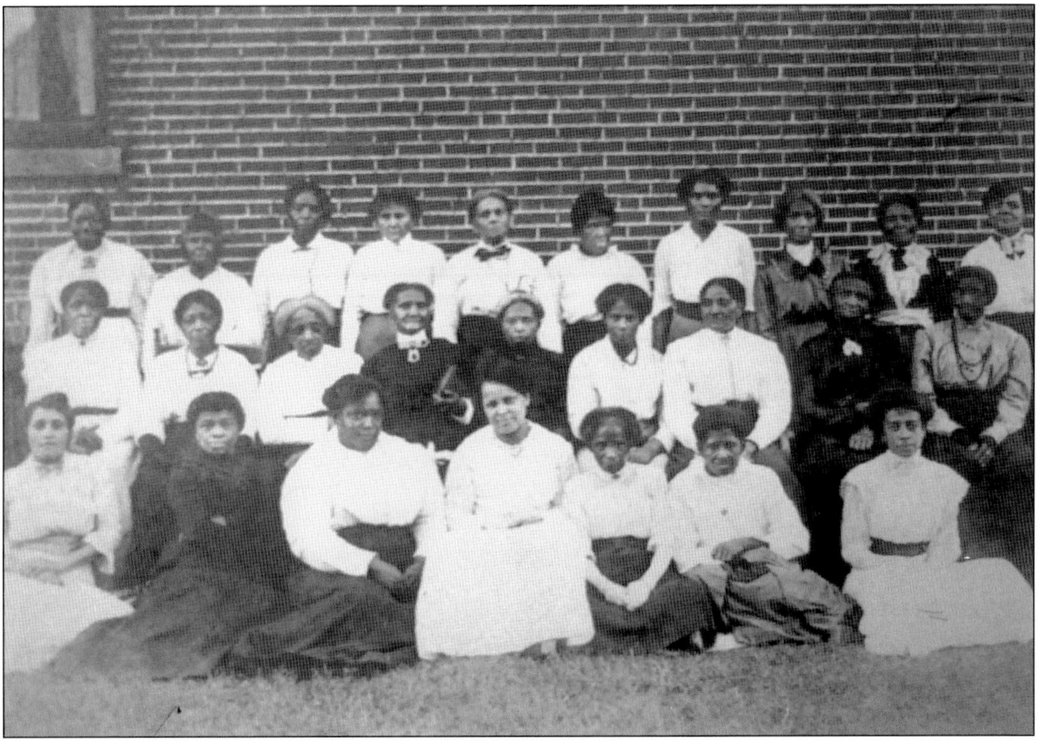

Antioch Baptist Church opened in 1884, to become the second church in The Ville. It was preceded by Elleardsville Church, an African-American Baptist Church located on Lambdin Avenue near St. Ferdinand Avenue. Pictured above are some of the members of an Antioch women's group. (Photo courtesy of Antioch Baptist Church.)

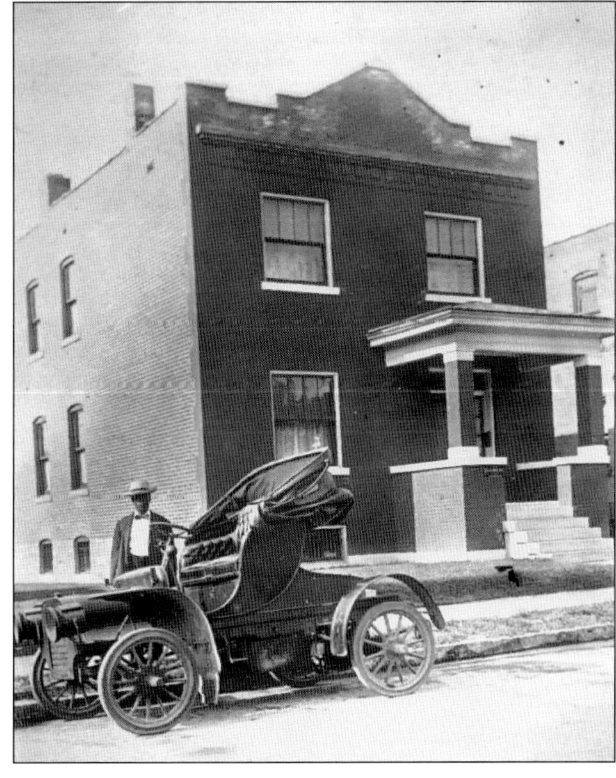

The Ville afforded many African-Americans an opportunity to purchase nice homes such as the one here. Rev. William Perry is pictured outside his home at 4452 Kennerly Avenue. Rev. Perry, who was also a physician, was pastor of Antioch Baptist Church from 1907–1945. (Photo courtesy of Antioch Baptist Church.)

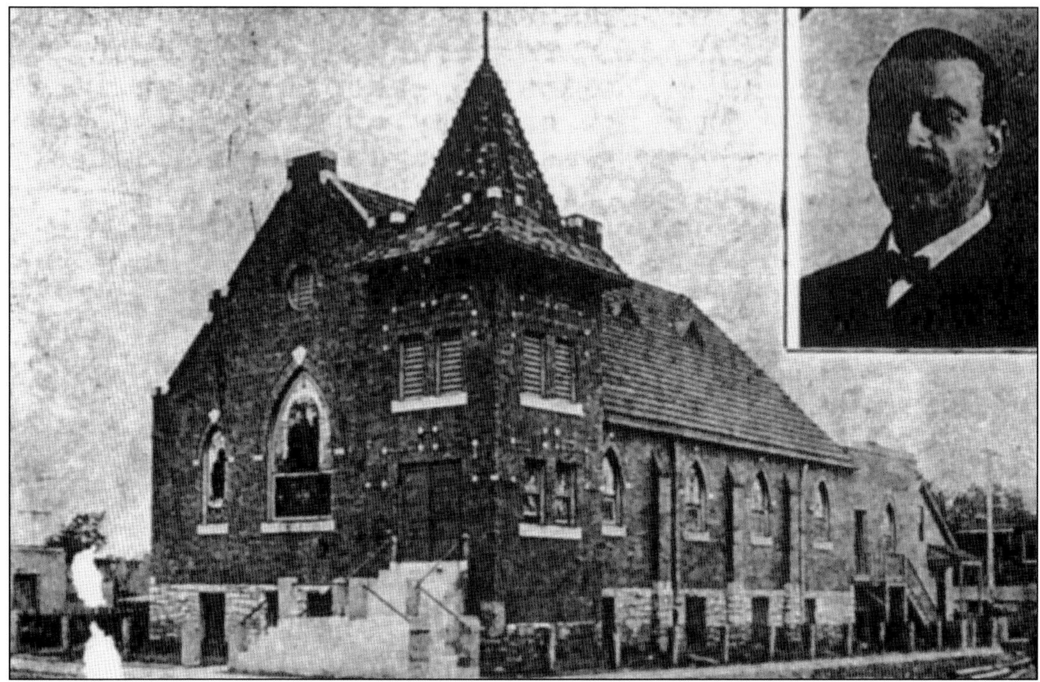

In 1885, St. James A.M.E. Church became the third known African-American church to open in The Ville. The church is pictured here with its pastor Rev. W.C. Williams in 1902, at its second location. (Photo courtesy of Odessa Farrell and St. James A.M.E. Church.)

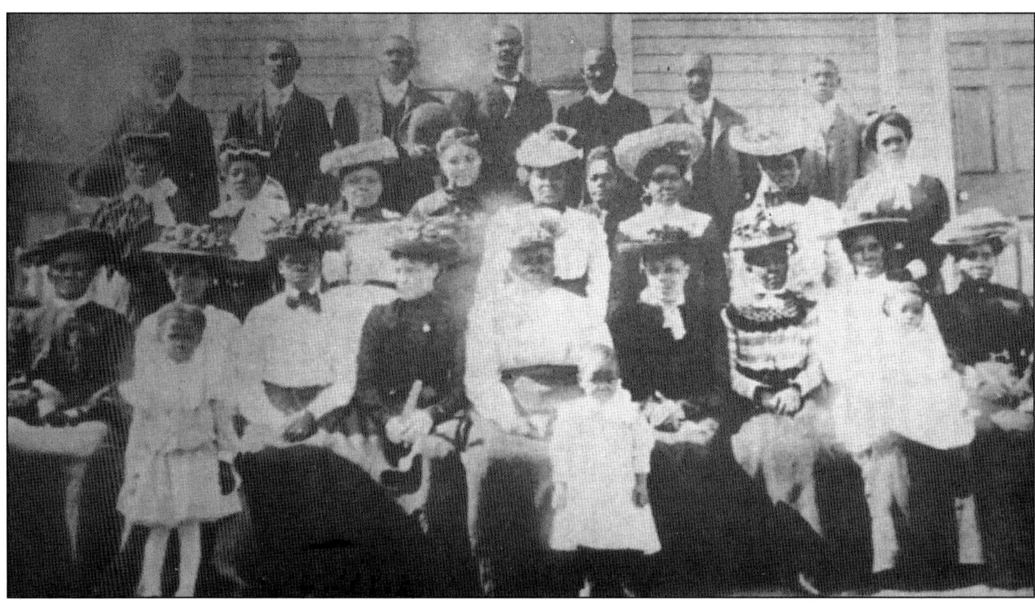

This group of well dressed and dignified looking African Americans, photographed in 1890, are members of St. James A.M.E. Church. They are, from left to right: (top row) Oliver Avery, Henry Rhone, James Gray, James T. White, Charles Scott, George Scott, and B.A. Walton. The other members are unidentified (Photo courtesy of Odessa Farrell and St. James A.M.E. Church.)

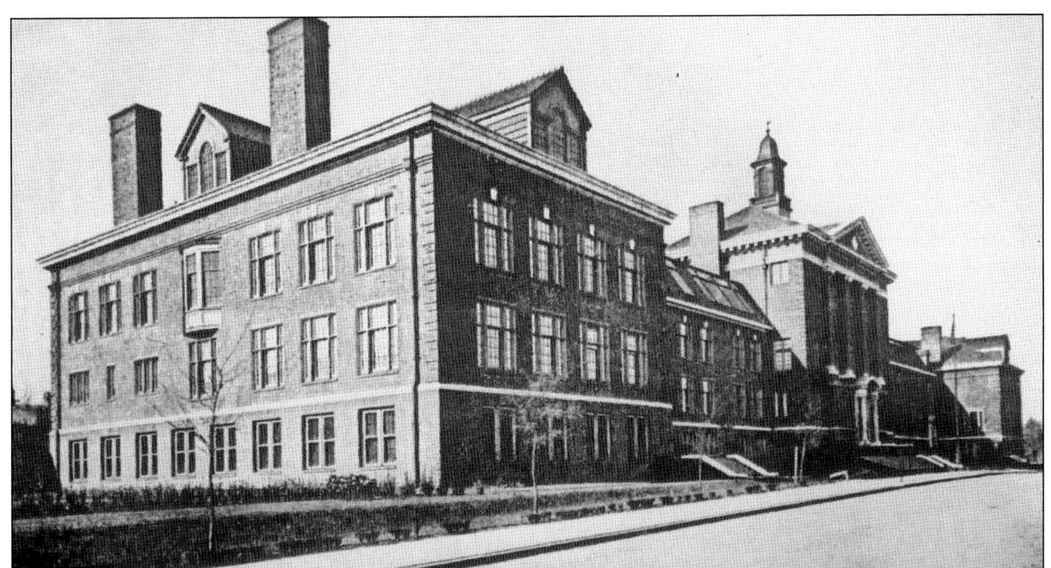

Sumner High School, the first high school west of the Mississippi River for African Americans, is pictured here after it opened in The Ville in 1910. Despite strong opposition from the white residents in the area, African Americans successfully pressured the St. Louis Board of Education to build Sumner High School in The Ville instead of downtown close to the Collier Lead Works and houses of prostitution. (Photo courtesy of the St. Louis Landmarks Association.)

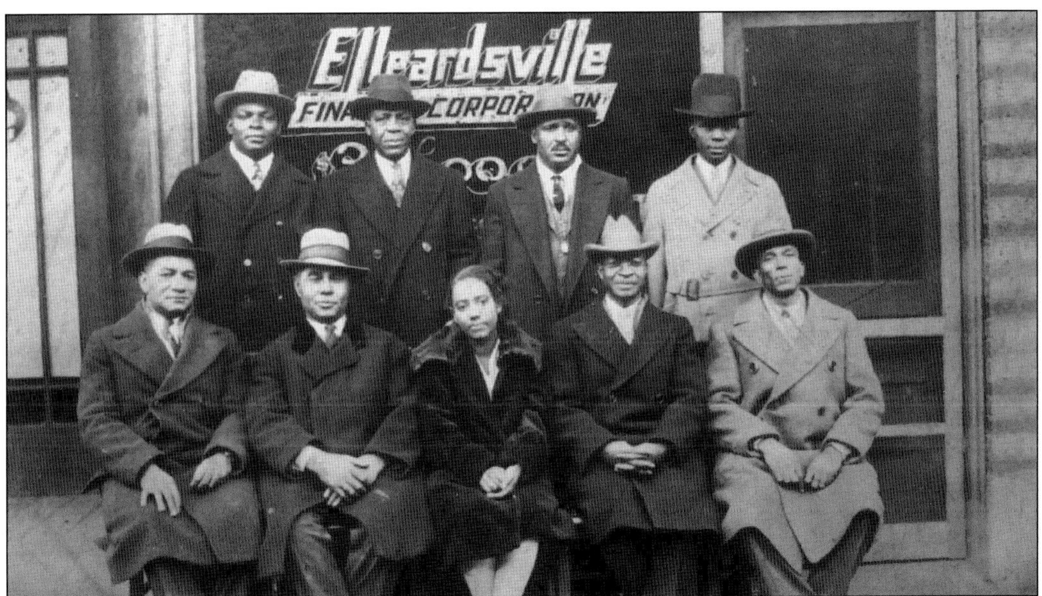

As more and more African Americans began to move into The Ville community, there was a need for the new residents to acquire loans for construction and to repair their homes. To meet that need, Joseph J. James, John E. Keen, Arthur Flagg, Herman Dreer, Hubert Burce, Henry Porter, Thomas Sanders, and Oral S. McClellan, M.D. put up $15,000 of their own assets to form the Elleardsville Financial Corporation in 1926. The building was located at 4214 W. Easton Avenue (now Dr. Martin Luther King Drive). (Photo courtesy of Vivian Dreer.)

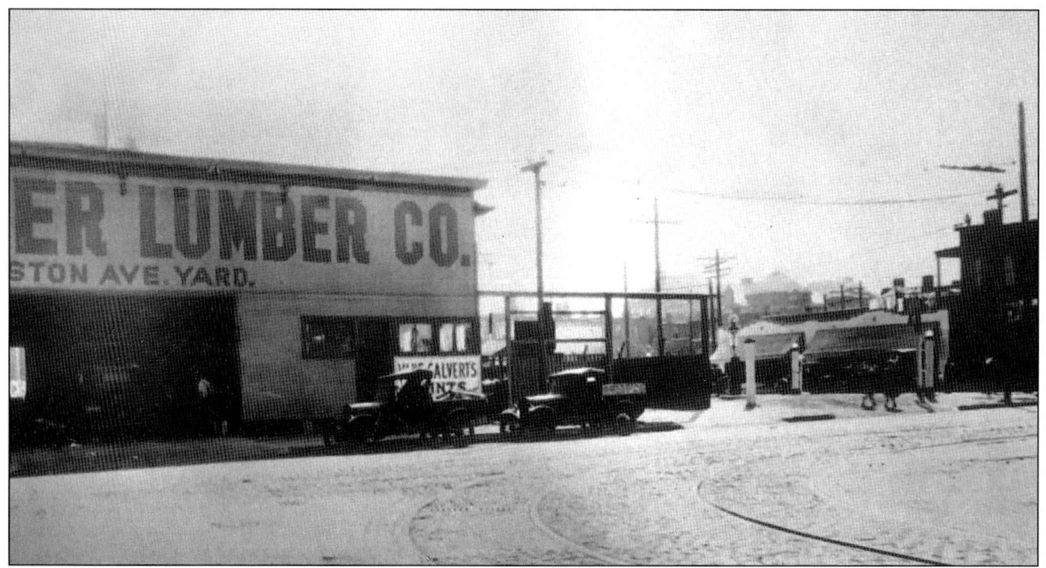

A growing Ville population also increased the number of businesses owned by both African Americans and Europeans. This picture of the lumber company at Easton (now Dr. Martin Luther King Dr.) and Sarah avenues was taken at the turn of the century. While the streetcar tracks in the picture provided easy access for transportation, they also provided a barrier on three sides of the community to contain the black residents. (Photo courtesy of the St. Louis Public Library.)

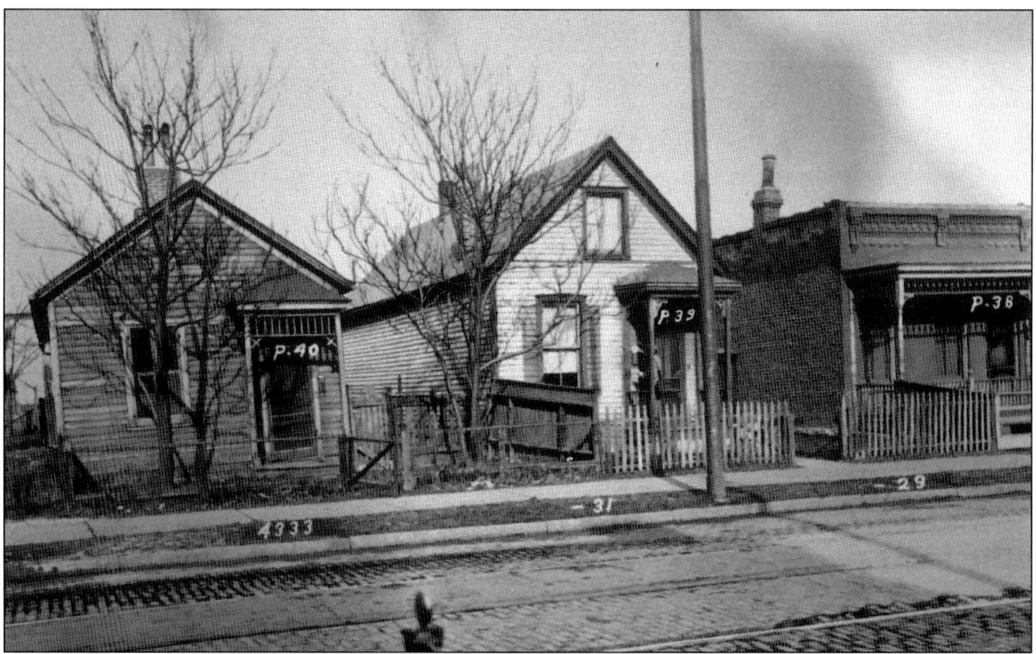

Along the streetcar tracks on the north side of the community and scattered throughout, one could find shotgun homes such as these on St. Louis Avenue, photographed at the turn of the century. These dwellings were one room wide to accommodate narrow urban lots. (Photo courtesy of the St. Louis Public Library.)

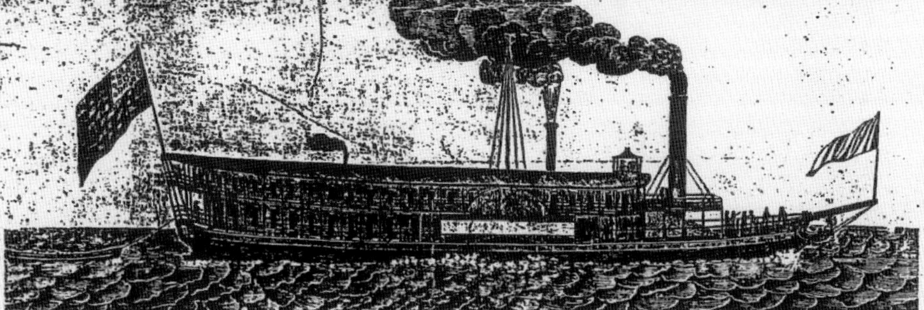

Racial tension throughout the history of St. Louis has been one of the contributing factors that has pushed African Americans to find and build supporting communities such as The Ville. Although blacks were free to move in any part of the city prior to the turn of the century, they were concentrated in only a few wards. Incidents such as the one involving Francis McIntosh, a free mulatto who was chained to a tree and burned to death in 1836, and the sideshow of the execution of four blacks on Duncan Island on this poster in 1841, helped to foster the need for blacks to come together. After the execution on Duncan Island, the heads of the executed were placed on display in a downtown drug store. (Photo courtesy of the Elijah P. Lovejoy Society.)

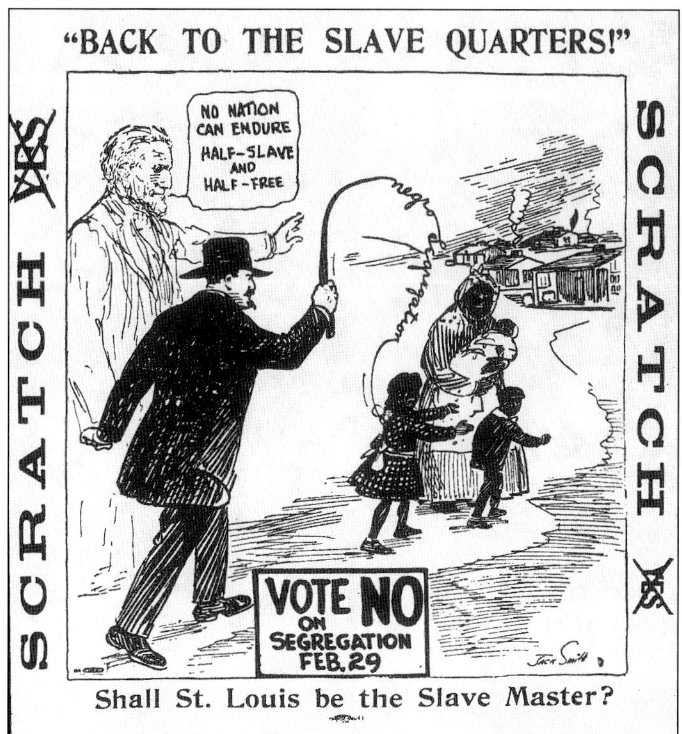

Between 1910 and 1920, the African-American population in St. Louis increased 60 percent. To prevent blacks from moving into white areas, the white citizens of St. Louis placed a segregation ordinance on the ballot in 1916. Black and white citizens passed out flyers such as the one shown here opposing the ordinance, but it passed anyway. When the Supreme Court later ruled the ordinance unconstitutional, white citizens escalated the use of race restrictive covenants to prohibit property owners from selling to minorities. (Photo courtesy of Elilah P. Lovejoy Society.)

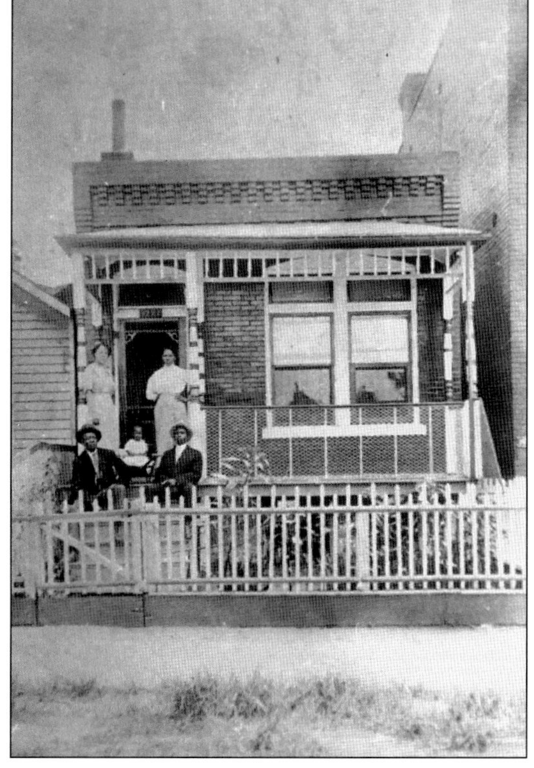

Odessa Farrell, the little girl in this 1907 photo, is shown here at her home at 3722 Fair Avenue outside of The Ville. After the passage of the segregation ordinance in 1916, and the enactment of restricted covenants, the movement of black families into white neighborhoods became restrictive. The Farrells later moved to The Ville and built a second home on Aldine Avenue. (Photo courtesy of Odessa Farrell.)

With the growth and support of African-American institutions in The Ville, blacks found the area a desirable place to live. Dr. Herman Dreer, pictured here with his family at 4335 Cote Brilliante Avenue, moved to the Ville in 1914 after he accepted a teaching position at Sumner High School. Dreer later became a well known educator, historian, minister, and strong civic leader. Both of his daughters, Clarice and Vivian, became accomplished educators in the community. (Photo courtesy of Vivian Dreer.)

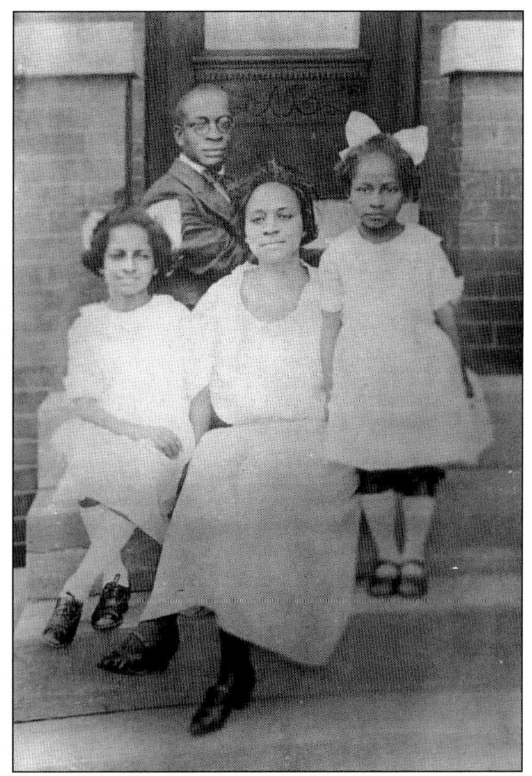

For entertainment and socializing, many of the women and men in The Ville formed clubs. The women in this photo were members of the Booklovers Club, founded in 1907. The Club's original eight members had grown to twenty-five by 1912, and the group decided that admitting any more members would crowd their living rooms. In 1925 at least sixteen Booklovers or their husbands were St. Louis school teachers or principals. (Photo courtesy of Vivian Dreer.)

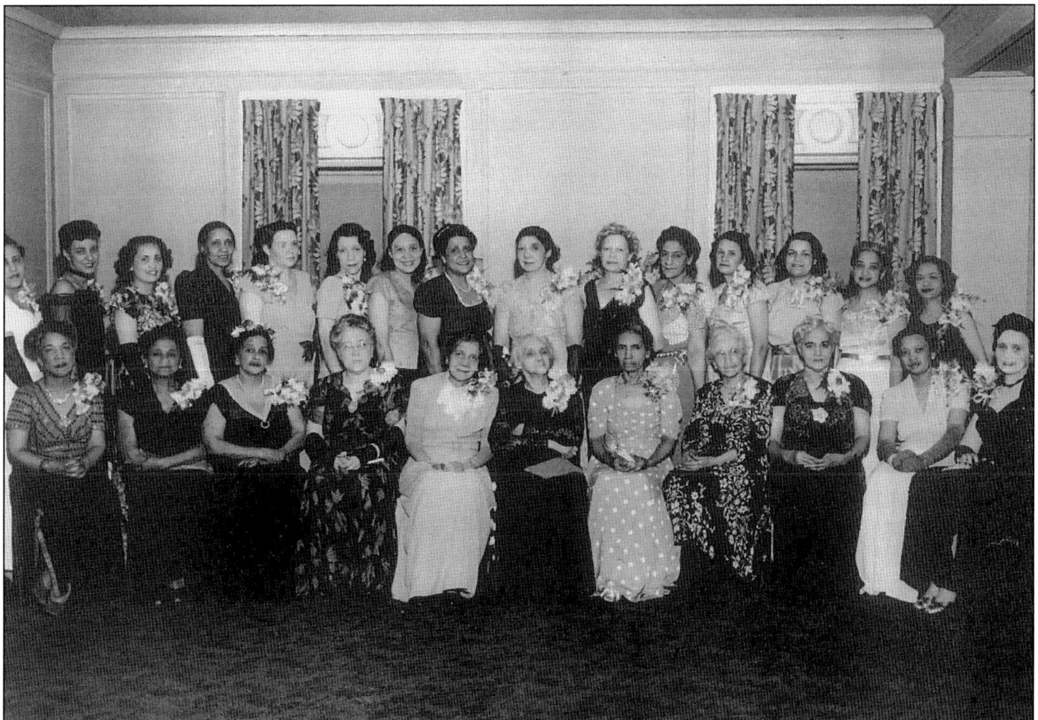

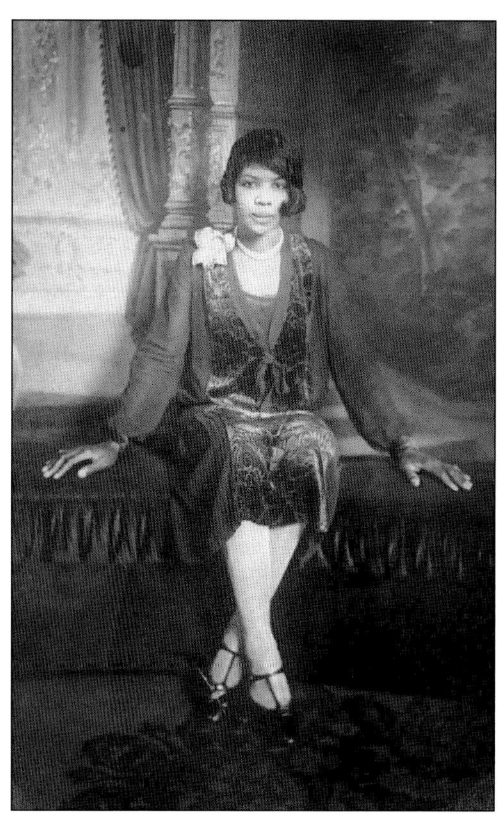

Beatrice Allen, pictured here, moved to The Ville in her teens from Jonesville, Louisiana, at the request of an uncle. Although she did not finish her elementary education, she became a charter member of the Negro Labor Council under A. Phillip Randolph and was its first female officer in St. Louis. She was also active with the NAACP and helped to organize the local group for the March on Washington in 1963. (Photo courtesy of John A. Wright.)

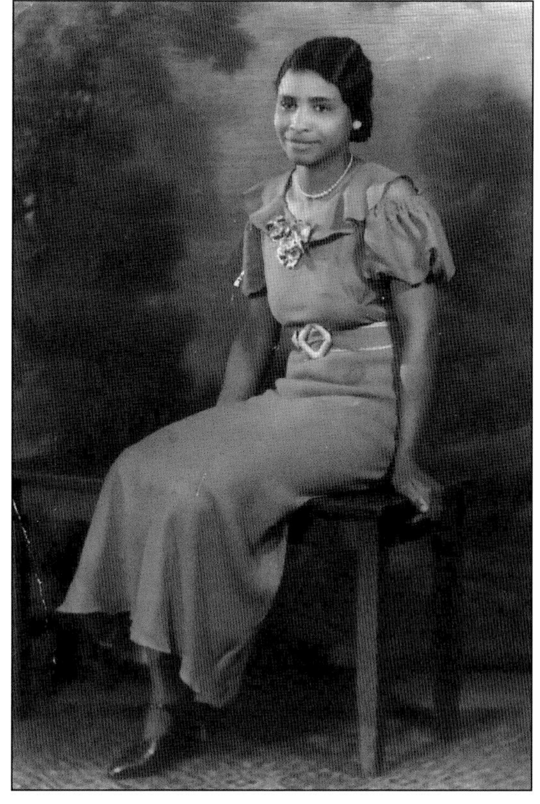

Elneal Allen, in this picture, was one of many, like her sister above, who left the rural south and came to The Ville during the 1920s in search of a better life. Allen did domestic work until she was hired as a dietary cook at Homer G. Phillips. The hospital provided many residents such as Mrs. Allen, a divorcee and single parent, with an opportunity to save enough money to purchase a home. Mrs. Allen not only purchased a home, but she was able to send her only child, a son, to college. He later became the superintendent of schools of the Kinloch School District in the City of Kinloch, Missouri. (Photo courtesy of John A. Wright.)

The Ville provided many African Americans an opportunity to go into businesses. Mattie Webster, pictured here, relocated to The Ville in the late 1920s from Georgia. After being in town for a while she opened a restaurant on Pendleton Avenue across from Poro College. The business closed after a few years and she went to work at the well known and popular Billy Burks Restaurant. (Photo courtesy of Thomas Webster.)

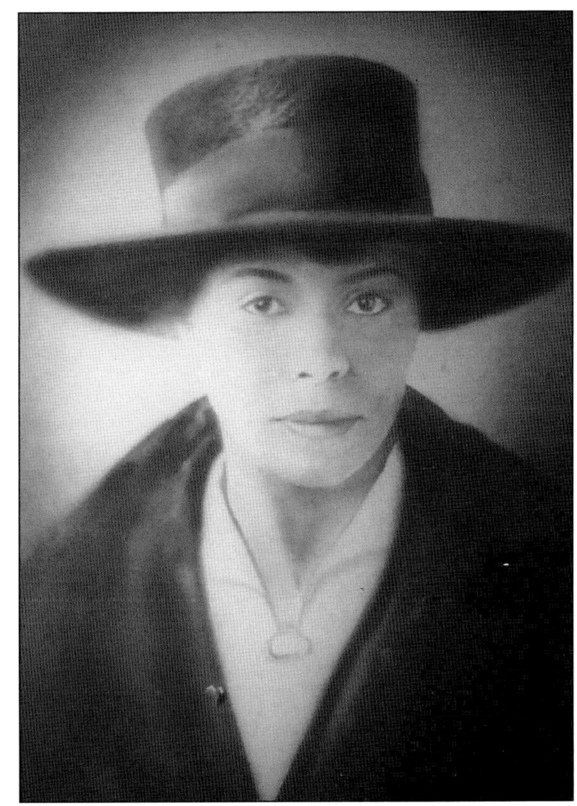

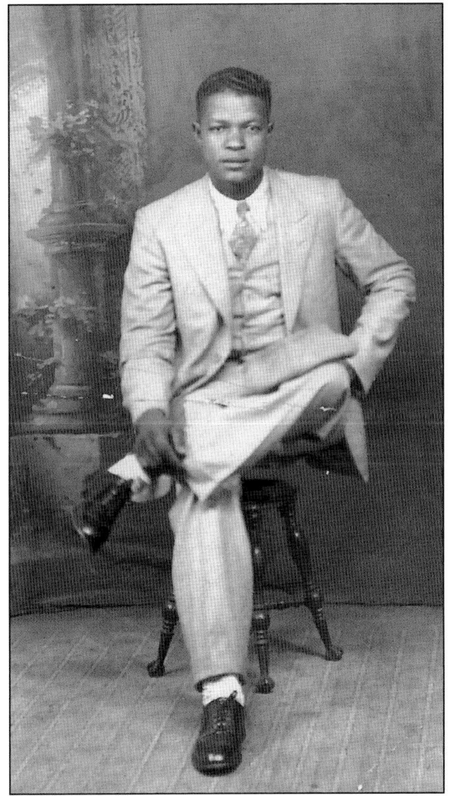

Many nonprofessional residents such as Dorsey Wright, pictured here, found the community an excellent place to branch out and to start their own business. He moved to The Ville from Georgia in the 1920s in search of opportunities and a better life. During his time in The Ville, he attempted several business ventures with some success. He lived several places in The Ville before purchasing a four family flat at 4260–62 St. Louis Avenue. This residence served as a way station for many of his relatives leaving Georgia heading north. (Photo courtesy of John A. Wright.)

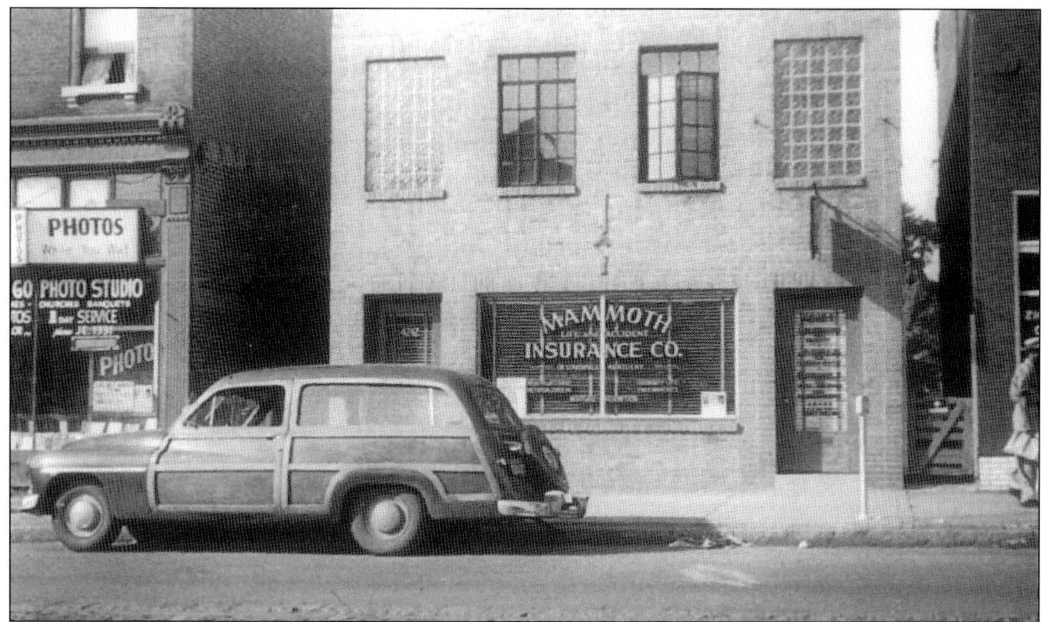

After restrictive covenants were placed on many of the streets surrounding The Ville community, it became very much a self-contained area. To serve the community more and more, entrepreneurs began to establish businesses. One such individual was Dr. Aldrich M. Brooks, D.D.S., who constructed this building in the 4200 block of Easton Avenue (now Dr. Martin Luther King Dr.). Brooks used a suite of offices upstairs for his practice and rented the facilities downstairs. (Photo courtesy of Sandra Lois Wallace.)

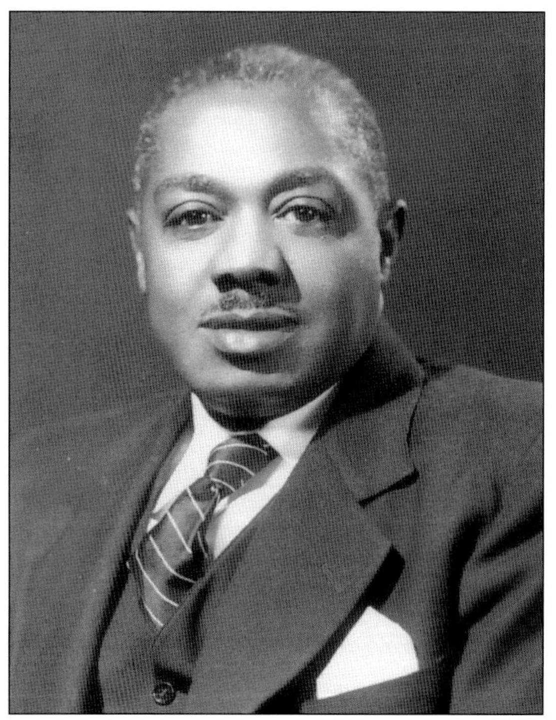

Dr. Aldrich M. Brooks, D.D.S., pictured here, came to St. Louis in 1933. He volunteered his services to the patients of City Hospital No. 2 (later named Homer G. Phillips Hospital). In 1937, he was named Head of the Department of Dentistry when Homer G. Phillips Hospital opened. Among the young graduate dentists who interned under Dr. Brooks were Luther A. Forrest, Donald Suggs, Kenneth Powell, William Gibson Jr., Charles Quigless, William G. Gregory, Etta M. Gopaul, Jack Miller, and Leon P. O'Hara. (Photo courtesy of Sandra Lois Wallace.)

Two

EDUCATION
A TRADITION OF EXCELLENCE

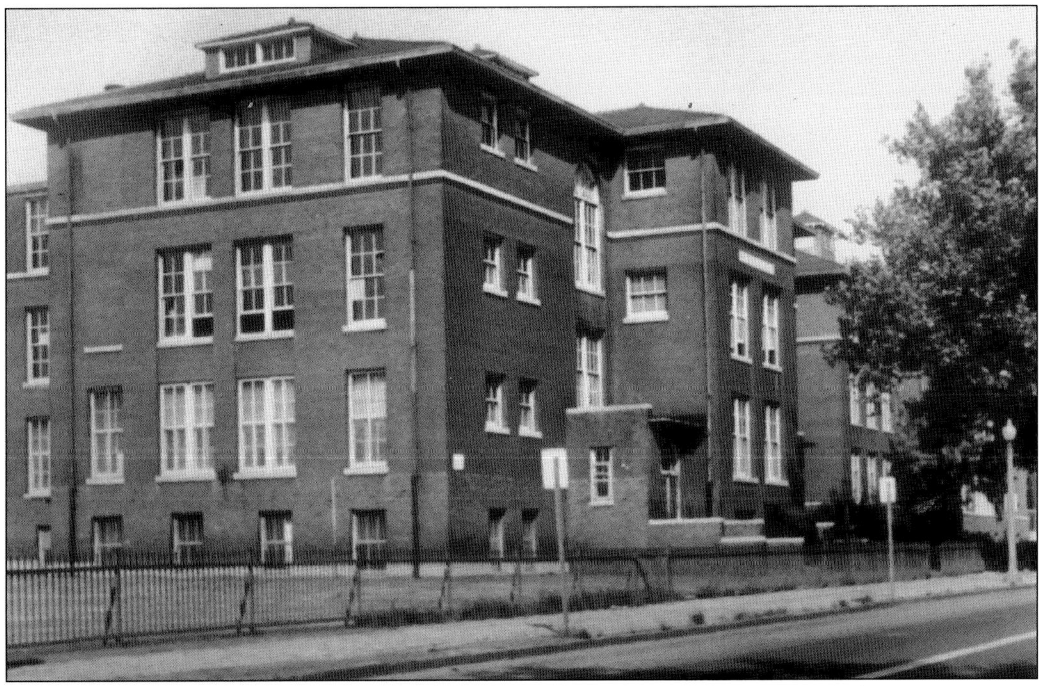

When Elleardsville Colored School No. 8 (later renamed Simmons) opened here in 1873, it marked the recognition of an African-American population in The Ville. This brick building was constructed in 1891 to replace a two-story frame building. The school's enrollment grew from 53 when it opened to 492 in 1900. (Photo courtesy of the St. Louis Public School Archives.)

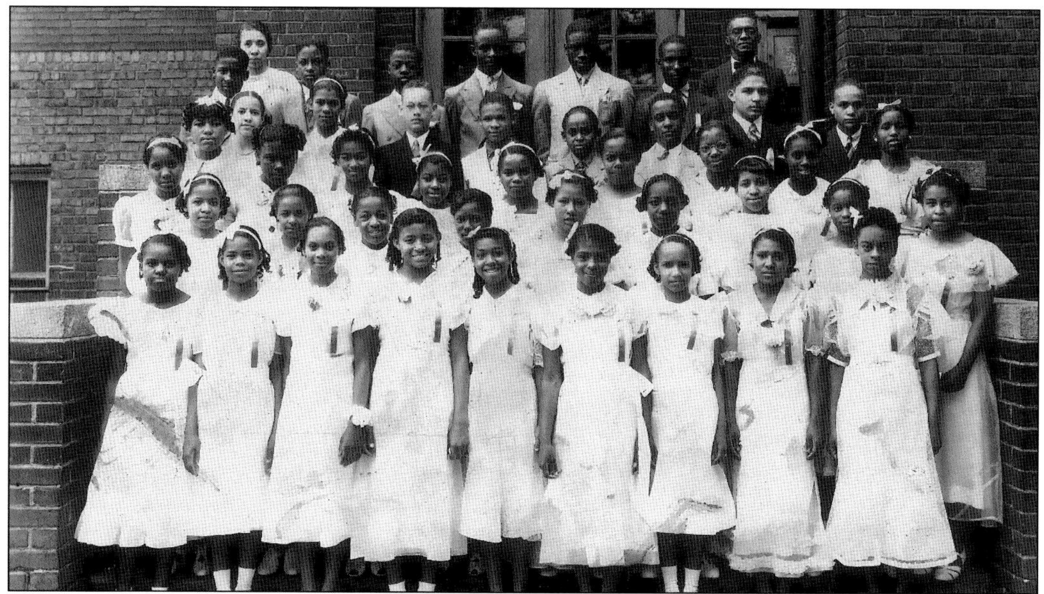

This photo is of the 1937 Simmons' eighth-grade graduation class. Upon graduation, these students went on to Sumner High School in The Ville or Booker T. Washington Technical High School in downtown St. Louis at 814 North Nineteenth Street. (Photo courtesy of Julia Davis Library.)

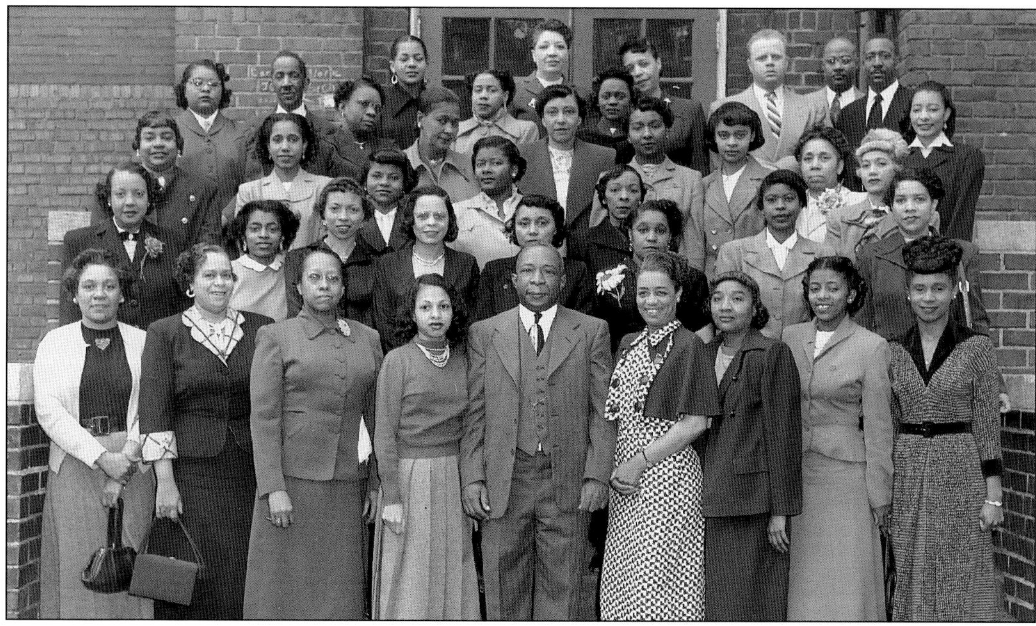

Throughout its history, Simmons has attracted many outstanding faculty members. Many of them, in this 1957 photograph taken outside of the school with Principal William T. Smith (fifth from right, first row), went on to become administrators in the St. Louis Public Schools. From 1928 to 1940, Simmons was the home of Stowe Teachers College, and a Junior College between 1933–38 through Lincoln University in Jefferson City under WPA funding. (Photo courtesy of the St. Louis Public Schools Archives.)

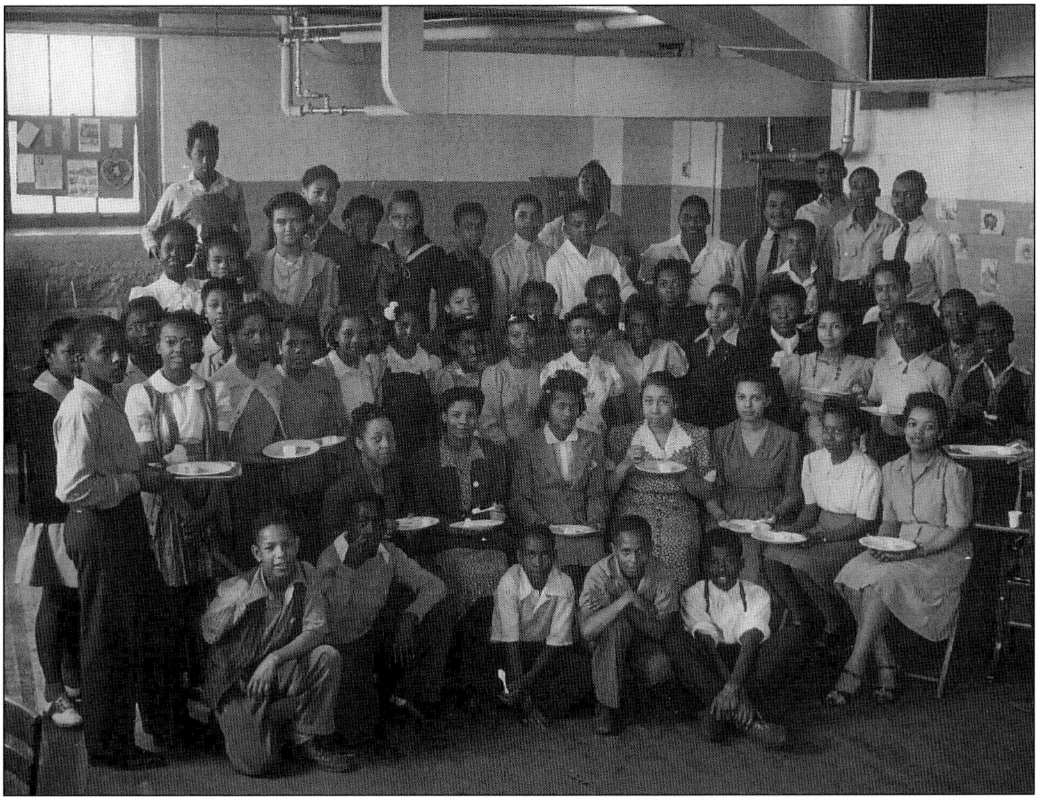

Since many of the Simmons School teachers such as Julia Davis (seated fifth from the left, second row.) lived in the community, a strong relationship developed between the teachers, students, and the community. The eighth grade students and parents in this picture are giving Ms. Davis a surprise birthday party. (Photo courtesy of the Julia Davis Library.)

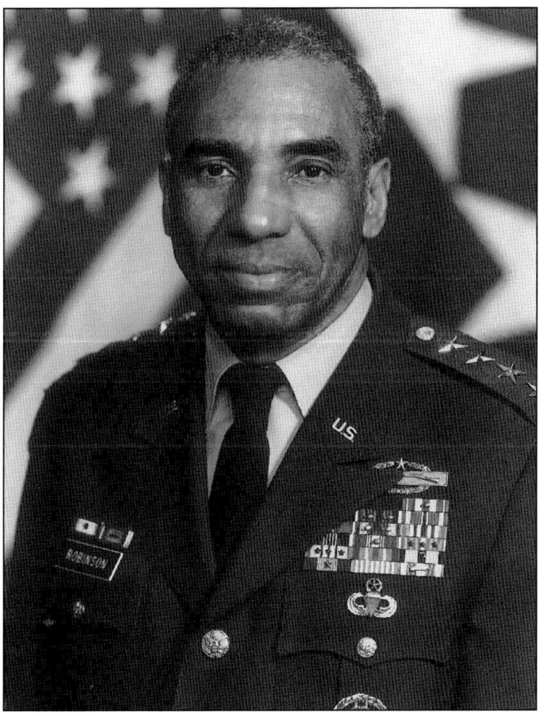

Many Simmons graduates such as Roscoe Robinson Jr., went on to do great things locally, nationally, and internationally. Robinson, pictured here, became the first black four-star General of the United States Army and a major role-model for thousands of soldiers who recognized his leadership and service to the country. Can you recognize him in the picture at the top of the page as an eighth-grade student? (Photo courtesy of Janet Bosley.)

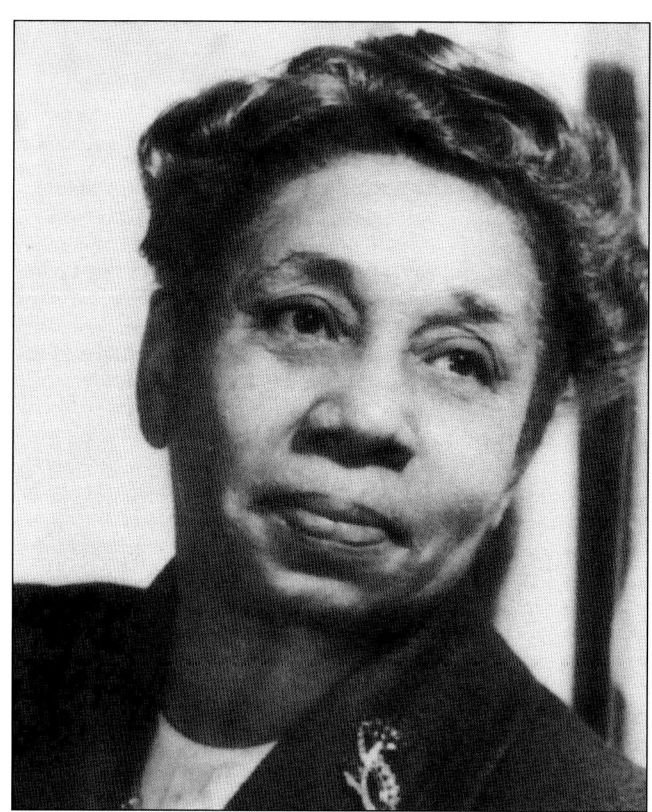

Simmons had many outstanding faculty members, but Julia Davis has been the one that has stood out over the years. She taught in the St. Louis Public Schools from 1913 until 1961. Thirty-five of those years were spent at Simmons. She was born in 1891, and received her education in the St. Louis Public Schools. Davis has a library named in her honor near the Ville area where she lived and worked most of her career. (Photo courtesy of University of Missouri-St. Louis, Western Manuscript Collection.)

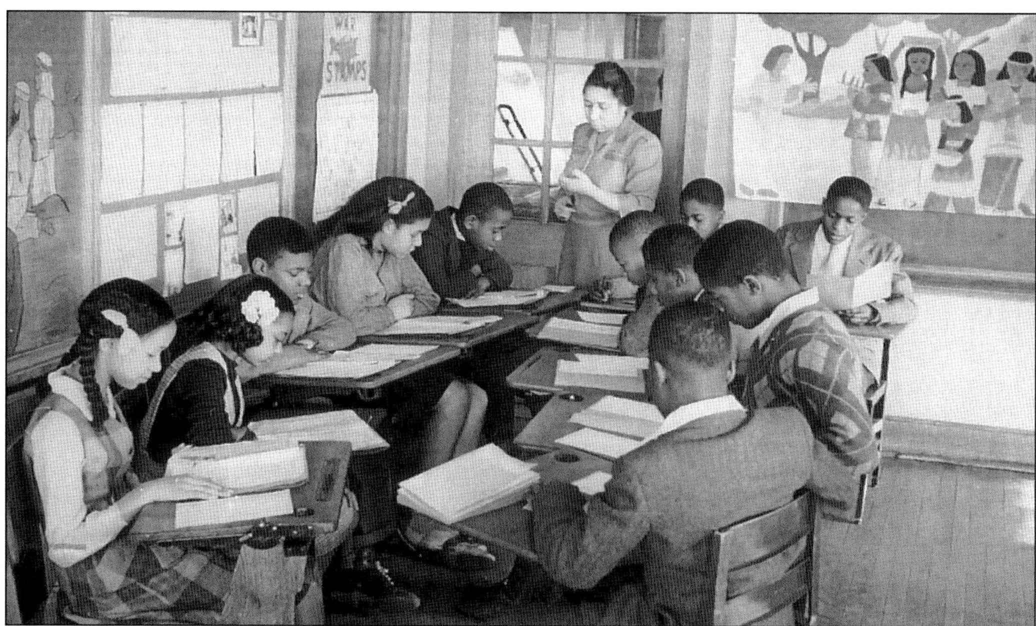

Julia Davis is shown here in her classroom doing what she did best: teaching. Davis believed in and worked to make sure that African-American culture and achievement was fully integrated into every aspect of her curriculum. (Photo courtesy of the Julia Davis Library.)

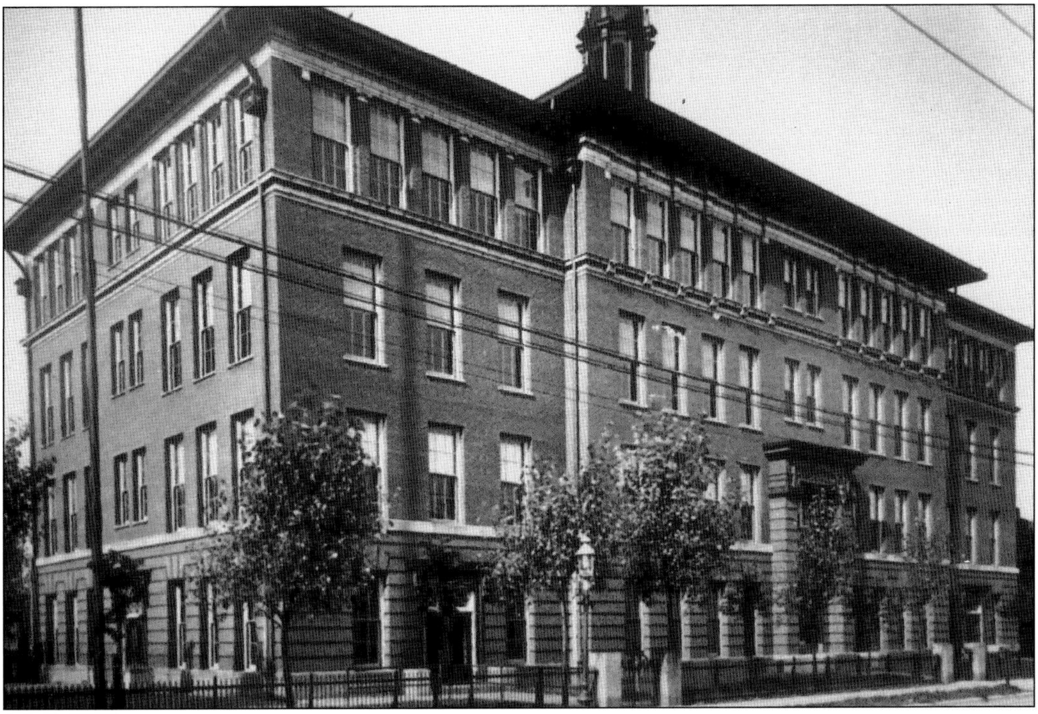

John Marshall Elementary School, pictured here, is the only school in The Ville that was not originally intended for African-American students. The building was constructed in 1900, and turned over to African Americans in 1918 as a middle school. It has been used as an elementary school since 1927. John Mercer Langston became the school's first black principal in 1919. The first teachers were Misses Maurice Williams, Mamie Hall, Bea Thomas, Sophoronia Richardson, Felicia Alexander, Helen Armstrong, Nannie Whitman, Marjorie Vashon, Selena Collins, and the Messrs. Sylvester Duvall, Madison Gray, and Frank B. Wilson. (Photo courtesy of the St. Louis Public Schools Archives.)

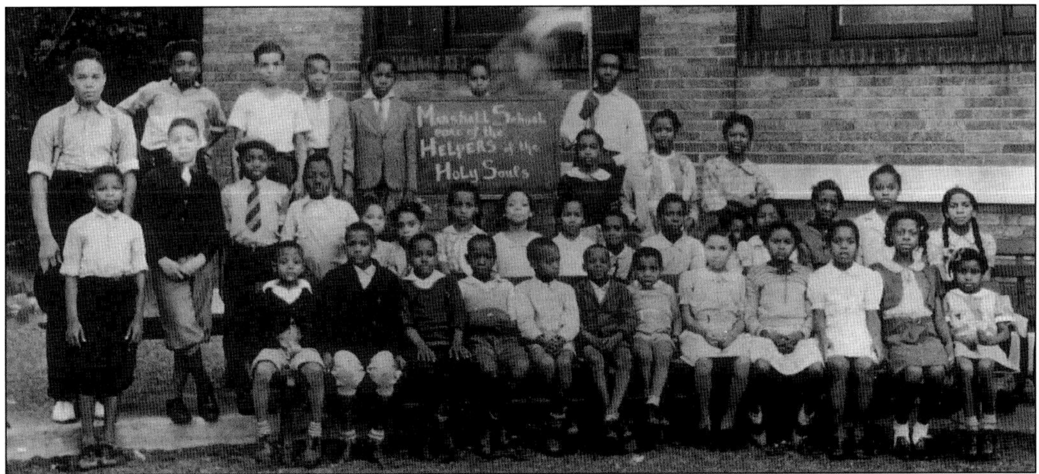

During the early 1940s, St. Louis Public School students took time out from their studies periodically to receive religious instructions. These John Marshall students are shown at the St. Benedict Center, 3950 West Bell Avenue. (Photo courtesy of Sister Patricia Hottinger.)

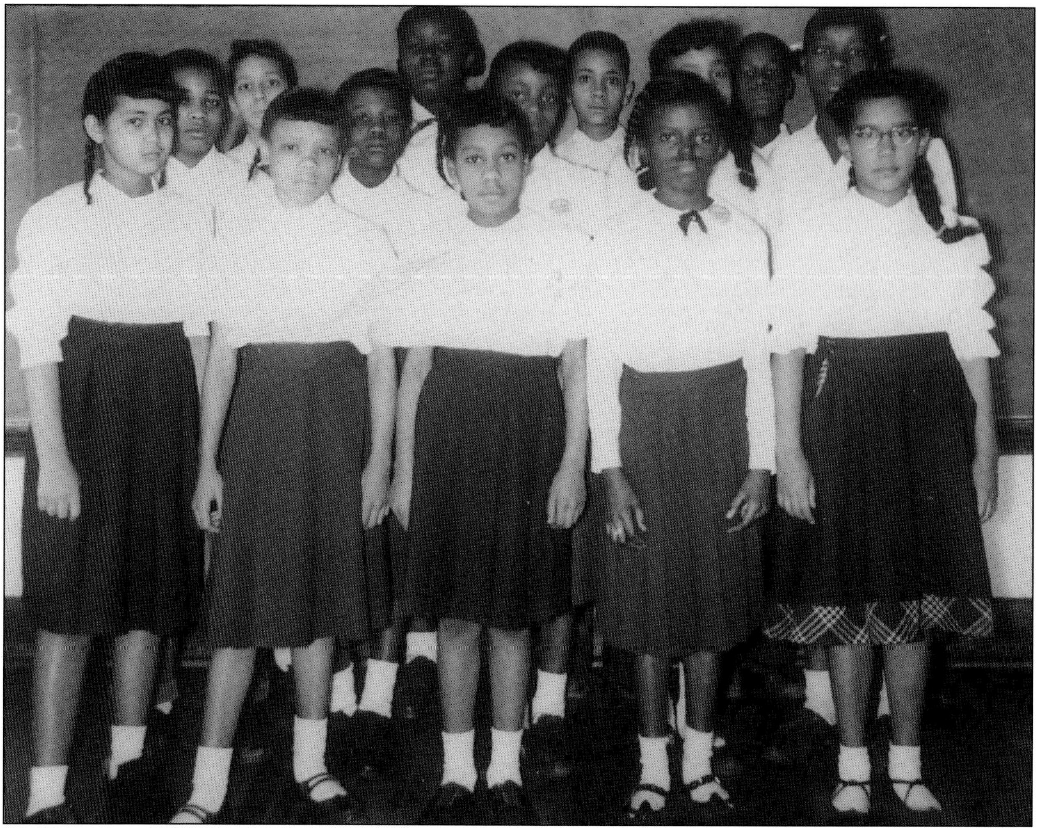

In the 1950s, Rosetta Chinn saw a need to provide young people with an opportunity to develop their leadership skills and organized the John Marshall Elementary School Student Council. This picture of members was taken during the council's beginning. Two members were chosen by the students from each grade level. (Photo courtesy of Rosetta Chinn.)

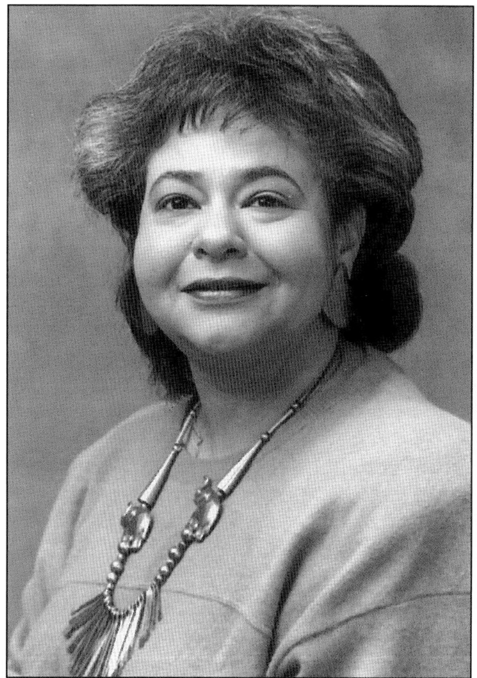

Marshall alumna Ida Goodwin Woolfolk returned to Marshall to teach after graduating from Harris Teachers College. She later was appointed assistant to the superintendent for Community Outreach. Ms. Woolfolk is a nationally recognized consultant in the areas of human relations, stress management, and race relations. Ida serves as planner for many stellar events, including the National Conference of Black Mayors. She has received numerous awards and is known about town as the "Toastmaster General!" (Photo courtesy of Ida Goodwin Woolfolk.)

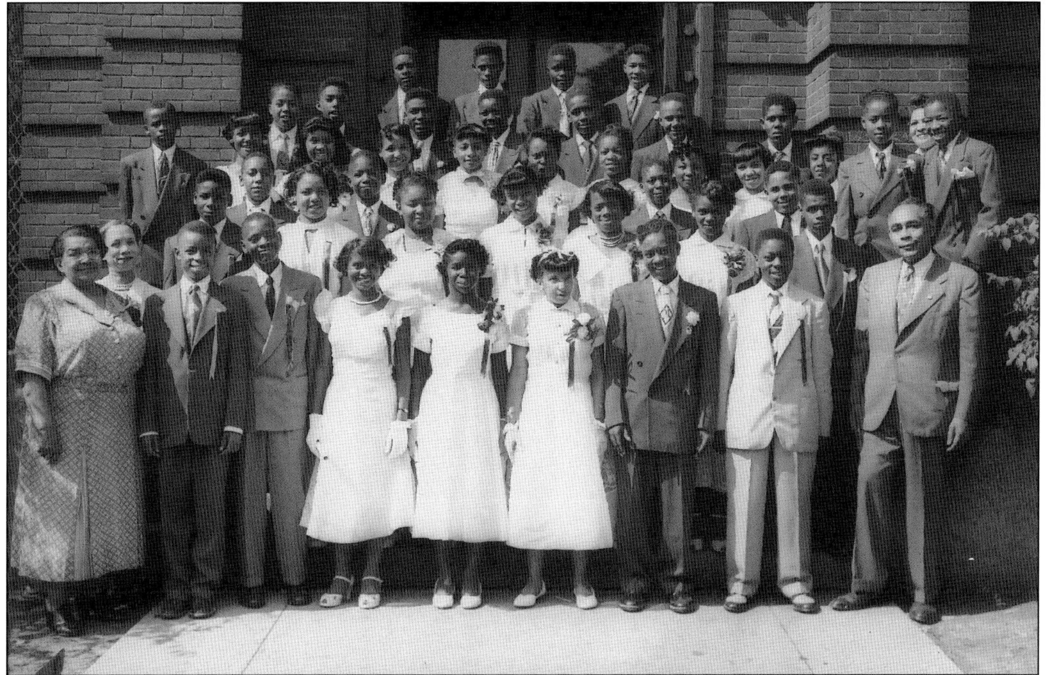

These 1951 John Marshall Elementary School eighth-grade graduates, all dressed up, are standing outside the school with their teachers Viola Clay, Lillian Randle, and Principal Dr. George Mann. Dr. Mann had a reputation as an outstanding administrator and scholar. Not only did he earn a Ph.D. in Education Administration, he also earned a law degree. (Photo courtesy of the St. Louis Public School Archives.)

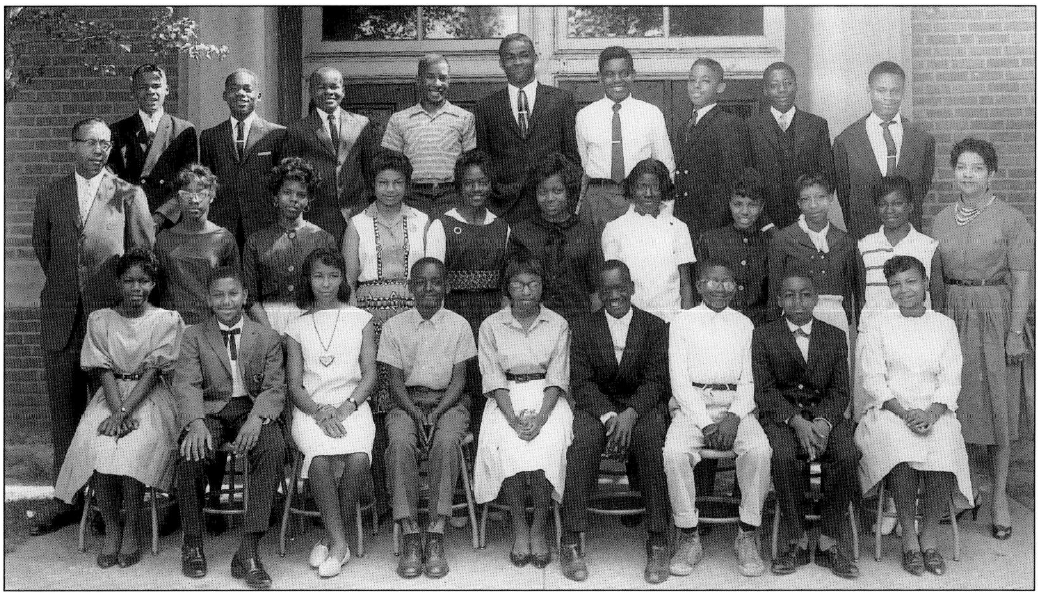

Like many other John Marshall School graduates, these 1962 eighth graders are dressed for the occasion and ready to accept the challenge of high school. (Photo courtesy of Betty Jean Henley Johnson.)

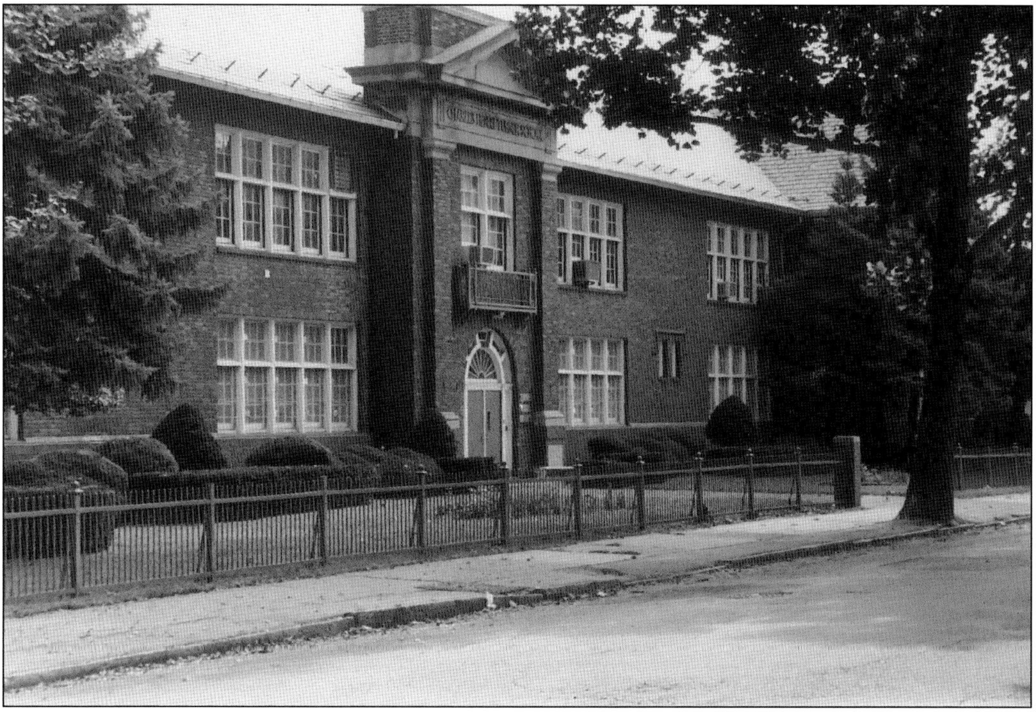

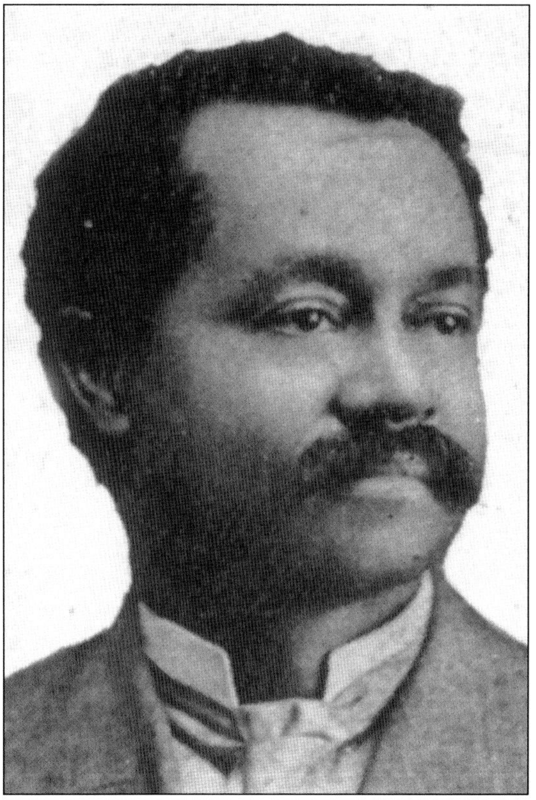

Turner Middle School, formerly Charles Henry Turner Open Air School for Handicapped Children, opened in 1925 at 4235 West Kennerly Avenue. It was the first school of its kind for African Americans in the United States. Prior to 1924, there were several special schools for crippled and handicapped white children but none existed for black children. The school attempted to show the public that the children were also human beings, not to be pitied, but given a chance to perform to their capacity. (Photo by John A. Wright.)

This picture is of Charles Henry Turner for whom the school for the handicapped children was named. Turner, who lived at 4540 Garfield Avenue, was a distinguished entomologist with numerous scientific publications to his credit. His was the first African-American Ph.D. at the University of Chicago. Turner was a biology teacher at Sumner High School from 1908 to 1922. (Photo by Nathan Young. Courtesy of the University of Missouri-Western Manuscript Collection.)

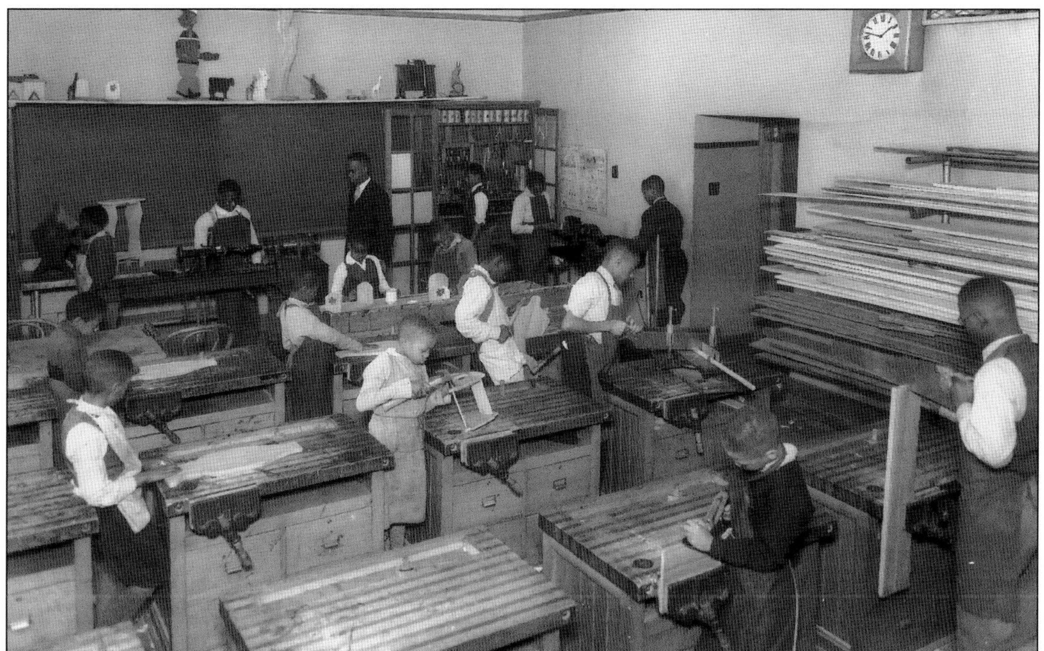

The courses offered at the Open Air School were comparable to regular school courses. The goal of the school and each teacher was to keep the child at grade level with regular and appropriate academic work and performance, and to see that their bodies and minds were improved. The students in this picture are participating in manual training. (Photo courtesy of the St. Louis Public Schools Archives.)

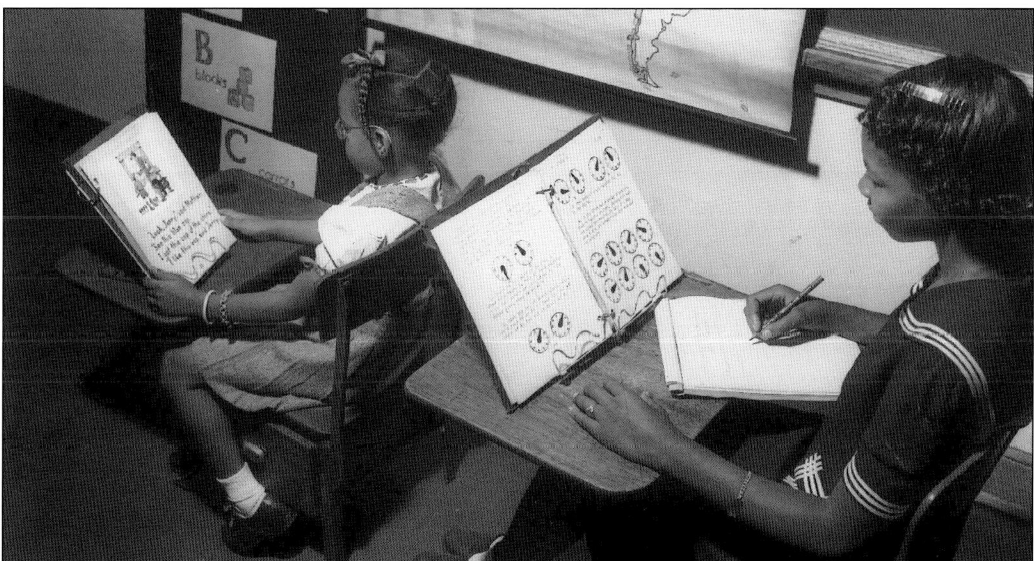

The children who attended the Open Air School came from a variety of backgrounds and graduated from the school to become doctors, teachers, cabinet makers, commercial artists, mechanics, and lawyers. These students are taking their lessons in a site conservation class to help improve their vision. (Photo courtesy of the St. Louis Public School Archives.)

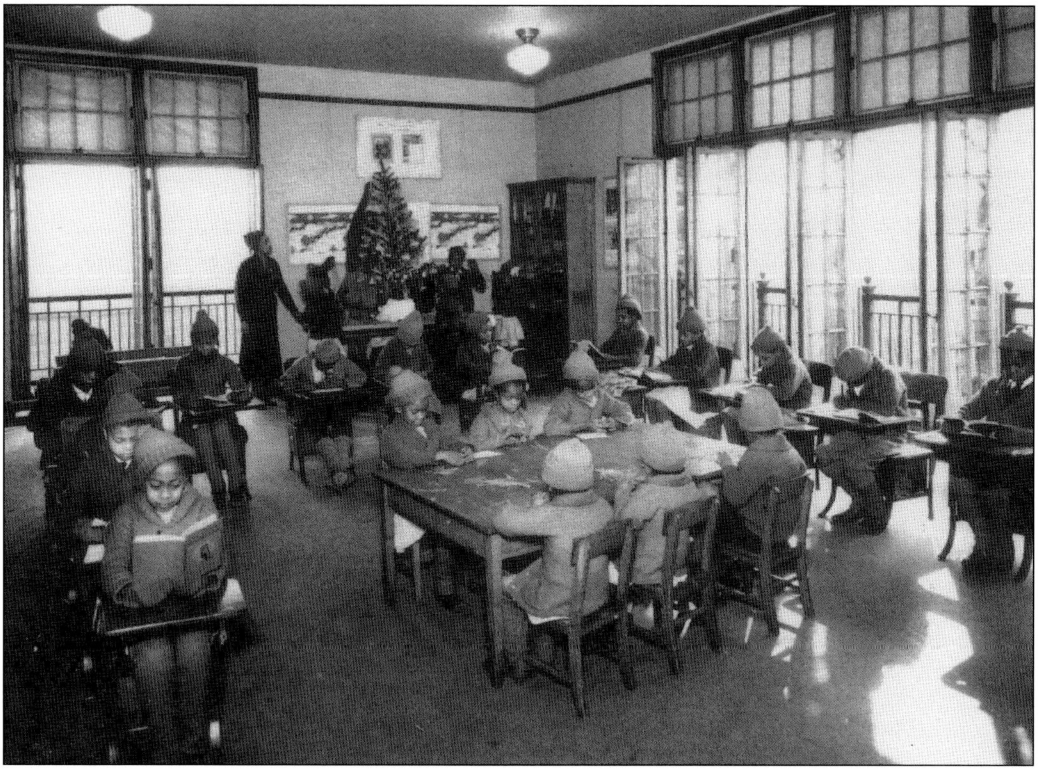

The Open Air School was equipped with French doors that were kept open throughout the school, often requiring teachers and children to remain warmly clad in coats, gloves, hats, and wool leggings, as the students in this picture. The tuberculosis-exposed children were given three meals per day: cereal and milk in the morning, full meal at lunch, and milk and crackers for a snack before leaving school. (Photo courtesy of the University of Missouri-St. Louis, Western Manuscript Collection.)

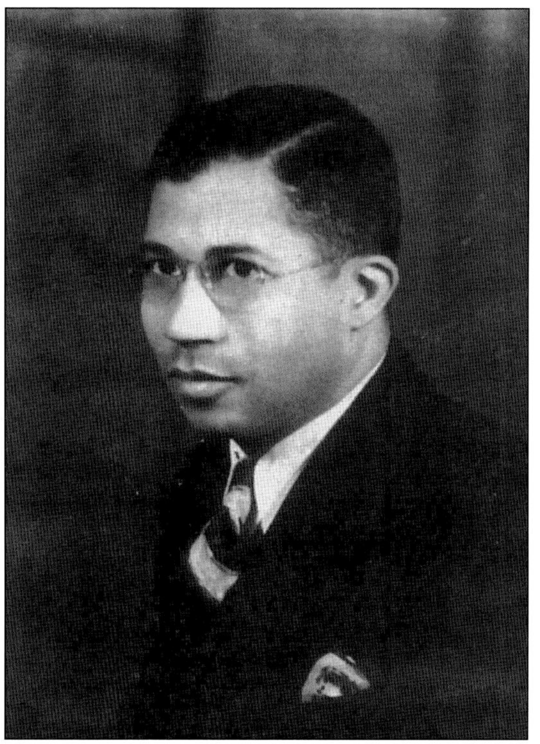

Turner Open Air School had many outstanding educators throughout its existence. Everett Colbert, pictured here, was principal from school years 1939–40 to 1952–53. (Photo courtesy of Berenice Colbert .)

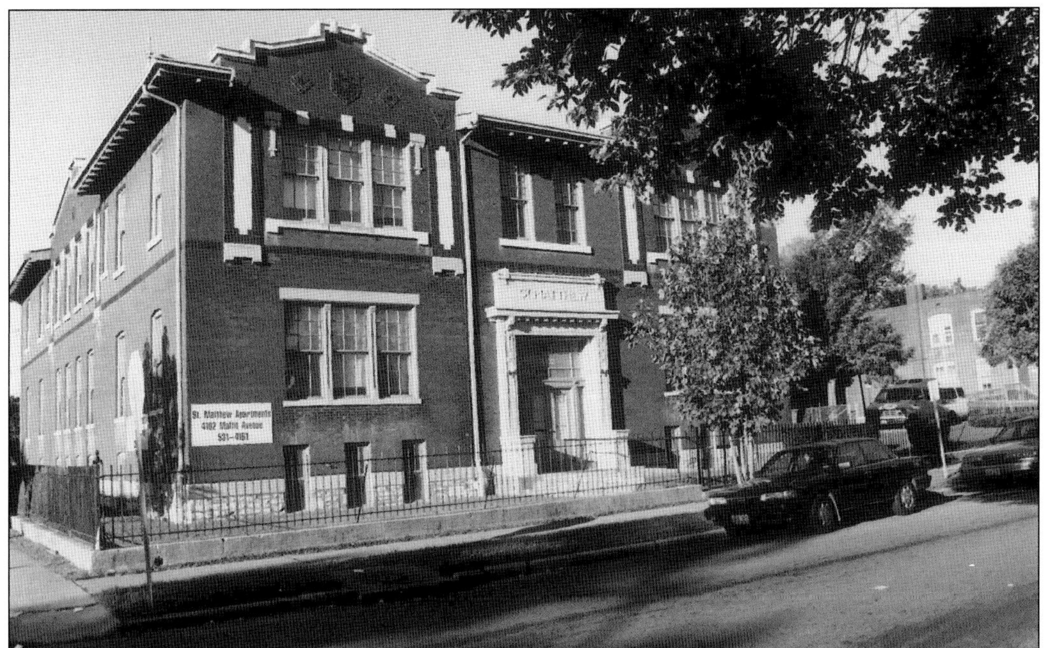

St. Matthew Elementary School opened in 1902 in a one story building designed for 100 students. As the parish and school grew rapidly, so did the need for constructing the school in this picture. Although the parish and school were in the community, the school's first African Americans did not enroll until 1951. (Photo by John A. Wright.)

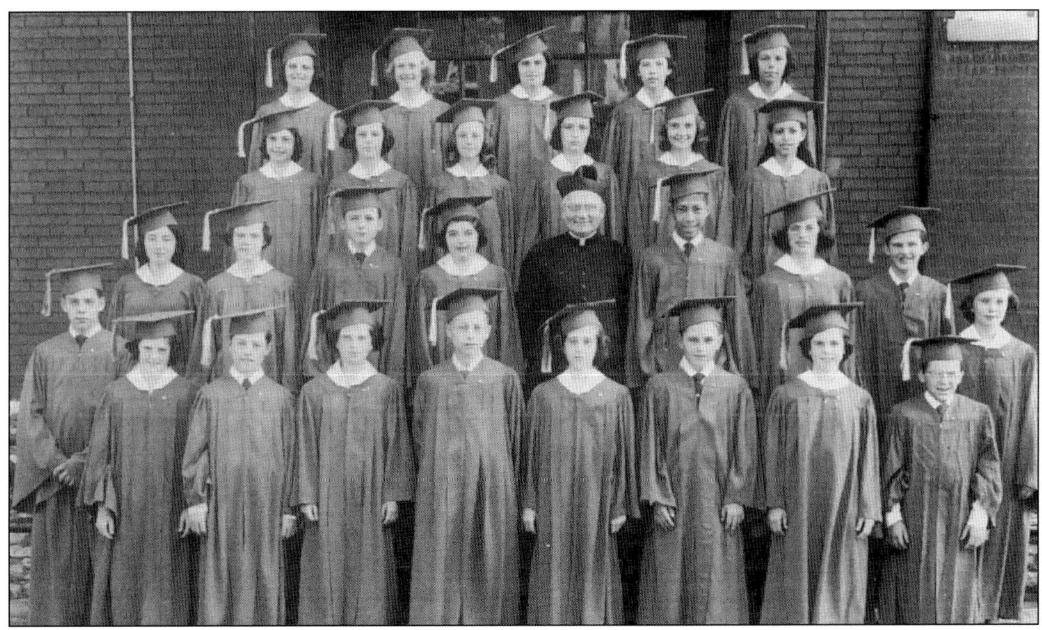

Father Craig is pictured here in 1953 with St. Matthew's first integrated class. When St. Theresa and St. Alphohsus Schools closed in 1959, their students were transferred to St. Matthew's. Sadly, in 1984, St. Matthew's was forced to close its doors when the parish could no longer support the parish school. (Photo courtesy of St. Matthew Catholic Church.)

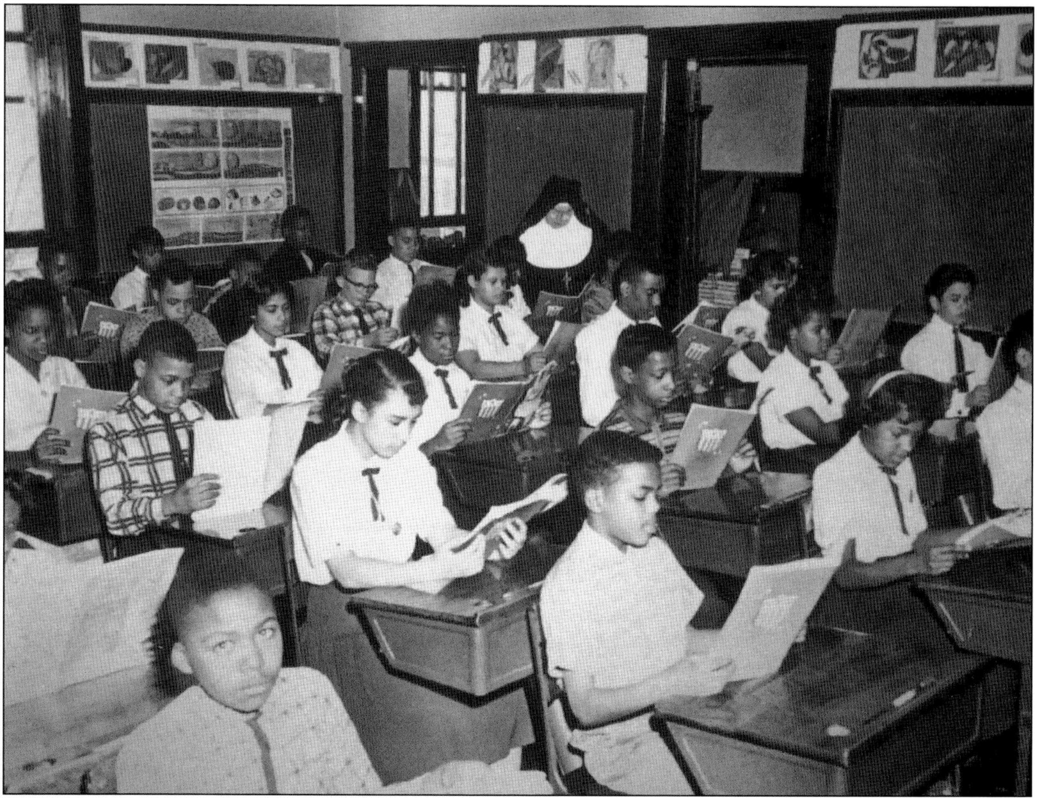

The students at St. Matthew's are pictured here with one of the Sisters of St. Joseph who staffed the school throughout its existence. The school's first principal was Sister Amarietta Jennings, C.S.J., and the last principal was Sr. Kathleen Murphy, C.S.J. (Photo courtesy of the Sisters of St. Joseph of Carondelet.)

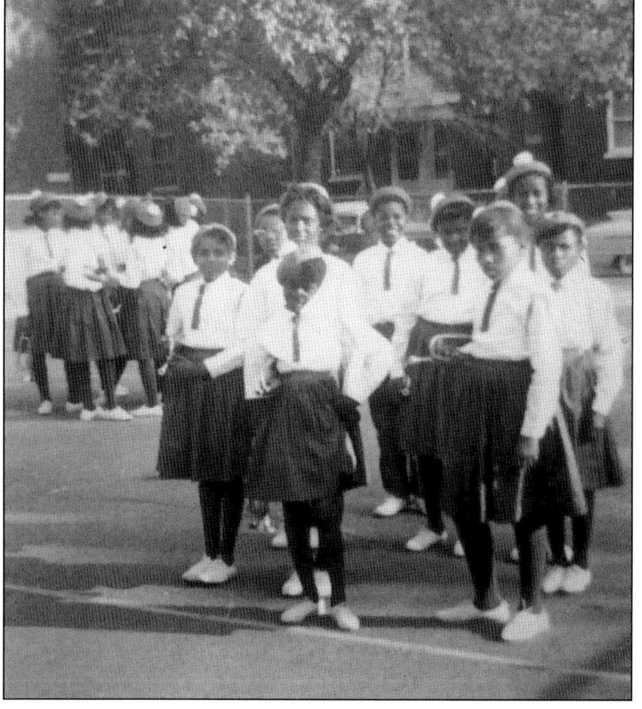

These students are part of St. Matthew's 1964 bugle corps. The corps was made up of the following members: Cassandra Gillmore, Diane Kelly, Anita Rena Allen, Janet Gugisha, Sheely Lee, Lydell Carter, Karen Wade, Joyce Stack, and Ronald Hill. (Photo courtesy of the Midwest Jesuit Archives.)

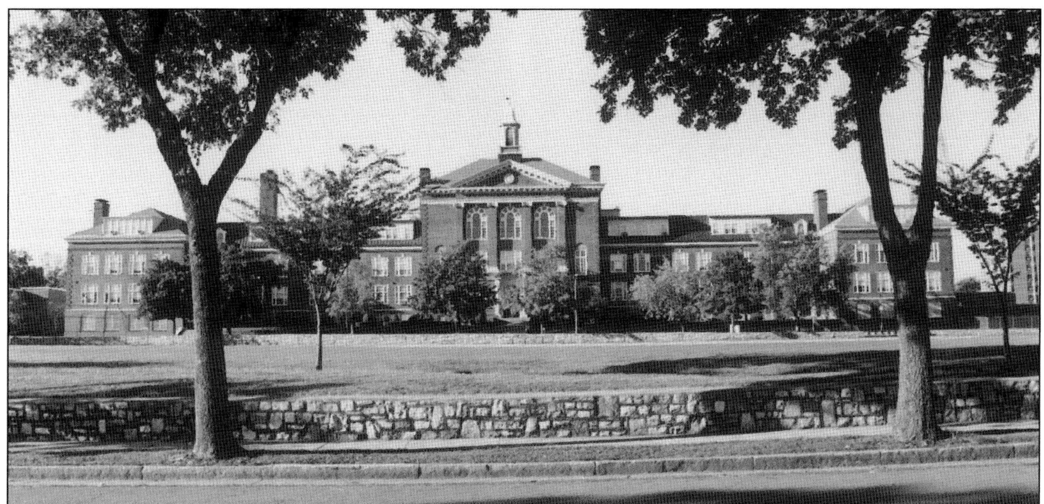

Sumner High School opened in 1875 as the first African-American secondary high school west of the Mississippi River. The school is named for Senator Charles Sumner who, in 1861, became the first prominent politician to call for full emancipation. To secure an education, African Americans came to The Ville from many county school districts to attend Sumner until 1954, when the Supreme Court made school segregation illegal. This picture is of Sumner at its present location, 4248 West Cottage Avenue. (Photo by John A. Wright.)

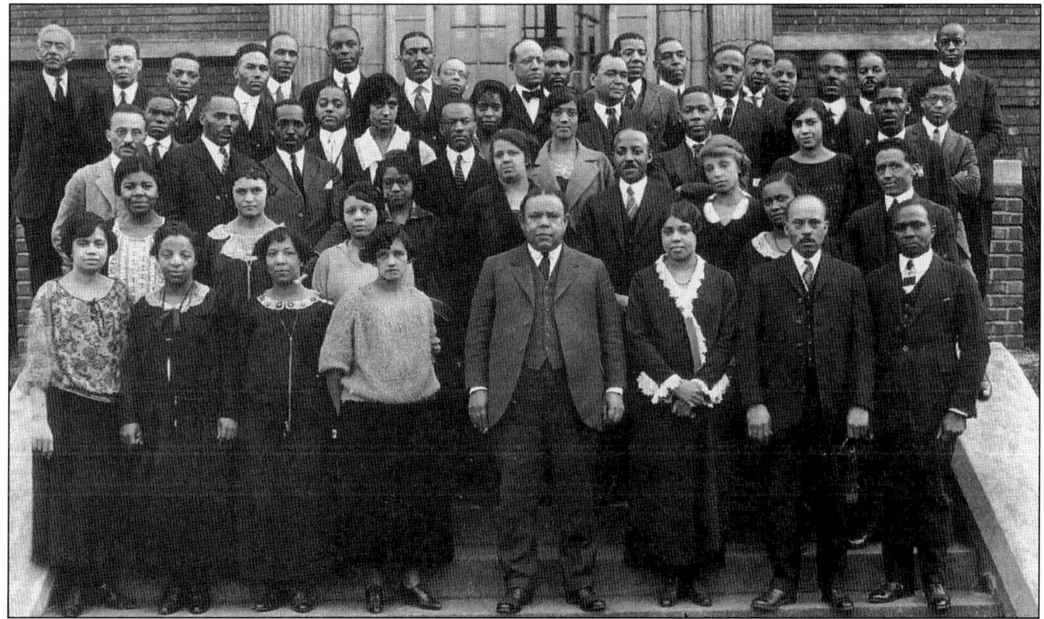

Because of limited opportunities for African-American professionals, Sumner High School attracted some of the best and brightest minds in the country. Frank Williams (fifth from the left in the first row) was principal of Sumner High School from 1908 to 1929. Williams sought and received two national affiliations in recognition of the excellence of the Sumner High School programs, namely accreditation by the North Central Association of Secondary Schools and Colleges, and membership in the National Honor Society. The Sumner chapter number 81 was issued in 1924. (Photo courtesy of St. Louis Public Schools.)

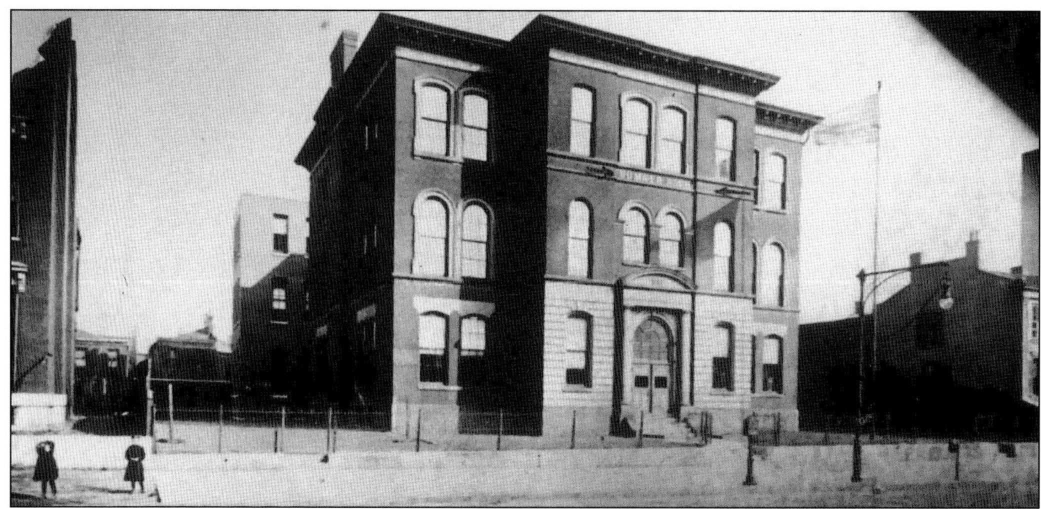

Sumner occupied two other locations prior to its move to The Ville. It was first located at Eleventh and Spruce streets and moved to the building in this picture at Fifteenth and Walnut streets during the 1894–95 school year. The school opened with 210 pupils, and had a graduating class of 27 in 1895. The building was an improvement over the earlier one, but it still lacked an assembly room, a gymnasium, a library, and other facilities. (Photo courtesy of the University of Missouri-St. Louis, Western Manuscript Collection.)

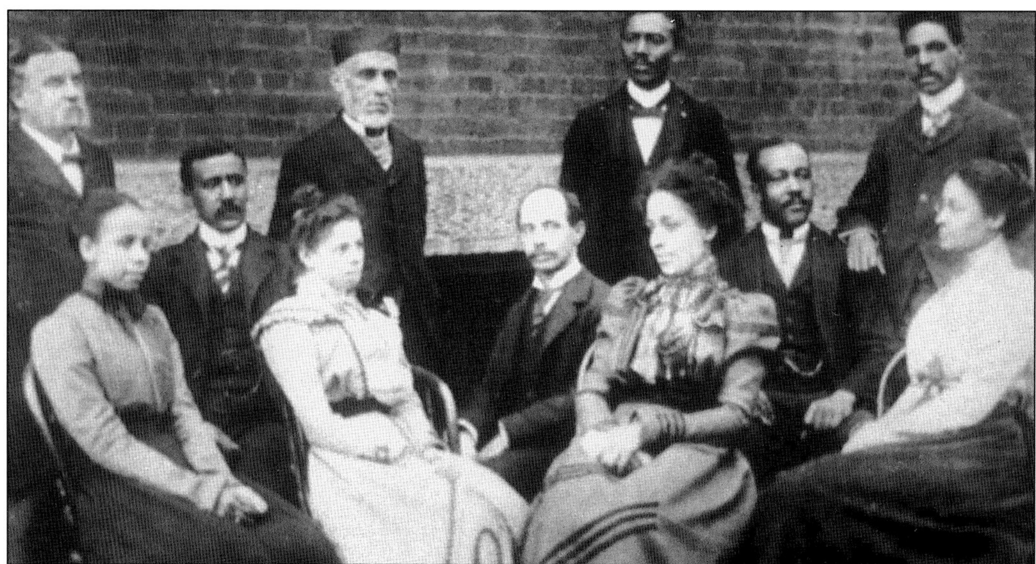

Sumner's 1900 faculty is pictured here, from left to right, outside the school: (seated) Araminta Parker, H.L. Usher, Alice Easton, D.J. Roberson, Helen Burrell, A.W. Scott, and Naomi Mitchell; (standing) Oscar M. Waring, P.H. Clark, A.J. Gossin, and E. Campbell. Oscar Waring, the principal, was one of the first blacks hired to teach in the public schools in St. Louis. In 1879, Waring became the first black to serve as principal of Charles Sumner High School. During his administration, John Pope and Emma Vashon were certified as the first graduates of the school. In 1890, Waring also established the Sumner Normal program to train teachers. (Photo courtesy of the University of Missouri-St. Louis, Western Manuscript Collection.)

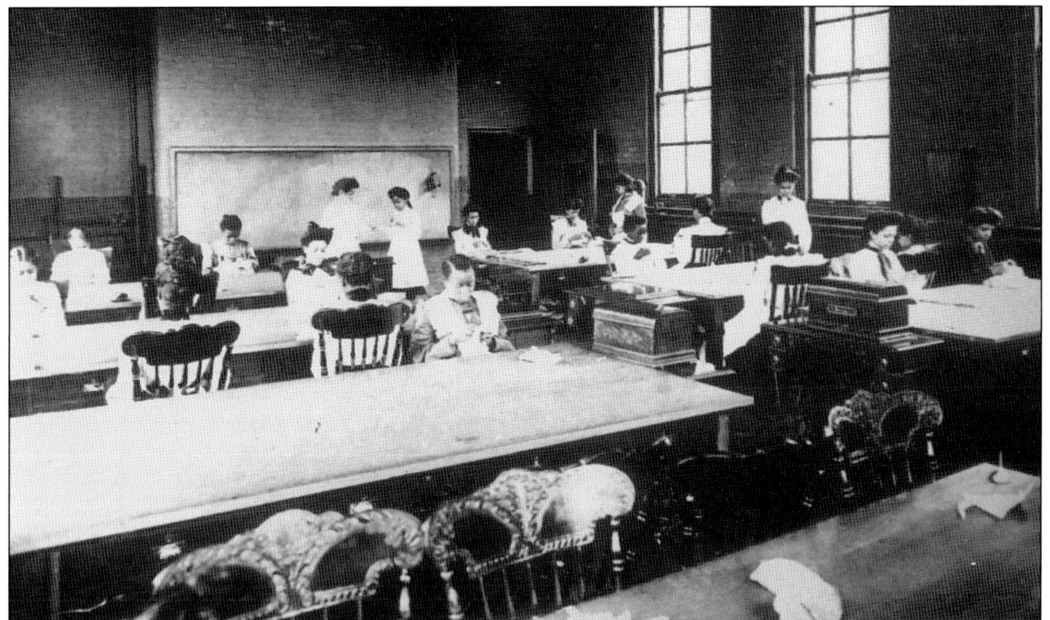

Sumner High School has offered a wide variety of course offerings to its students throughout the years. The students in this 1892 picture are involved in a sewing class. (Photo courtesy of the University of Missouri-St. Louis, Western Manuscript Collection.)

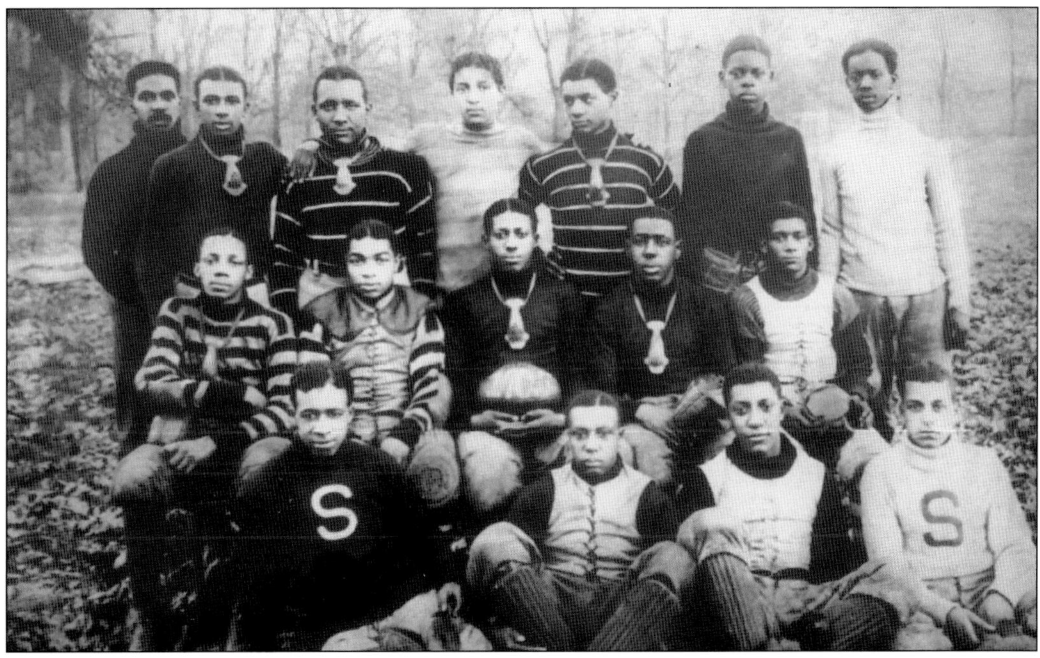

Football has been a vital part of Sumner High School's athletic program since 1900. In the early days, Sumner played colleges Fisk and Lincoln University. Lincoln was never able to beat Sumner. Eventually, the two schools met and Lincoln decided it was beneath the dignity of a college to play a high school. Members of Sumner's 1905 football team are pictured here. (Photo courtesy of the St. Louis Public Schools Archives.)

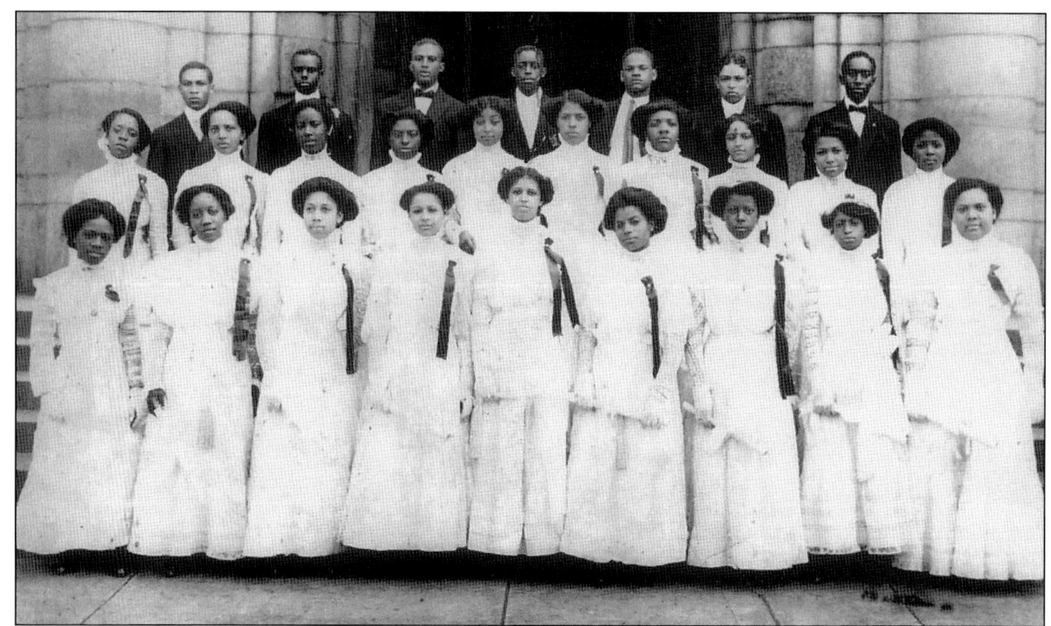

Pictured here is part of Sumner's 33 member graduation class of 1909. The graduates are, from left to right: (back row) George Overton, Robert Buck, Lorenzo Graham, Ira Williams, Walter Lowe, Artie Reed, and Earl Duke; (center row) Loveta Henson, Maudelle Clay, Edna Morrell, Eliza Hunt, Bessie Brown, Mabel Lewis, Sabra West Olivia Jones, Birdie Arbuckle, and Regina McMurray; (front row) Annabelle Dickson, Sarah Walker, Julia Davis, Irene Macklin, Percy Robinson, Lottie Wyatt, Emeely Harveson, Irene Kellogg, and Olive Thompson. By Sumners' 150th birthday in 1975, it had graduated 17,195 students. (Photo courtesy of the St. Louis Public Schools Archives.)

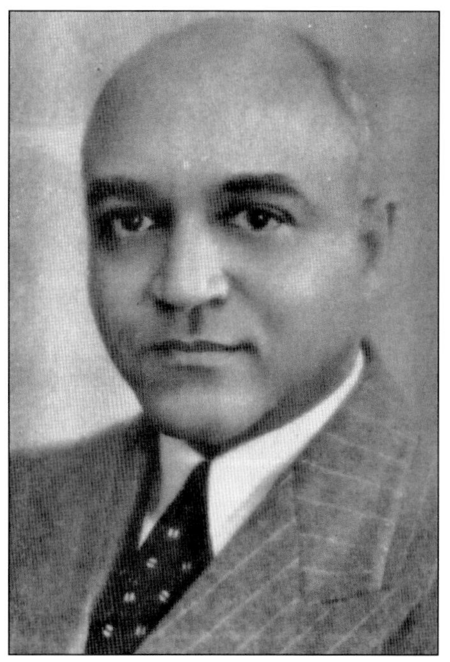

An early graduate of Sumner High School was Lester Walton, pictured here. Walton was appointed by Franklin D. Roosevelt as United States Minister to Liberia. While in St. Louis, he was a reporter on the old *St. Louis Star*, and one of two African Americans to hold such a position at that time with a St. Louis daily newspaper. He later found a position in New York on the liberal *New York World,* where he became a star reporter. (Photo by Nathan Young. Courtesy of the University of Missouri-Western Manuscript Collection.)

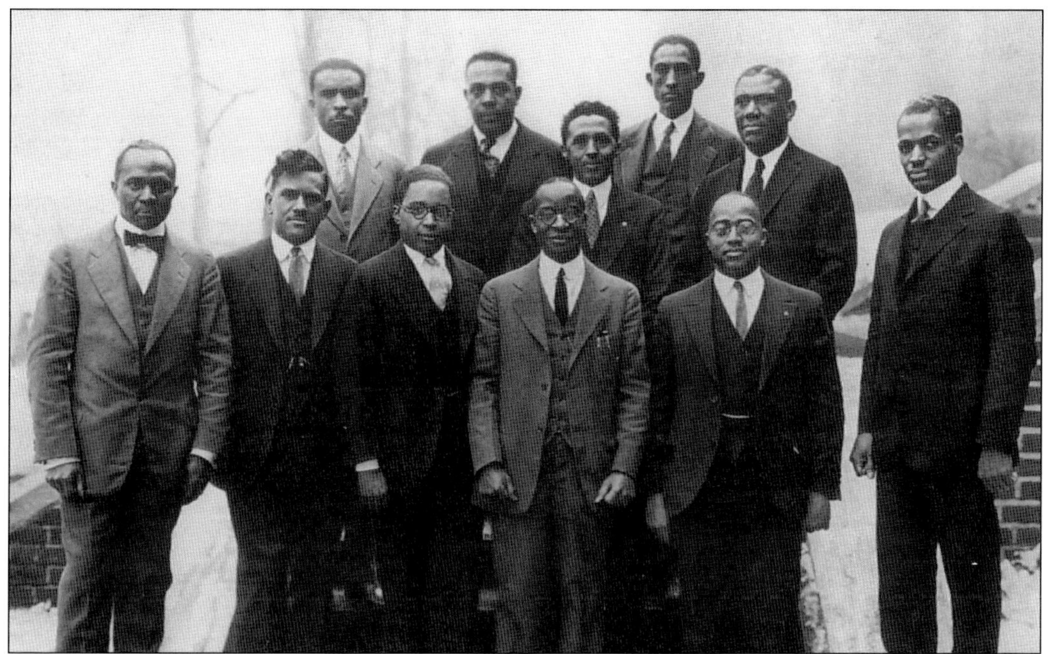

Sumner's male and female staff was known for their professionalism and professional appearance. Pictured here are members of the 1927 Faculty Glee Club. (Photo courtesy of the St. Louis Public Schools.)

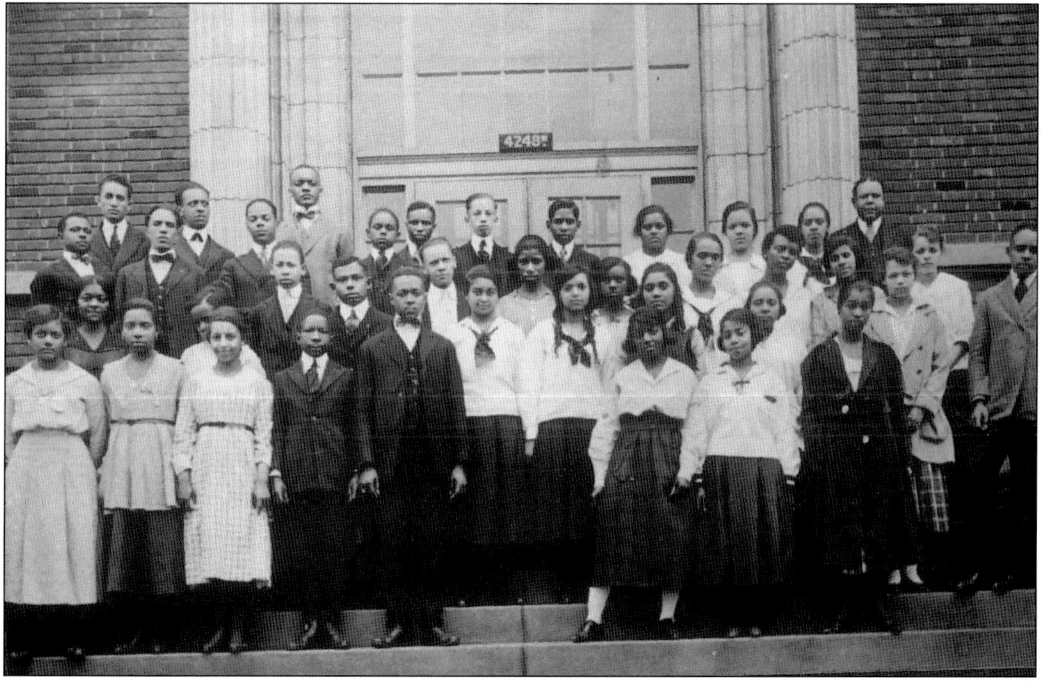

Sumner High School's students, like its faculty, were known for their dress and how they presented themselves. These well dressed students with their Principal Frank Williams (top row, far right) are part of the 1920 graduating class. (Photo courtesy of Berenice Colbert.)

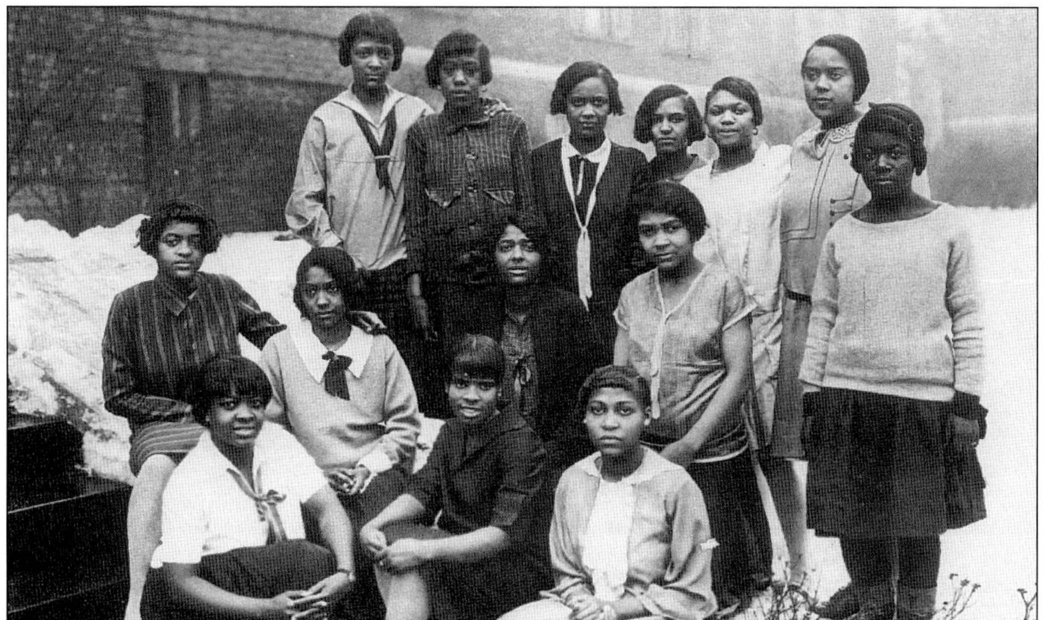

Sumner High School has provided many extra curricular activities for its students since opening in 1875. The girls pictured here in 1927 are members of the Modern Priscillas. (Photo courtesy of the St. Louis Public Schools.)

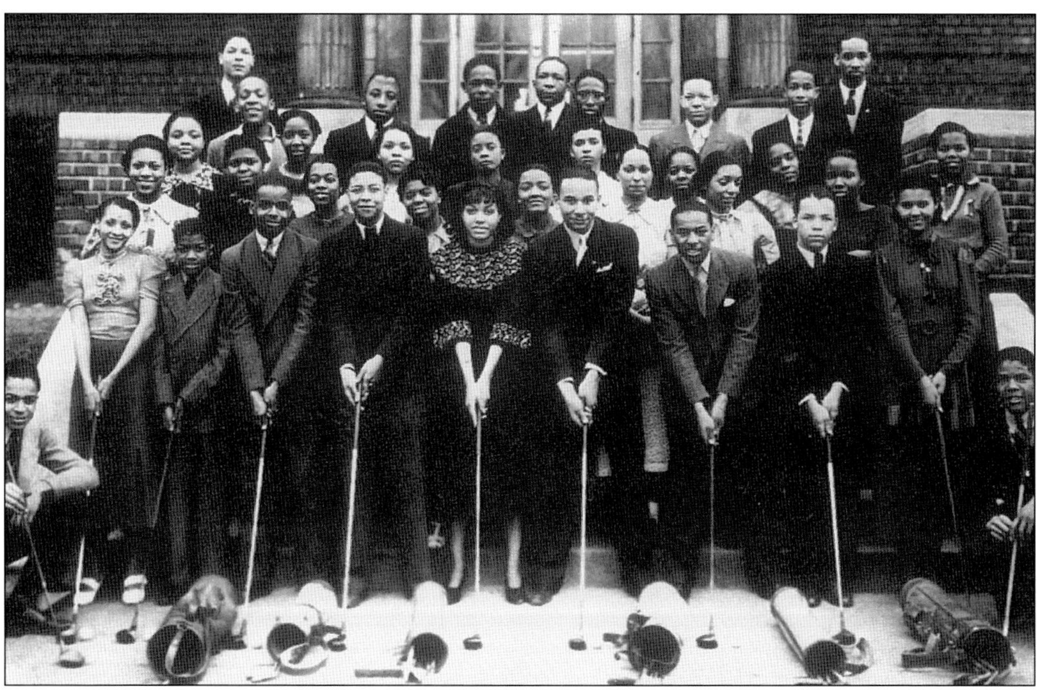

These African-American students were members of Sumner's 1938 Golf Club. Sumner students were provided with opportunities and exposed to learning that was not available to many students in other white or black schools. (Photo courtesy of the St. Louis Public Schools.)

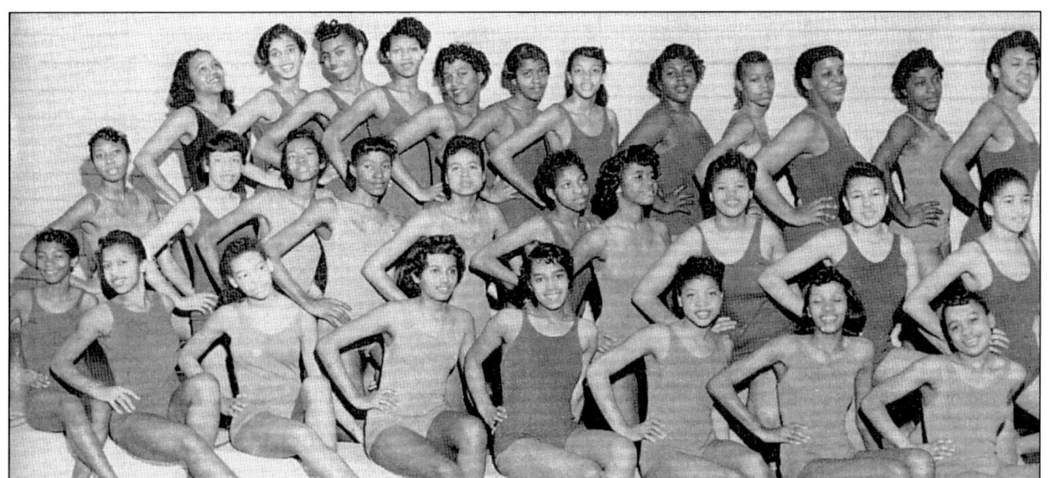

After the Sumner addition was added in the mid–1950s, swimming became an integral part of the curriculum. These girls are members of the 1958 Girls' Swimming Club that was organized in September 1957. They are, from left to right: (first row) Betty Garrett, Bernice Hamer, Rennee Adkins, (president) Geneva English, Doris Dangerfield, Mary Ellen Johnson, Joyce Henley, and Sylvia Overall; (second row) Brenda Buchanon, Barbara Tillis, Willetta House, Sylvia McConico, Reforce Jordan, Jane Cunningham, Jean Daniels, Alvetta Jackson, Barbara Green, and Evelyn Jacobs; (third row) Miss D.E. Owens, Karen Robinson, Fannie Davis, Patricia Byrd, Evelyn Bell, Azzie Lee Emerson, Nita Harris, Joan Gaines, Frances Brown, and Hattie Ballentine. (Photo courtesy of the St. Louis Public Schools.)

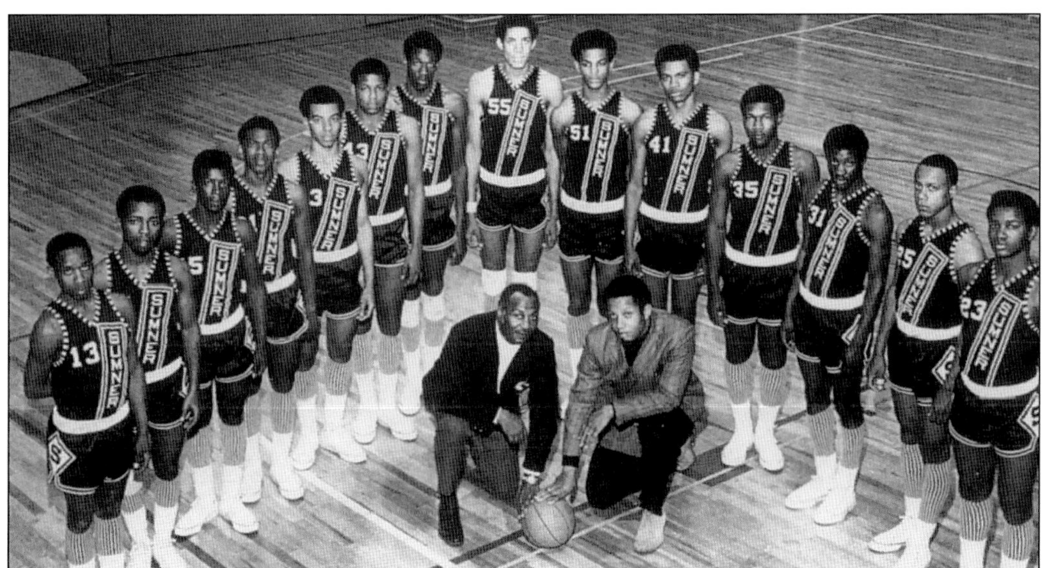

Under the leadership of coaches John Algee and Edward Clark, this Sumner Bull Dog basketball team continued to excel as the teams before them. Pictured here are the 1969–70 State Basketball Champions. Pictured, from left to right, are: (coaches) John Algee and Edward Clark; (team members) Emmett Costello, Lawrence Weathers, Jimmie Cook, Larry Burgess, Anthony Williams, Curtis DeBoe, Clarence Weavers, Davis Brent, William Westfall, Rickey Brown, Clarence May, Willie Battle, David Rupert, and Marshall Rogers. (Photo courtesy of the St. Louis Public Schools.)

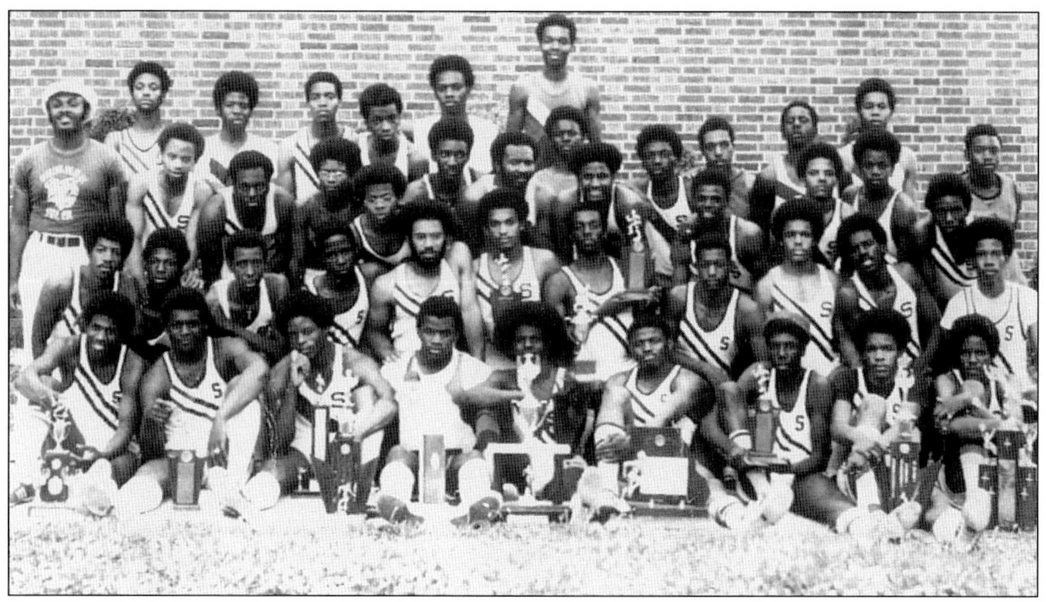

Pictured here is the 1974–75 Sumner High School track team which won the 1973–74 State Track championship. (Photo courtesy of St. Louis Public Schools.)

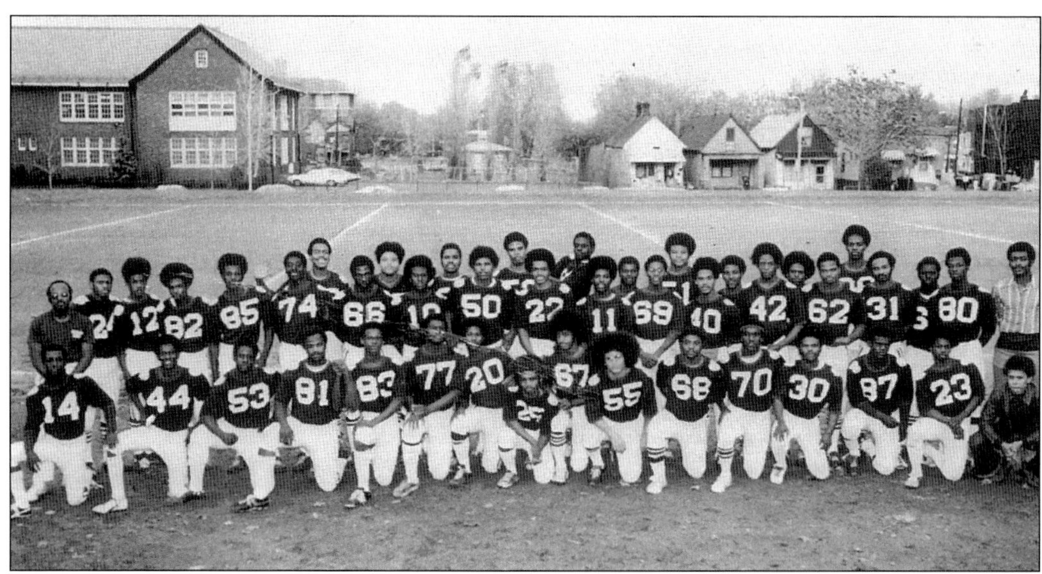

Sumner's 1973–74 State Football Champions are pictured here with their coach Lawrence Walls, a 1955 Sumner graduate. Under Walls leadership the Sumner Bulldogs won three state and numerous regional championships. (Photo courtesy of the St. Louis Public Schools.)

George Dennis Brantley, pictured here, was assistant principal of Sumner High School from 1927 to 1929, and principal from 1929 to 1968. He devoted 41 years of service to the pupils of Sumner High School, the longest tenure of any Sumner administrator. During his tenure, Sumner experienced a tremendous period of growth. In 1952, Sumner had an enrollment of 2,400 students, giving the school the largest secondary school enrollment in Missouri, and one of the largest in the North Central Association region. (Photo courtesy of the St. Louis Public Schools.)

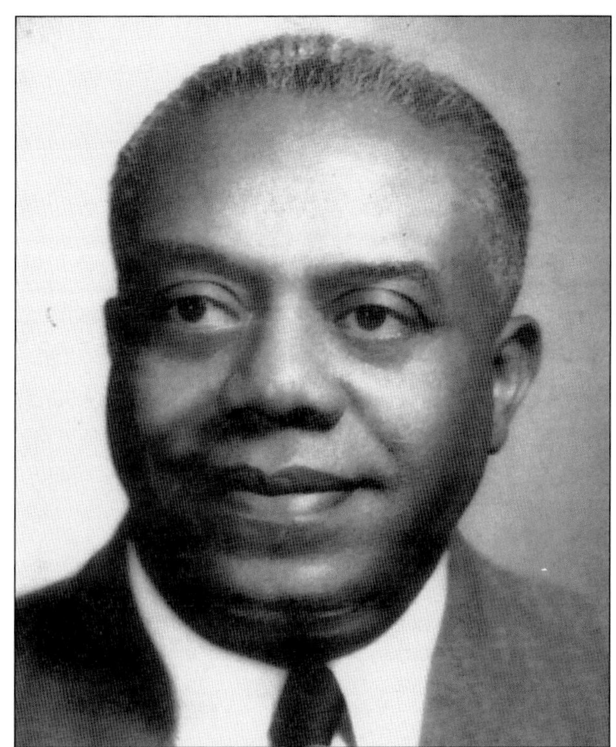

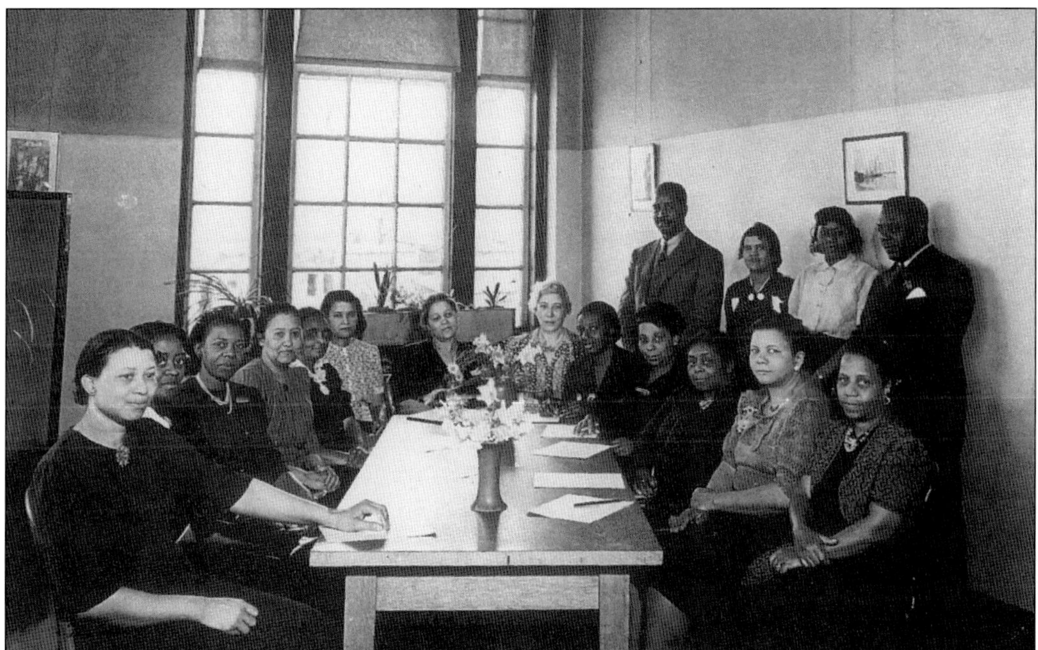

The Mothers Club at Sumner High School has always played a vital role in the school's operation by supporting its fund raising activities and scholarship funds. These women are some of the members of the 1940 Mothers Club. (Photo courtesy of the St. Louis Public Schools.)

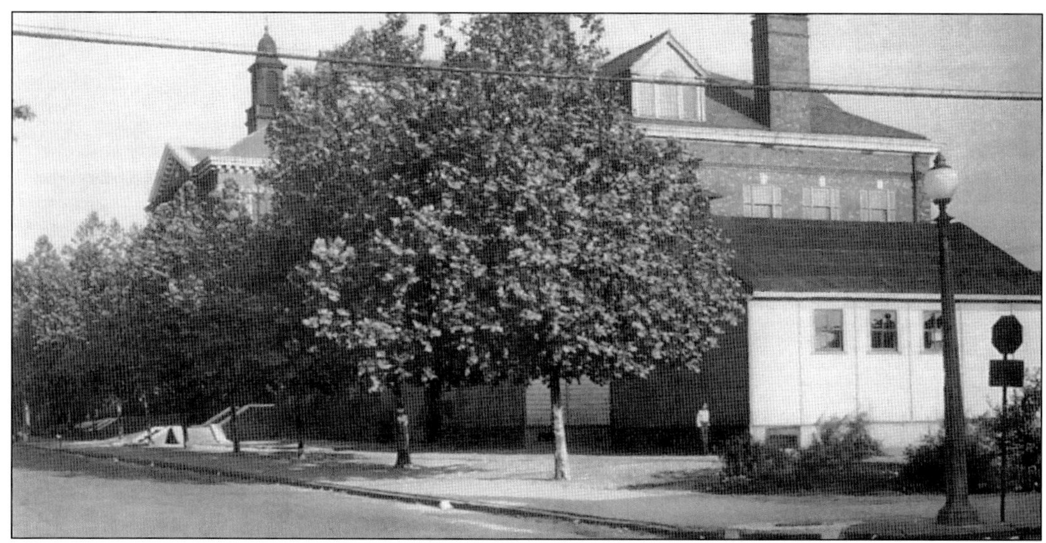

In 1914, nine portable classrooms were added to Sumner High School at Cottage and Pendleton avenues (now Billups Avenue). The facilities pictured here became the Cottage Avenue School, a demonstration school to train Sumner students who were attending Sumner Teachers College for teacher training. This college was the forerunner of Stowe Teachers College. In 1929, the college moved to the Simmons building and its name changed to Harriet Beecher Stowe Teachers College. (Photo courtesy of the St. Louis Public Schools.)

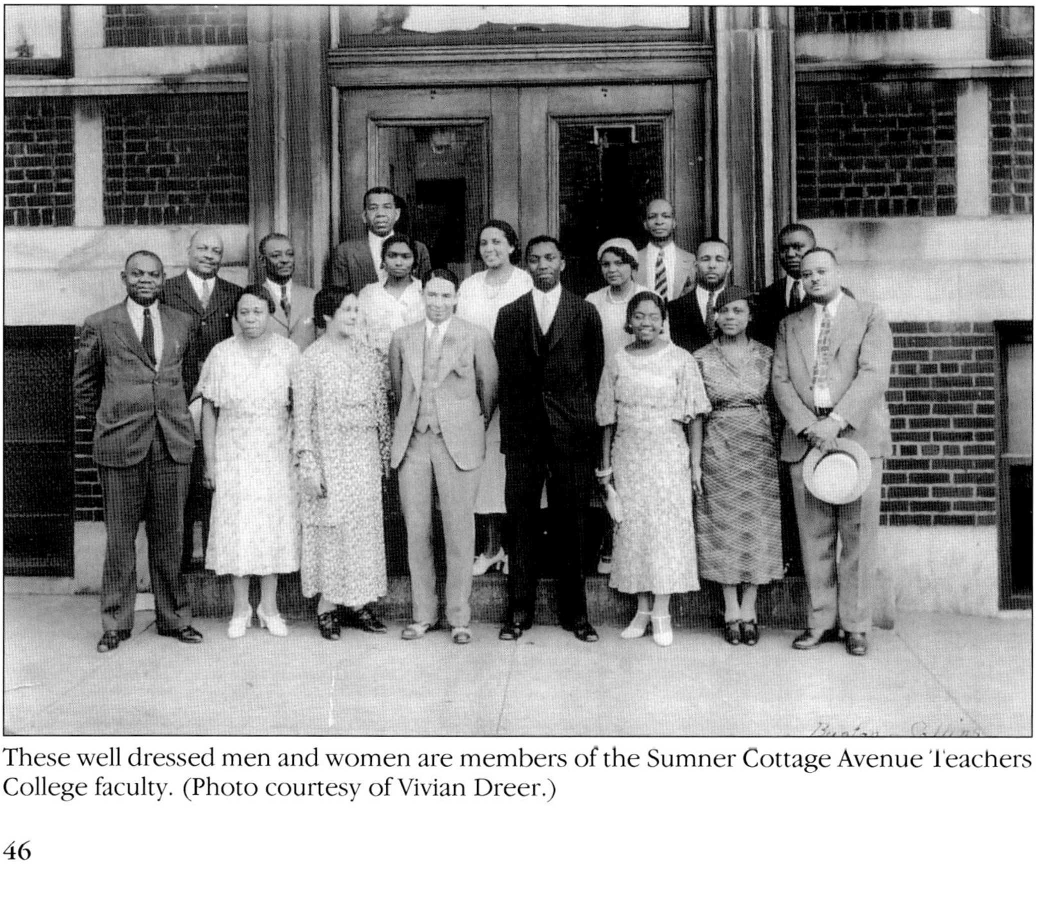

These well dressed men and women are members of the Sumner Cottage Avenue Teachers College faculty. (Photo courtesy of Vivian Dreer.)

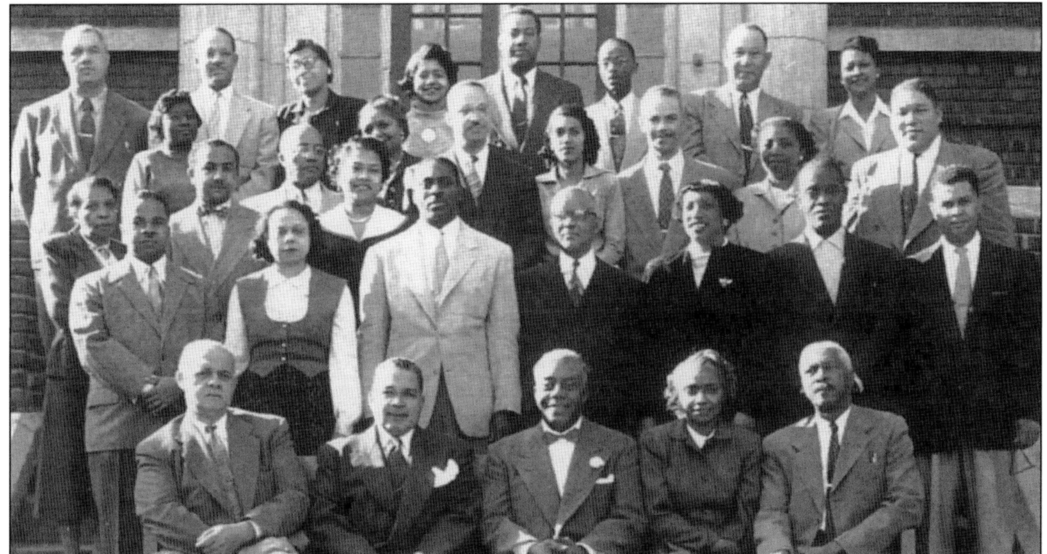

The members of Sumner's 1957 faculty pictured here, from left to right, are: (first row, seated) Mr. J.E. Anderson, Mr. A.S. Jackson, Mr. G.D. Brantley, Miss G.E. Crutcher, and Mr. C.H. Harper; (second row) Mr. N.C. Brown, Mrs. R.D. Hill, Mr. J.M. Brown, Mr. W.J. Beatty, Mrs. A.H. Fullwood, Mr. T.A. Catlin, and Mr. R.E. James; (third row) Miss G.R. Alford, Mr. J.W. Aldrich, Mrs. G.H. Freeman, Mr. P.D. Ingram, Miss A. Kimbrew, Mr. M.F. Lemmons, Miss M.E. Huff, and Mr. J. D. Buckner; (fourth row) Miss L.J. Bailey, Mr. U.S. Donaldson, and Mrs. A.C. Garrett; (fifth row) Mr. J.C. Carpenter, Mr. R.P. Carter, Mrs. C.W. Johnson, Miss E. Esters, Mr. K.B. Billips, Mr. M. Hamilton, Mr. E.T. Johnson, and Mrs. C.D. Davis. (Photo courtesy of John A. Wright.)

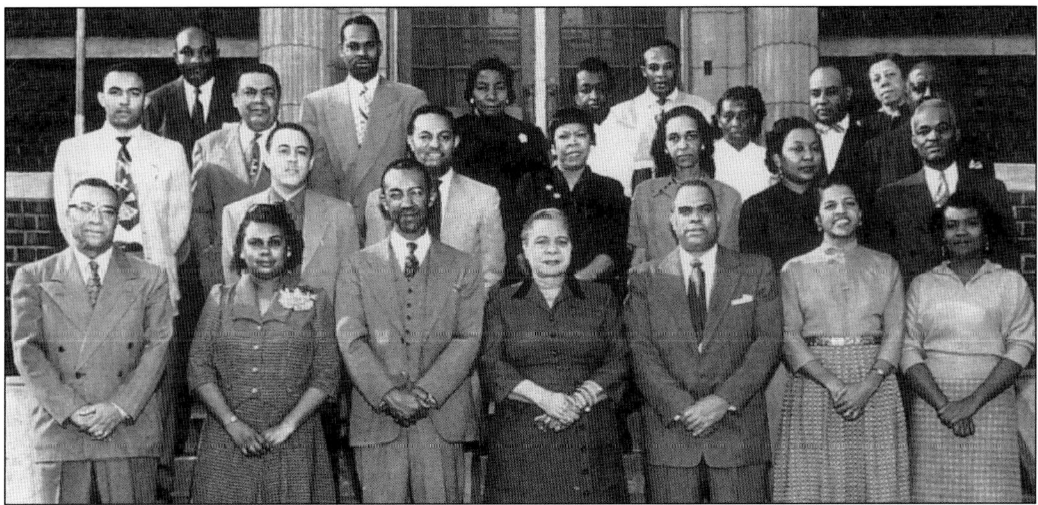

Other members of the 1957 faculty and staff are pictured here, from left to right: (first row) Mr. H. Payne, Miss J. Turner, Mr. H.C. Roberts, Miss M.C. Taylor, Mr. George Stafford, Mrs. M.N. Walker, and Miss A S. Harris; (second row) Mr. J.A. Whitfield, Mr. W. St. James, Mrs. S.G. Ward, Mrs. R.S. Morgan, Mrs. O.M. Perkins, and Mr. W.L. Skinner; (third row) Mr. E.V. Mosee Jr., Mr. G.P. Turnstell, Mr. J.E. Price, Miss W.E. Woods, Mrs. S.E. Smith, Miss H.J. Moore, Mr. J.A. Morrison, and Mr. W.L. Thompson; (fourth row) Mr. W.J. Brunson, Mr. W.L. McKinnie, and Miss N.E. Walton. (Photo courtesy of John A. Wright.)

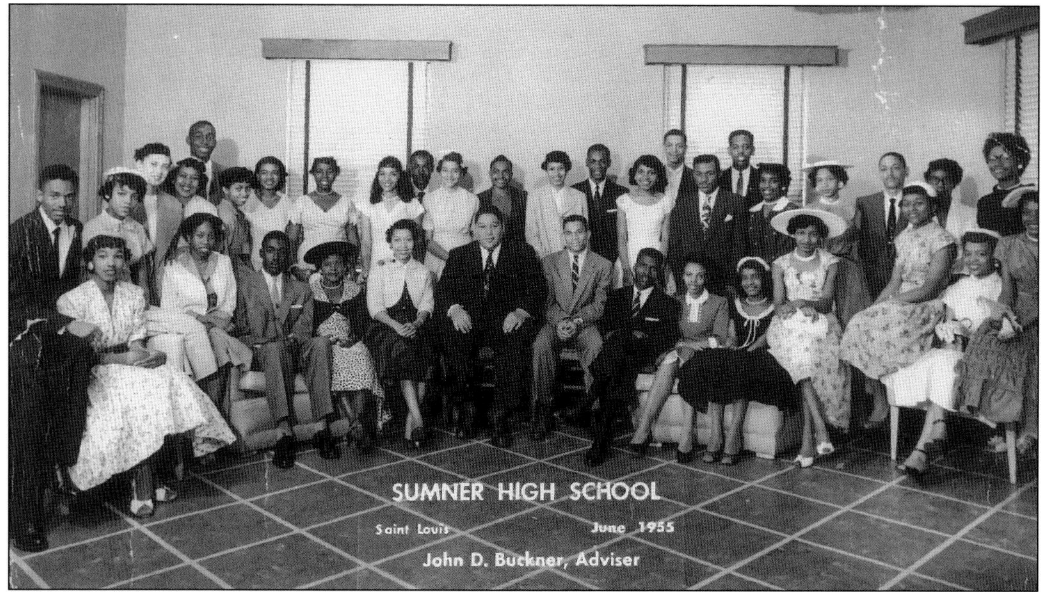

This group of students were part of a superior achieving students advisory program started by John Buckner in January 1952. The goal of the program was to encourage and prepare students to pursue higher education. Almost all of the students in this group continued their education and obtained advanced degrees. John Buckner, the advisor (sixth from the left), was one of the first male graduates of Stowe Teachers College. He later became principal of Sumner High School. (Photo courtesy of Sylvia Henley Wright.)

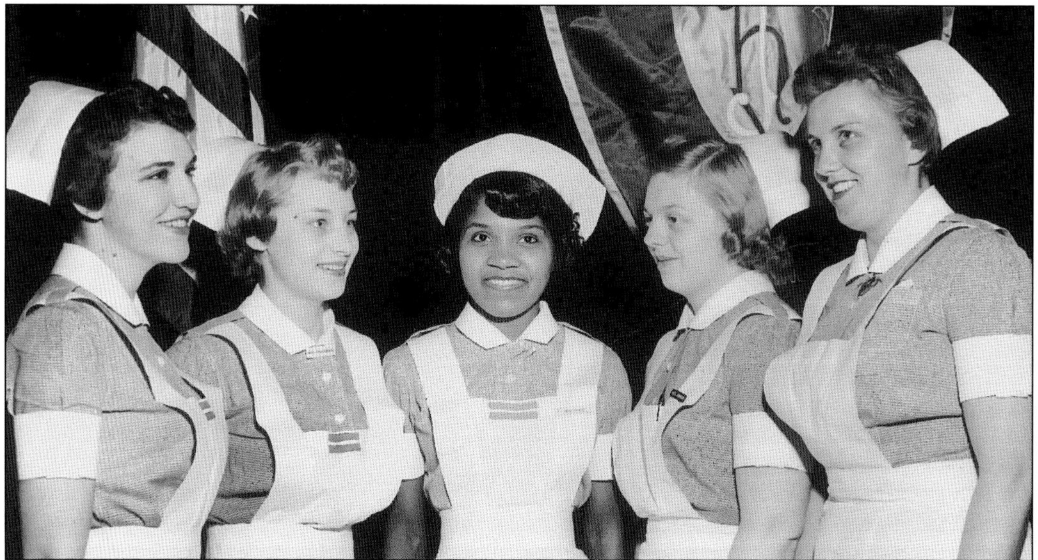

Pictured here is Sylvia Henley, one of the students in John Buckner's Accelerated Advisory Group. Sylvia was one of the first two African Americans to enroll in Jewish Hospital's School of Nursing in 1955. She later was elected student body president. After graduating from Jewish Hospital School of Nursing, she earned a B.S.N. and a M.S.N. in Psychiatric Nursing from Washington University, and a Masters in Education from the University of Missouri-Columbia. (Photo courtesy of Sylvia Henley Wright.)

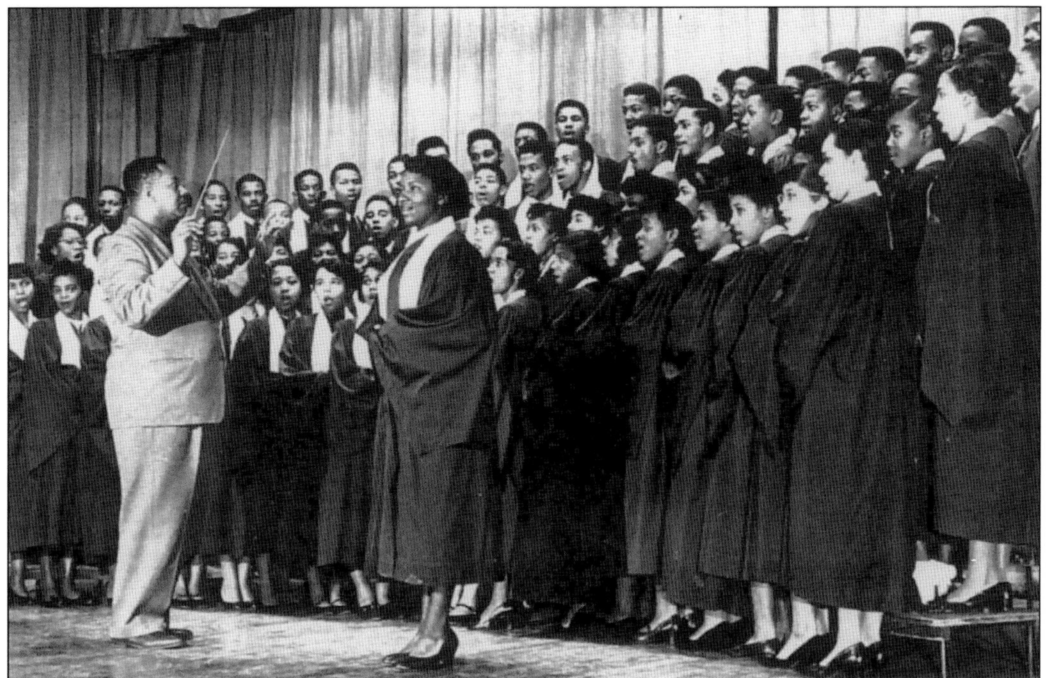

Faculty member Kenneth Billups is shown here directing the Sumner Acappella Choir with Grace Bumbry singing solo. Billups taught vocal music from 1943 to 1949 at Douglass High School in Webster Groves before coming to Sumner High School as the director of the Music Department. He was the founder and director of the Legend Singers, director of the Chancel Choir at Antioch Baptist Church, and president of the National Association of Negro Musicians. Pendleton Avenue in The Ville was renamed Billups Avenue in his honor. (Picture courtesy of St. Louis Public Schools.)

Sumner graduate Grace Bumbry, who lived at 1703 Goode Avenue (now Annie Malone Drive), pictured here, became an internationally acclaimed opera star. She gained national attention when she sang an aria on Arthur Godfrey's "Talent Scouts" television program. Ms. Bumbry's performance won her a scholarship to Boston University. She made her Carnegie Hall debut in 1962, and in the same year sang at a gala White House dinner given by President John F. Kennedy. (Photo courtesy of the St. Louis Walk of Fame.)

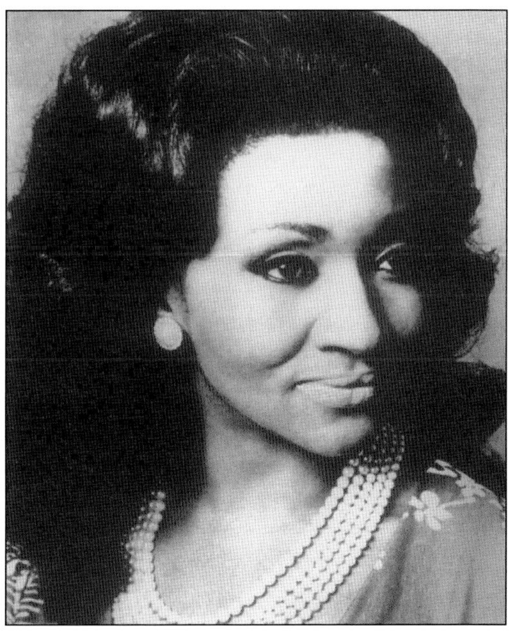

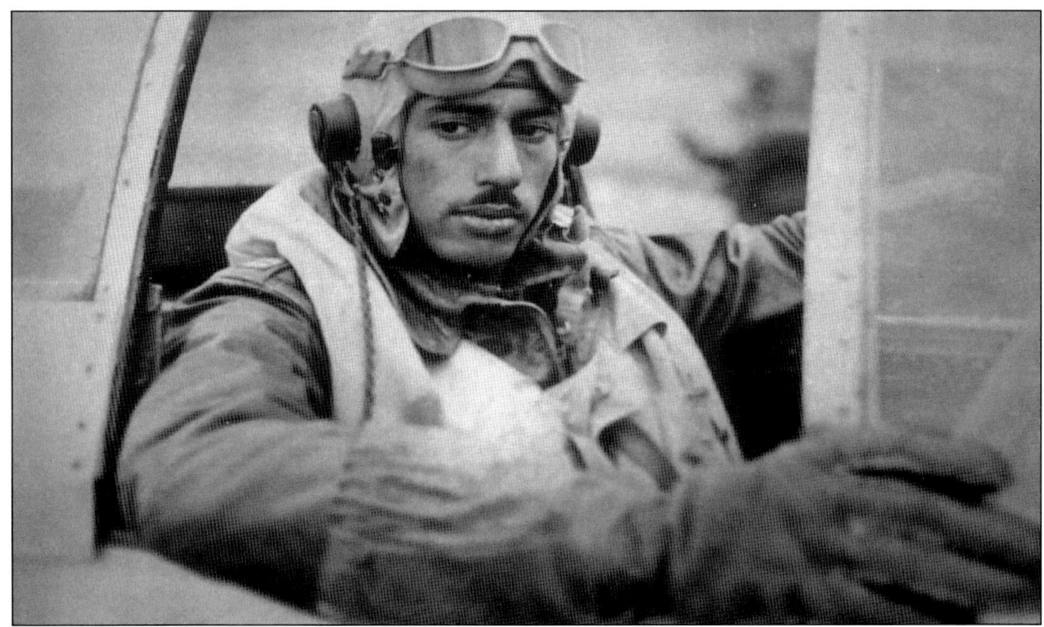

Sumner graduate Cpt. Wendell Oliver Pruitt distinguished himself as a member of the 32nd Fighter Group and the 99th Squadron. For his skill and courage in combat he was decorated with the Distinguished Flying Cross and the Air Medal with four oak-leaf clusters. Pruitt is pictured here in his plane. He can also be seen in the *Black Americans in Flight* mural at Lambert-St. Louis International Airport. Pruitt Military Academy in St. Louis is named in his honor. (Photo courtesy of Lincoln University.)

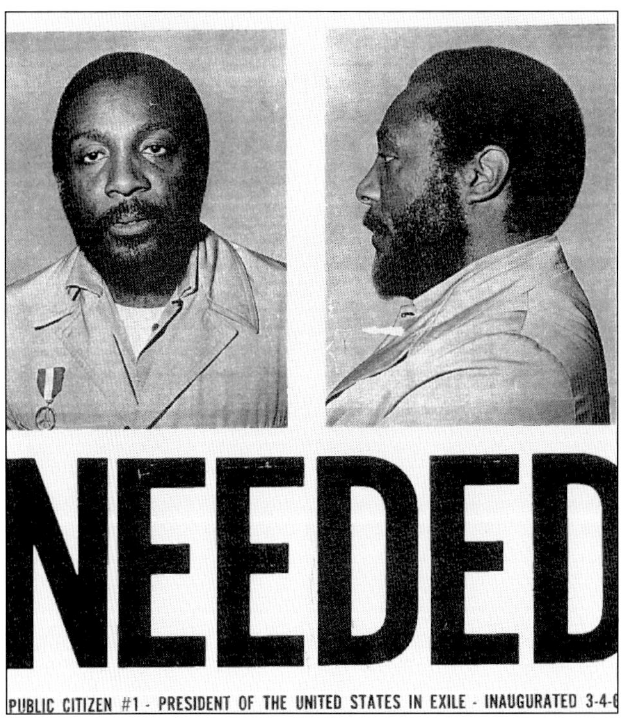

Richard "Dick" Gregory, another Sumner graduate, is seen here on his campaign literature when he ran in the 1968 presidential campaign. Gregory is a comedian, author, and entrepreneur. He has interrupted his successful stage career several times to fight for civil rights and the interests of African-Americans. Wagoner Street close to The Ville was renamed Dick Gregory Place in his honor. (Photo courtesy of John A. Wright.)

Rock n' roll great Chuck Berry was born at 2520 Goode Avenue (now Annie Malone Drive). While a student at Sumner High School he was a member of Antioch Baptist Church. Berry is pictured here with his guitar, an instrument that took him to the Rock and Roll Hall of Fame. Berry is known for many hits songs, including "Roll over Beethoven," "Maybelline," and "Johnny B. Goode." (Photo courtesy of St. Louis Walk of Fame.)

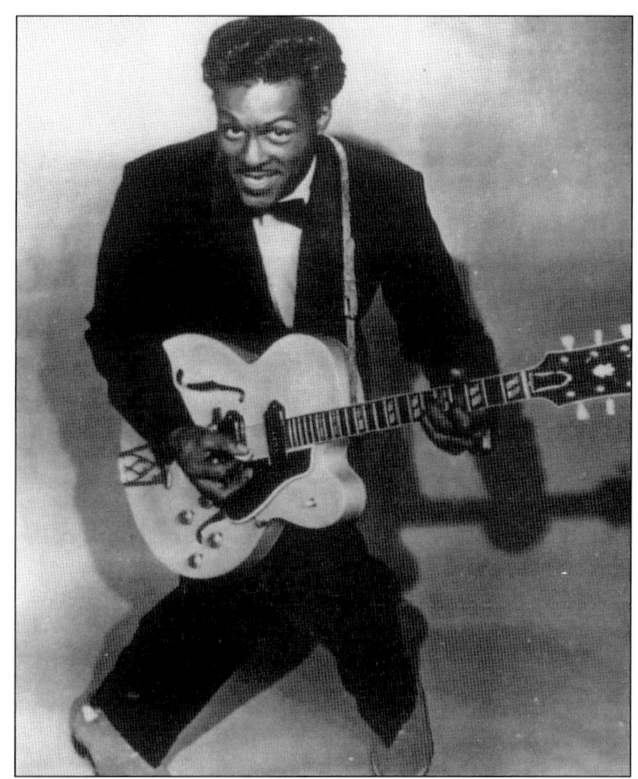

Members of the Fifth Dimension, founded by Sumner graduate LaMonte McLamore, was one of the most successful singing groups of the late 1960s and early 1970s. The group popularized a type of music that differed from the rock and roll images of their day. Member of the Fifth Dimension pictured here are: LaMonte McLamore and Ronald Townson, both Sumner graduates; Marilyn McCoo, Florence LaRue, and Billy Davis. (Photo courtesy of Willa and Lloyd Townson.)

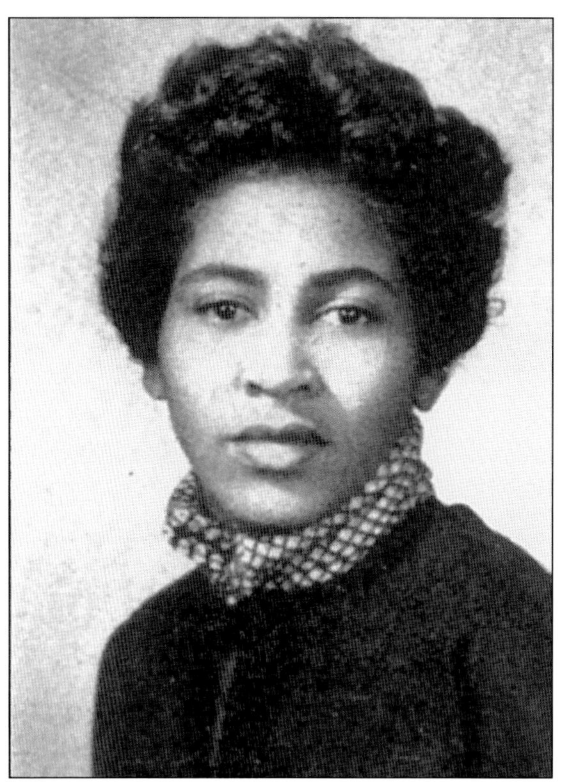

Tina Turner, the former Annie Mae Bulock, is pictured here during her high school years as a Sumner High School student in the late 1950s. Turner went on to become an internationally known popular singer, dancer, and actress. As a teenager, she began singing with Ike Turner's "King of Rhythm" in East St. Louis, Illinois. Her career took off after her solo album in 1984 *Private Dancer* which sold more than 10 million copies around the world, and her follow up album, *Break Every Rule*, which sold over a million copies. (Photo courtesy of Joyce and Andrew Pruitt.)

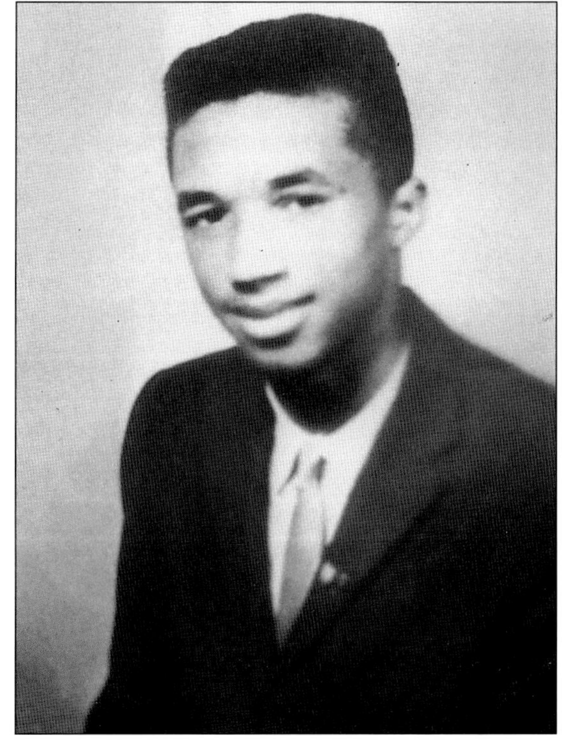

This young man is Authur R. Ashe, one of the greatest tennis players. Ashe came to St. Louis to attend Sumner High School and to be tutored by Richard Hudlin, a Sumner faculty member. Hudlin was the first black team captain at the University of Chicago. After graduation, Ashe went on to win the United States Hard Court Singles Championships, including the Wimbledon in 1975, and the Davis Cup. (Photo courtesy of St. Louis Public School Archives.)

Julius Hunter, the award winning St. Louis news anchor for the CBS KMOV-Channel 4, is a Sumner graduate and one of the city's best known faces. He has earned countless awards for journalism, including five St. Louis Emmy Awards. Hunter is the only St. Louis reporter, and one of the few journalists in the nation, who has conducted exclusive television interviews with five United States presidents. He is also the author of five literary works, and has conducted a variety of musical groups including the St. Louis Symphony. (Photo courtesy of the St. Louis Public Schools Archives.)

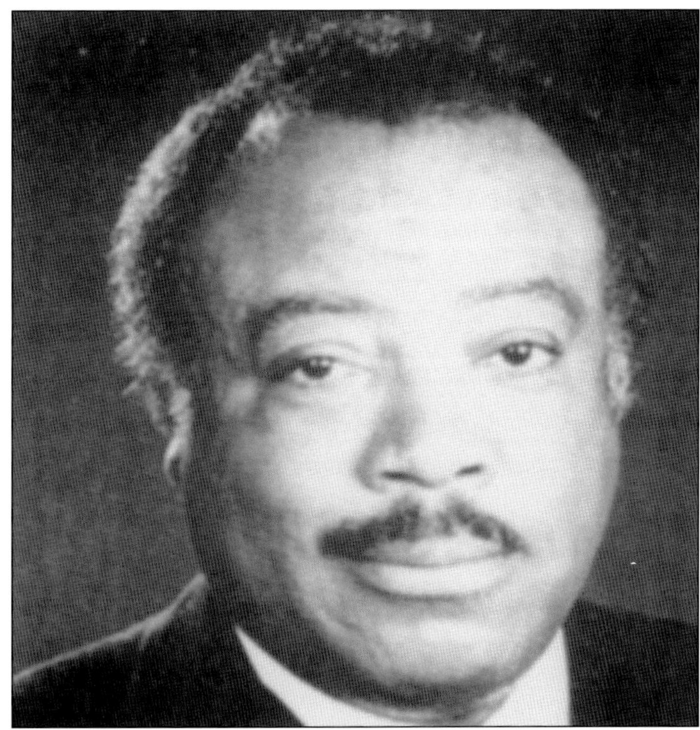

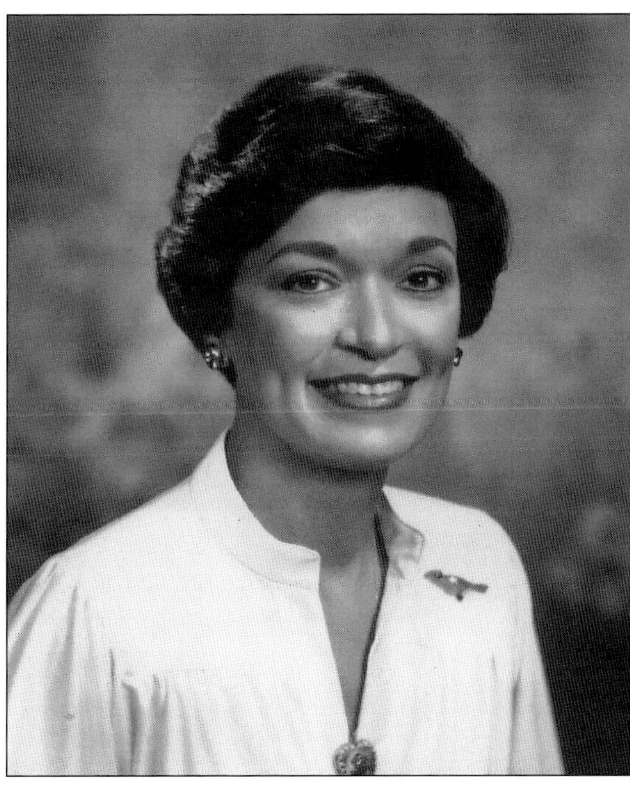

Sumner graduate Dianne White, shown here, is known as a pioneer in breaking down racial barriers in St. Louis. She was the first African-American model at major St. Louis department stores, including Stix-Baer and Fuller and Saks Fifth Avenue. In 1962, she became the first African-American television meteorologist in the nation. Her career at KSDK-TV spanned more than 26 years from features to hard news. (Photo courtesy of Dianne White.)

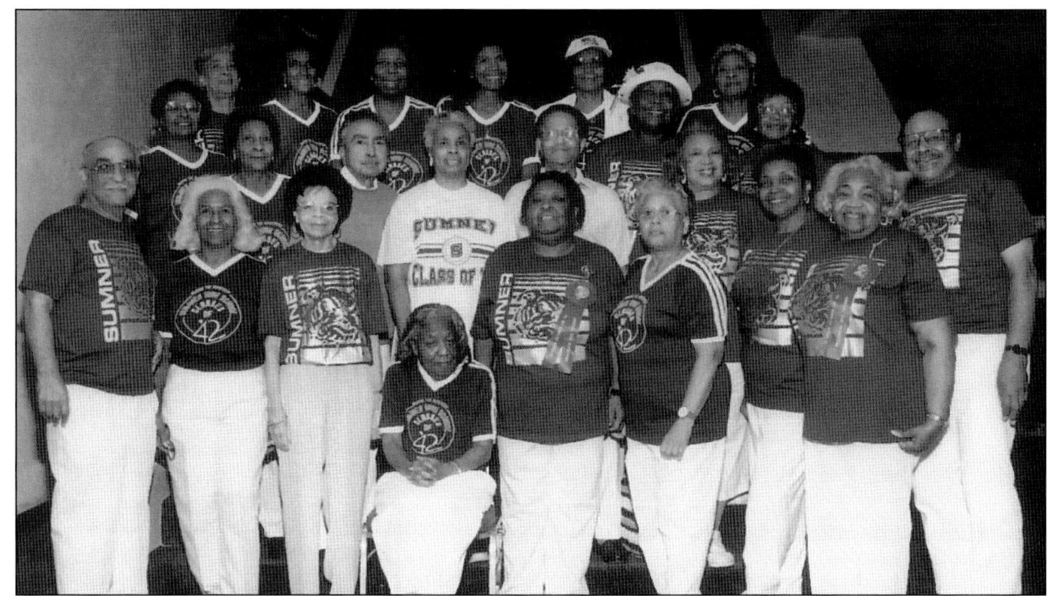

Once a Sumner graduate always a Sumner graduate. These members of the classes of 1942 above, and 1957 below, have come together on a regular bases since graduation to enjoy each other and reflect on their special place in time at Sumner High School. Most have gone on like others before them to assume leadership roles in the community. Members of the 1942 class above are, from left to right: (first row) Bertram Jones, Billy Phillips, Virgina Brown, Alese Hammonds, Virgina Morris, Juanita Webb, Marion Mitchell, and Amina McPherson; (second row) Audrey Gooch, Almarie Bunn, Donald Hammonds, Ethel Price, Raymond Hammond, Mary Virgina Carwell, and Al Lane; (third row) Caroline Fischer, Marie Taylor, Doris Toney, Hazel Lee, Olivia Malone, Arzella Abernathy, Ardella Lewis, and Clothilde Garrett. (Top photo courtesy of Hazel Lee, and bottom photo courtesy of John A. Wright.)

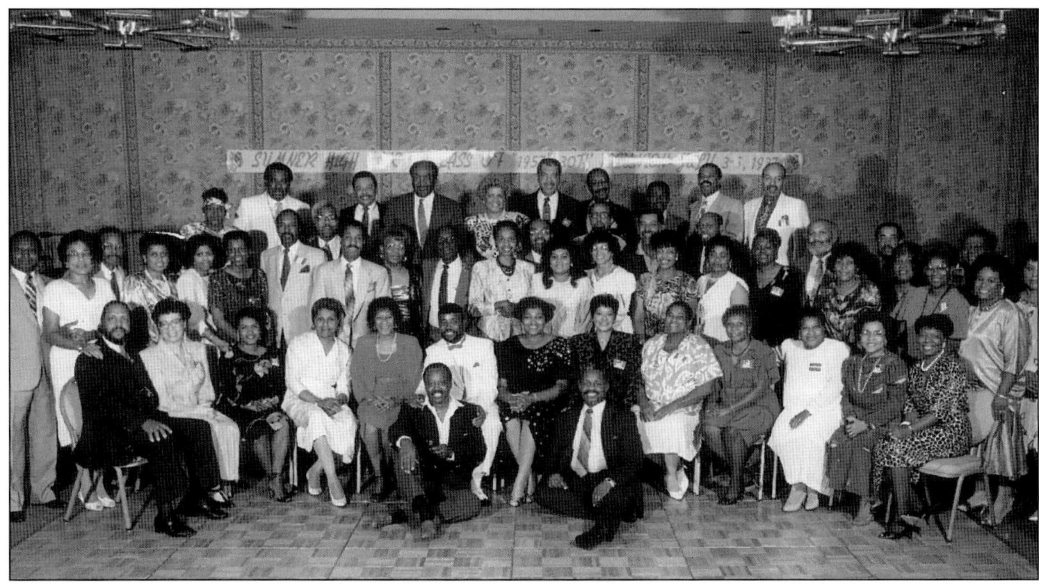

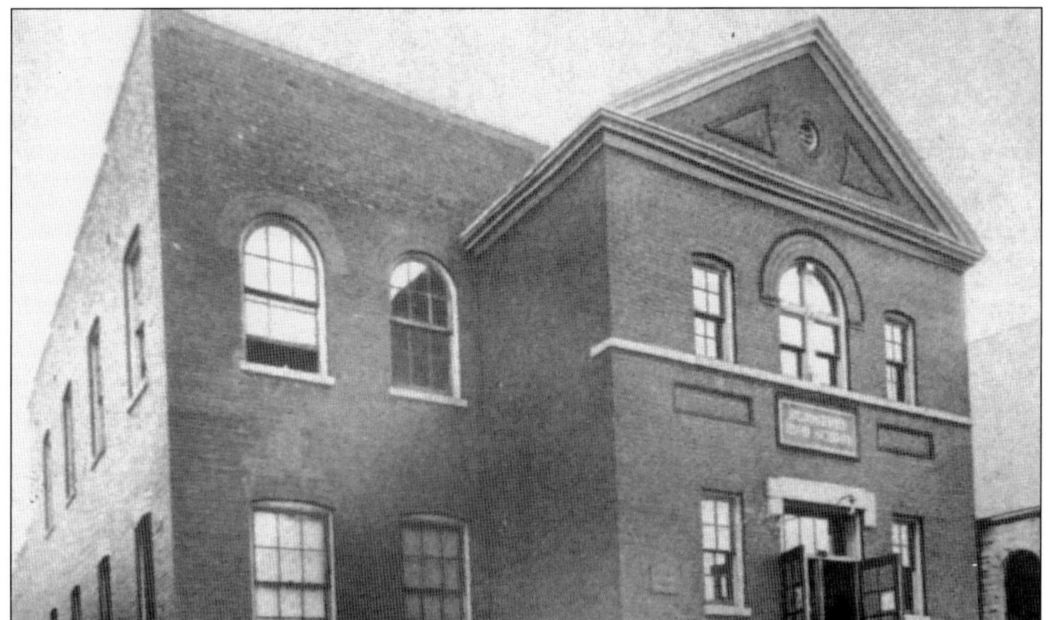

While Sumner High School had been available for African-American pubic school students since 1875, there was not a Catholic high school open for African-American Catholic students in St. Louis or St. Louis County until St. Joseph's High School opened in 1937. The school opened at Father Dunn's Newboys Home, with two Sisters of St. Joseph of Carondelet and 13 students. It later moved to 3954 West Belle and finally to 4132 Page Blvd., the building in this picture, to accommodate its swelling enrollment in 1939. (Photo courtesy of the Sisters of St. Joseph of Carondelet.)

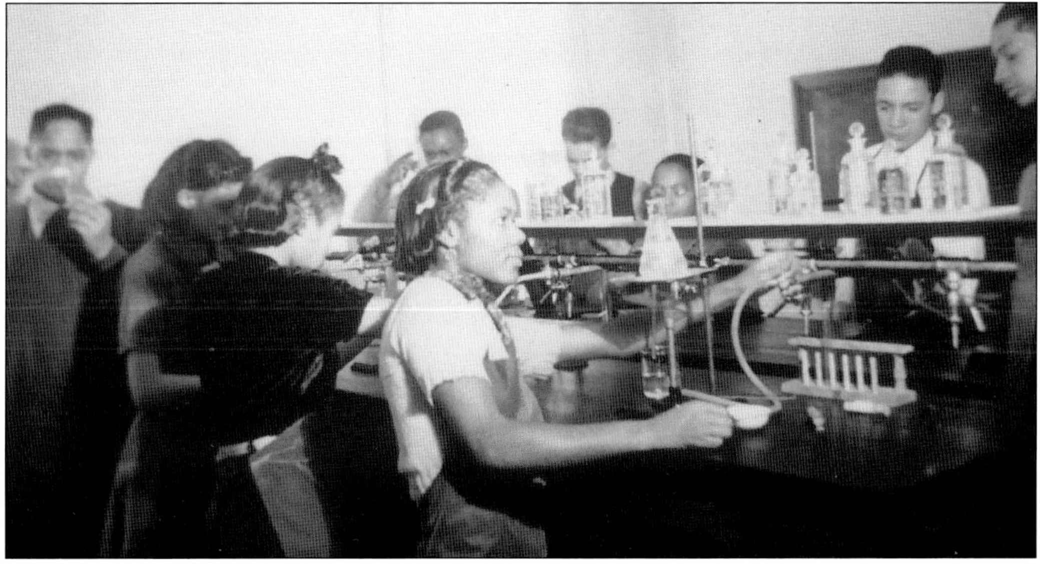

After the school got fully underway more and more courses were added to the curriculum and by the 1940–41 school year, St. Joseph became the first accredited four-year high school for Catholic African Americans in the state of Missouri. The students in this picture are working in the science laboratory. (Photo courtesy of the Sisters of St. Joseph of Carondelet.)

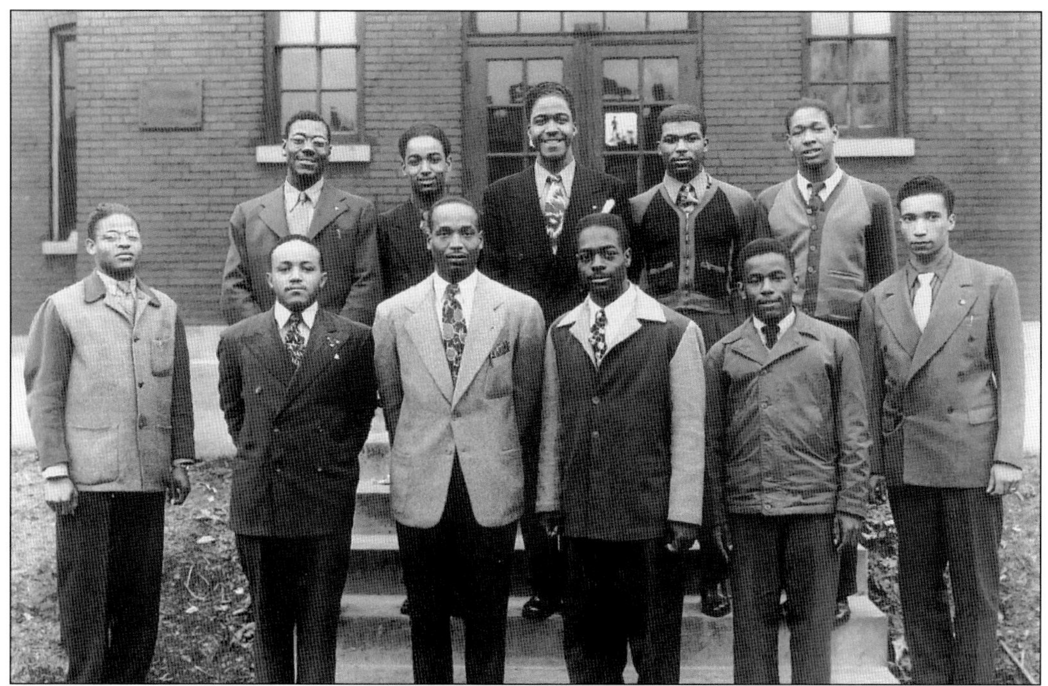

The veterans in this photograph returned to St. Joseph to complete their high school education. (Photo courtesy of the Archdiocese of St. Louis Archives.)

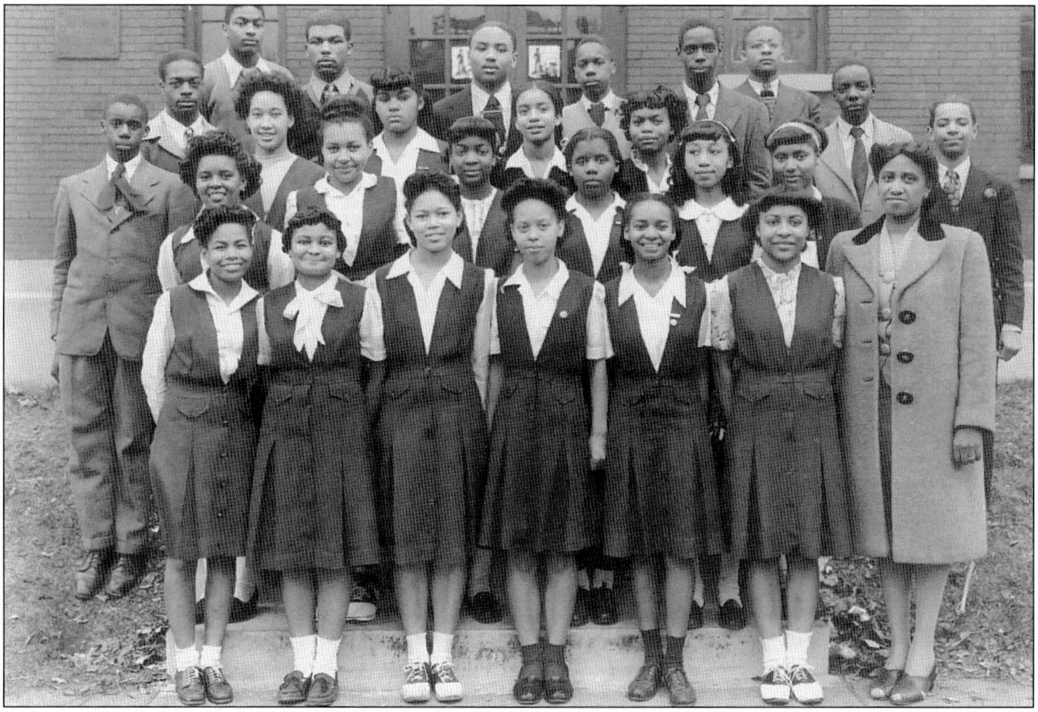

Members of the St. Joseph's High School Choir are pictured here outside of the school with their teacher, Thelma Lewis. (Photo courtesy of the Archdiocese of St. Louis Archives.)

Through the efforts of Father Patrick J. Malloy who coached the boys in sports, St. Joseph's played a dramatic part in opening integrated activities between schools. This is a copy of a letter Father Molloy received from the Missouri High School Athletic Association which stated they were unaware they were approving integrated athletics. (Document courtesy of Monsignor Patrick J. Malloy.)

H. R. DIETERICH, Pres.
Maryville
JAMES F. MILLER, Vice-Pres.
Gideon
CARL BURRIS, Sec'y-Treas.
Clayton
H. R. SHEPHERD
Kansas City
LESLIE V. CAHILL
St. James
CLYDE W. McCONNELL
Ozark
DAVIS H. ACUFF
Clarence
J. S. MAXWELL
Warrensburg

MISSOURI STATE HIGH SCHOOL
ATHLETIC ASSOCIATION

Member National Federation of State
High School Athletic Associations

CARL BURRIS, Secretary
P. O. Box 312
Office Phone, PArkview 8231
Res. Phone, PArkview 0734

CLAYTON (5), MO.

Sept. 26, 1944

Rev. P. J. Molloy,
St. Joseph High School,
St. Louis, Missouri

Dear Mr. Molloy:

Receipt for your dues is enclosed herewith.

I think the way we made the mistake on the location of your high school was that we were assuming it to be in the County the same as the church from which you are accustomed to write me. We know of course that 4132 Page is in St. Louis. We shall keep it correct in the future.

Yours truly,

Carl Burris

Carl Burris, Secretary

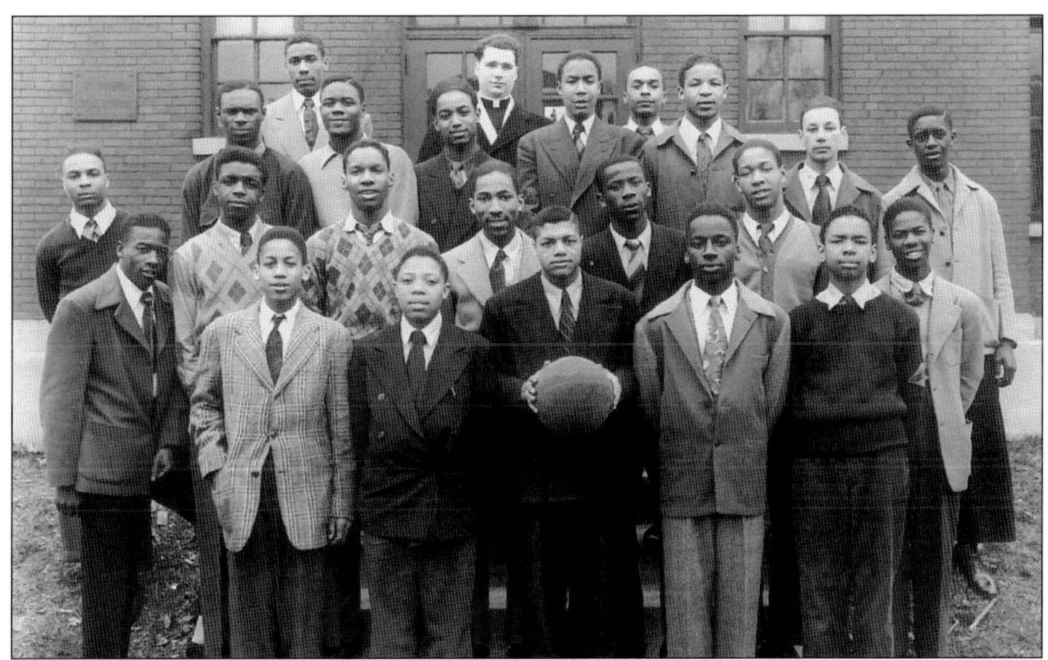

St. Joseph's High School eventually became the home of the first African-American basketball, baseball, football, and track teams in integrated high school competition. The school was also the place where the first African-American team gained membership in the Missouri State High School Athletic association, and the first African-American basketball team to compete in a state tournament with 550 other teams, all white. Pictured here are members of St. Joseph's 1946 basketball team. (Photo courtesy of the Archdiocese of St. Louis Archives.)

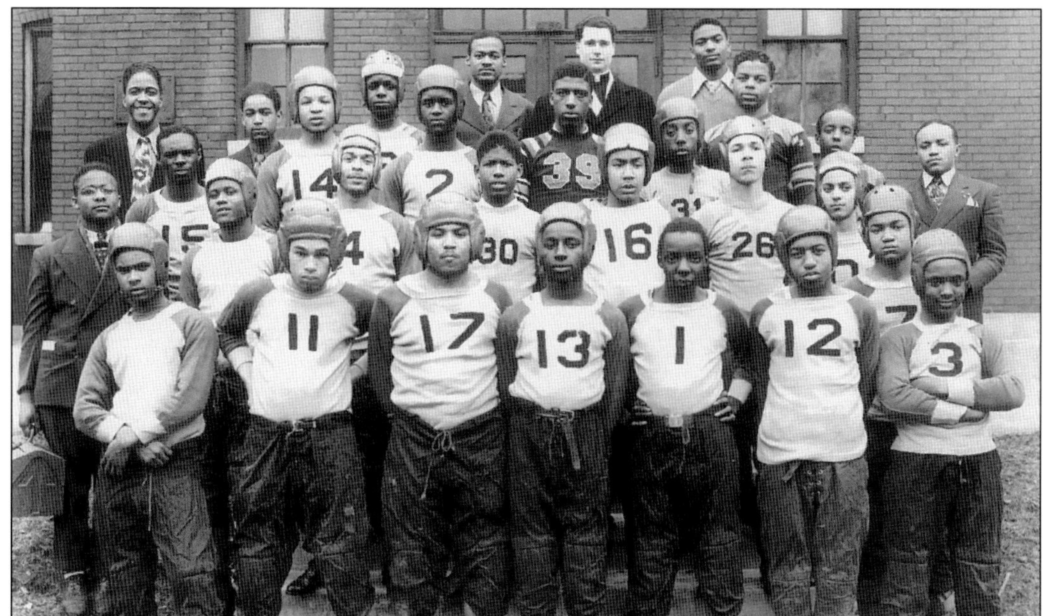

Father Patrick Malloy was able to get St. Joseph's into the Catholic School's League by asking its members to vote by mail instead of at a meeting on St. Joseph's admission to the league. Many members had feared for their jobs. The vote passed when members were able to keep their vote a secret. Members of the 1946 St. Joseph's football team are pictured here outside the school with Father Patrick J. Malloy. (Photo courtesy of the Archdiocese of St. Louis Archives.)

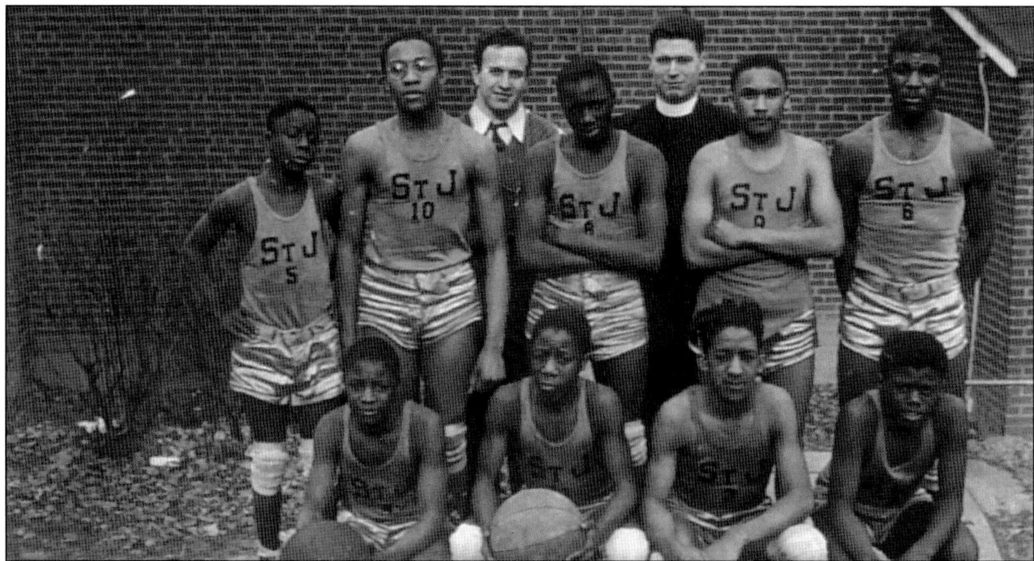

Pictured here are members of St. Joseph's basketball team with Father Patrick J. Malloy. From left to right, they are: (first row) Finis Massey, Joe Quinn, Marion Miller, and Donald Thomas; (second row) Fred Quinn, Guy Pollard, Ernest Parker, Jerome Boone, and unidentified; (top row) Bob Englebreit, and Father Patrick J. Malloy. (Photo courtesy of Monsignor Patrick J. Malloy.)

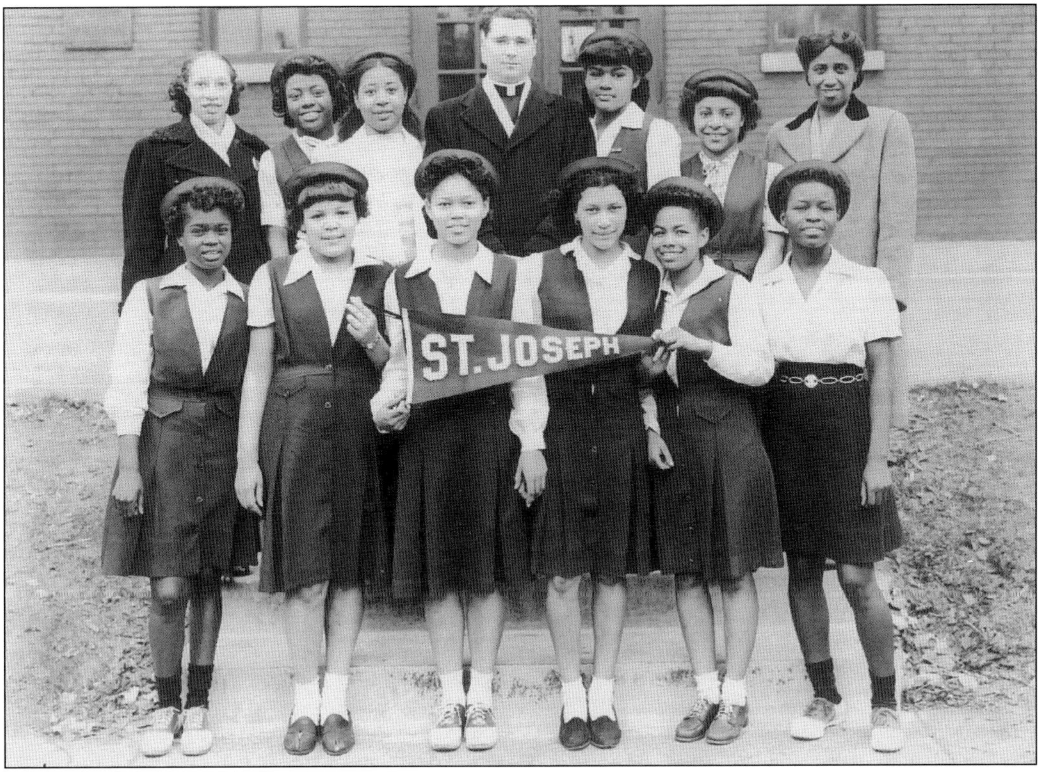

These members of St. Joseph's Booster Club were actively involved in school events cheering the school's teams on to victory. (Photo courtesy of the Archdiocese of St. Louis Archives.)

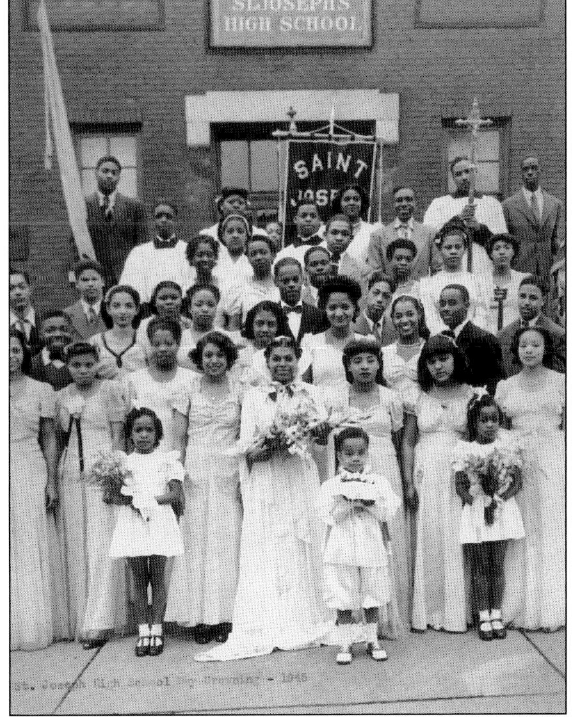

St. Josephs' students are pictured outside the school on May 6, 1945, during the celebration of their May Day Crowning. (Photo courtesy of the Sisters of St. Joseph of Carondolet.)

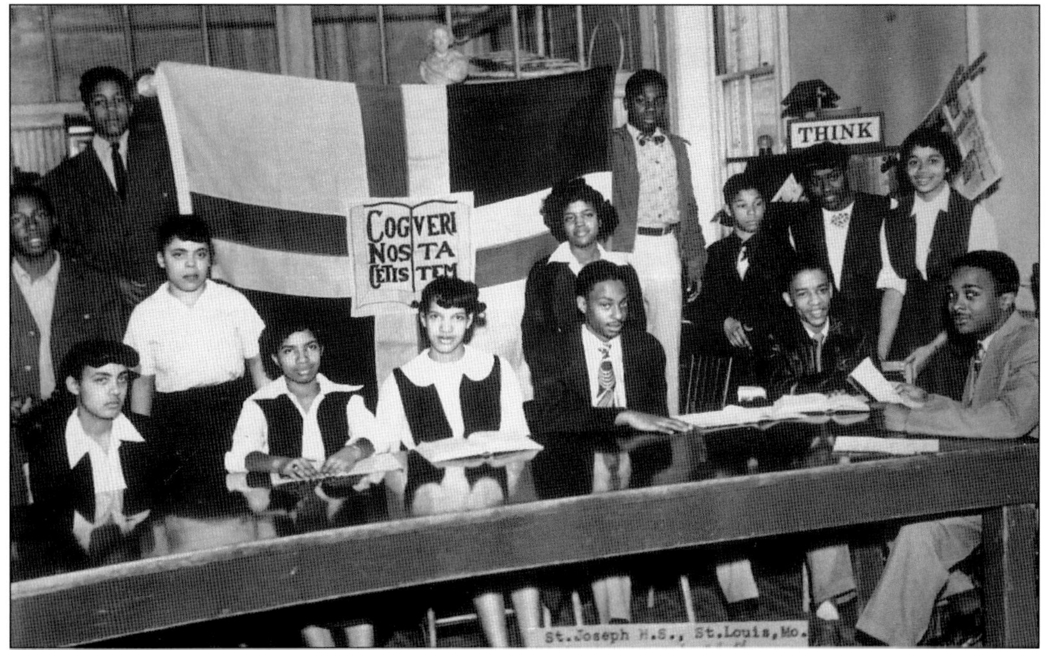

Members of St. Joseph's 1949–50 Student Mission Crusade are pictured here during one of their meetings. From left to right, these memebers are: Rosemary Fowler, Inez Frior, Irene Wilson, Rose Jones, Earl Gaskin, and Joe Reynolds; (standing) Monte Widdle, Clifford Wells, Adrian Thomas, Rebecca King, William Brooks, James Vincent, Juanita Young, Margaret Brinsford, and Willard West. (Photo courtesy of Sisters of St. Joseph of Carondolet.)

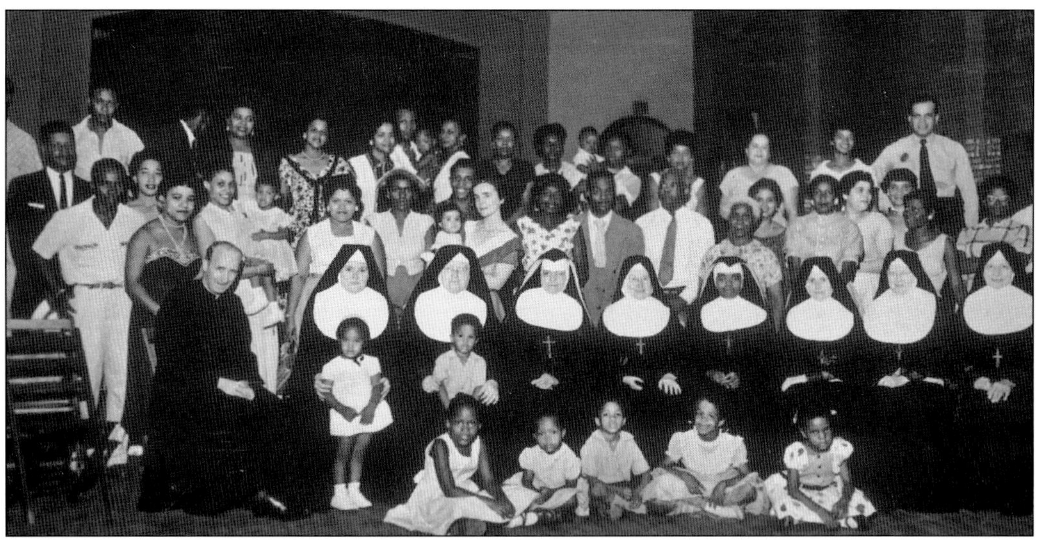

St. Joseph's High School closed in 1951, four years after Archbishop Joseph E. Ritter laid down the policy for integrating Catholic schools. In 1966, St. Joseph's alumni, teachers, six sisters of St. Joseph, and a priest came together at Visitation School, 1421 North Taylor Avenue, to reminisce and celebrate their place in time and attendance at St. Joseph's High School. This photograph was taken at that gathering. (Photo courtesy of the Sisters of St. Joseph of Carondolet.)

In May of 1940, Stowe Teachers College moved into this new building on Pendelton Avenue. The following year, men were admitted to Stowe Teachers College for teacher training for the first time. When the spring semester started, these young men were admitted: Warren J. Brunson, John D. Buckner, Odell Clark, Chester Hodges, George H. Hyram, Calvin Price, Walter Ray, and Ogie Wilkerson. (Photo courtesy of Geraldine Johnson.)

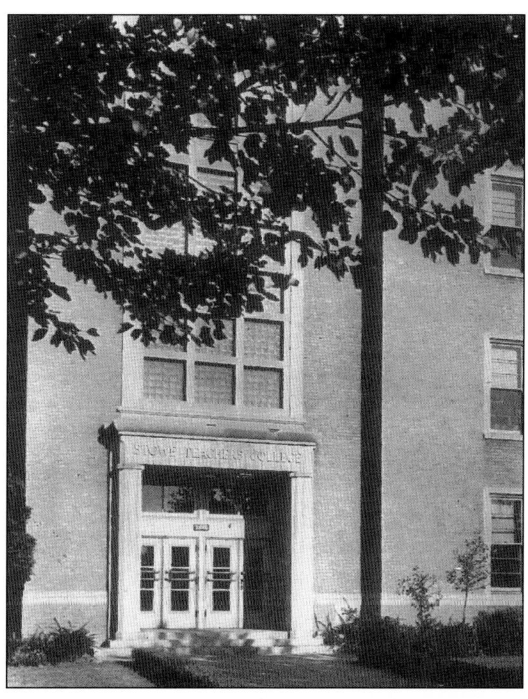

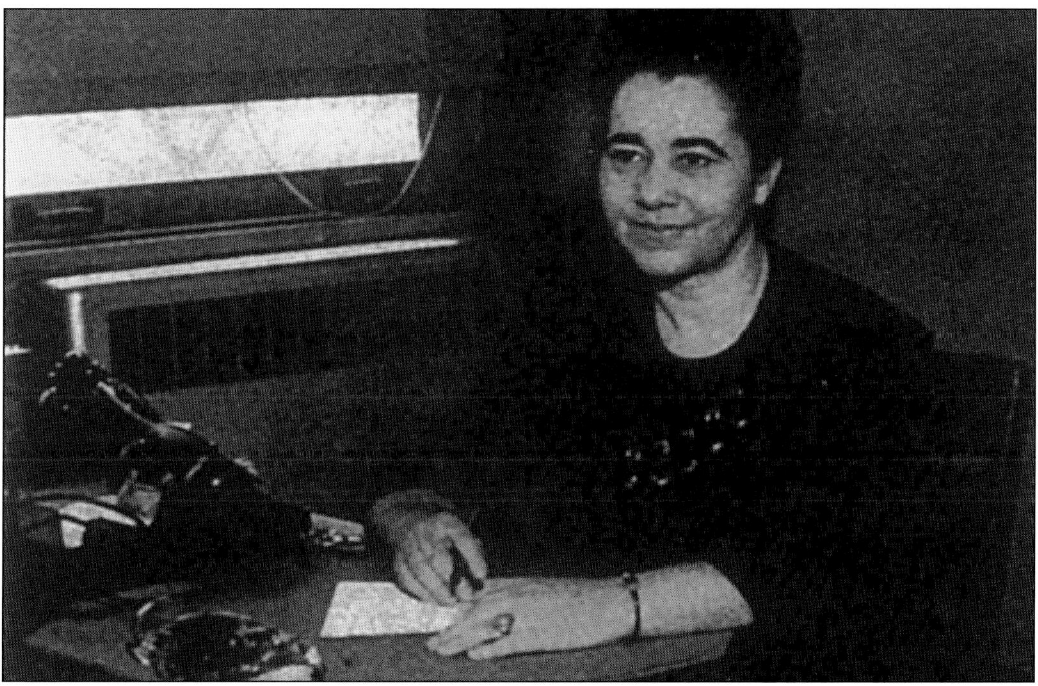

In 1940, Dr. Ruth Harris, pictured here, was appointed President of Stowe Teachers College, a position which she held until the merger with Harris Teachers College in 1954. Dr. Harris was a teacher at the Cottage Avenue Demonstration School and at Sumner Teachers College before she became Dean of Women at Stowe. (Photo courtesy of Geraldine Johnson.)

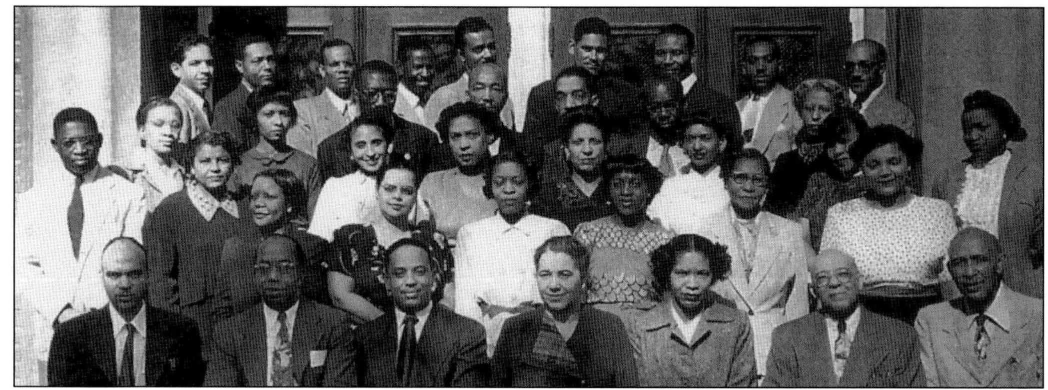

Members of the Stowe Teachers College faculty, from left to right, are: (first row) Mr. Morton F. Offett, Dr. Harry S. Blackiston, Mr. James W. Bailey, Dr. Ruth M. Harris (president), Miss Pelagie A. Greene, Mr. Fred P. Blair, and Dr. S.H. DuValle; (second row) Mrs. Alberta E. Douglas, Dr. Florence R. Brown, Miss Helen Flowers, Mrs. Helen Diamond, Miss Ophelia Shepard, and Miss Clara Robnett; (third row) Mr. E.E. Thorpe, Dr. Alice M. Smart, Mrs. Dorothea W. Anderson, Mrs. Blanche J. Lee, Mrs. Thelma Sutton, Mrs. Ellene Nash, Miss Ethel B. Huffman, and Mrs. Ozelie M. Stephens; (fourth row) Miss Clayda J. Williams, Miss Sarah M. Morrison, Mr. Josiah C. Cox, Dr. Lawrence Nicholson, Mr. Meriwether R. Martin, Dr. John H. Windom, and Miss Leah N. Guthrie; (fifth row) Dr. Lincoln Diuguid, Mr. Leonard D. Nelson, Dr. Frederick W. Bond, Mr. H. Ray McNeil, Mr. Carl F. Flipper, Mr. George O. Bynum, Mr. George Elliott, Dr. John B. Ervin, and Mr. Nathaniel Watlington. (Photo courtesy of Geraldine Johnson.)

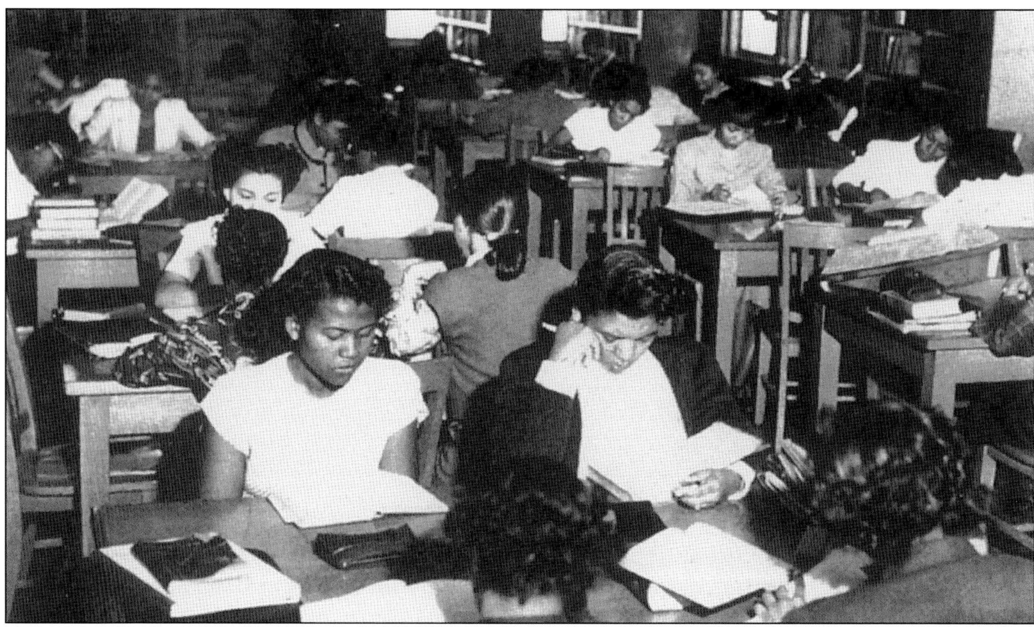

The faculty at Stowe brought out the best in their students. Many students went on to assume leadership roles in the St. Louis Public Schools. The students in this picture are putting in the needed study time required for them to pass the national teacher's examination and to complete their four and a half year program on time. (Photo courtesy of Geraldine Johnson.)

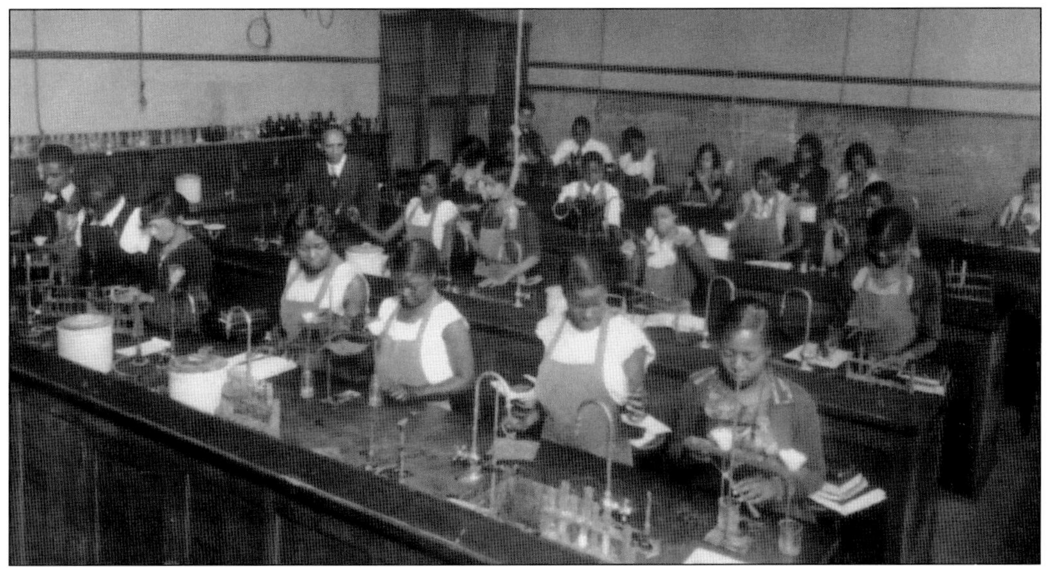

The students in these pictures are fully engaged in their science lesson. The basic difference in the 1931 picture at the top of the page, and the 1940s picture at the bottom, is that the one at the bottom has male students in the class room and the top one does not. Male students were first admitted to the Junior College Division of Stowe in 1930, and to the Teacher College Division in 1941, after a search of the Missouri legislation and other regulations showed that there were no statutory reasons why men could not be admitted to elementary school teacher education training. (Top photo courtesy of the St. Louis Public School Archives, and the bottom photo courtesy of Geraldine Johnson.)

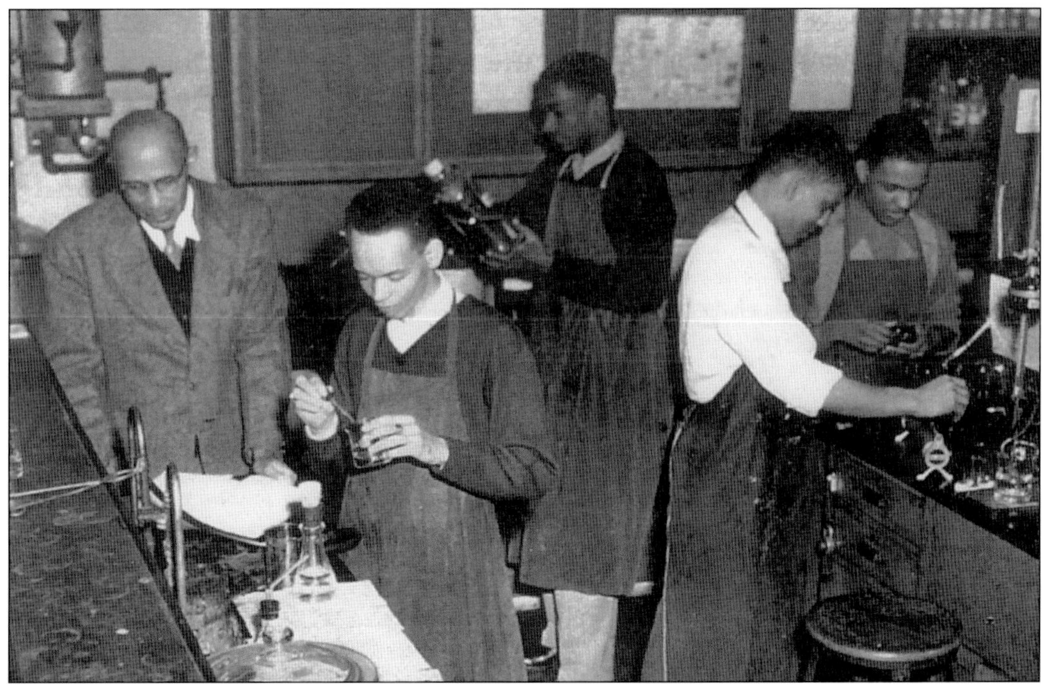

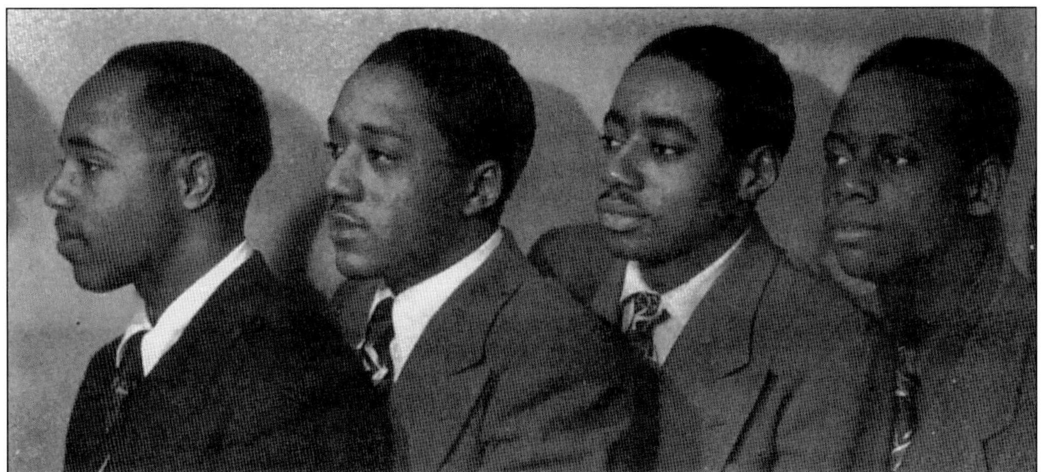

Stowe's faculty and students were proud of the Rhythmaires Quartet, the young men in this photograph. They brought much praise to the college's Music Department. As well as participating in various assembly programs, the Rhythmaires represented the college twice on the television station KSD. Members of the quartet were, from left to right: Earl Taylor—bass, Ben Johnson—second tenor, Clyde Turner—first tenor, and Charles Gladney—baritone. (Photo courtesy of Geraldine Johnson.)

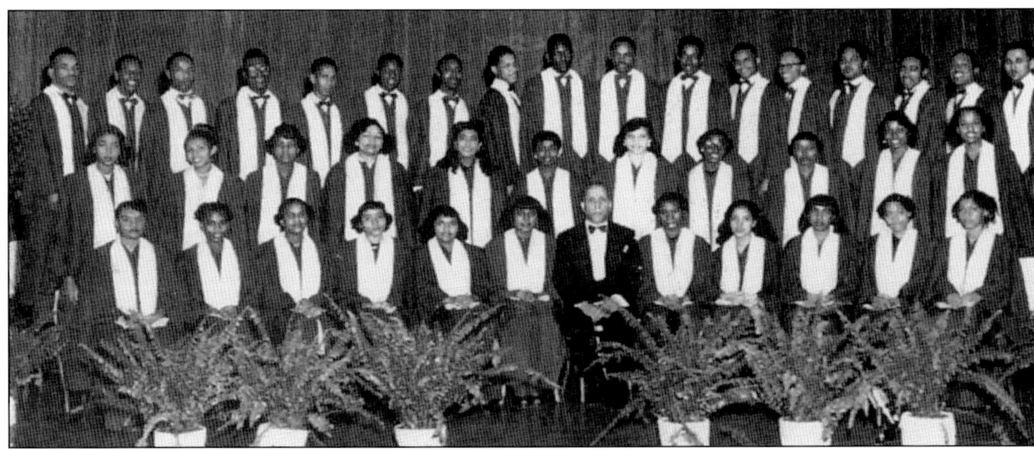

The Stowe Glee Club was the oldest musical organization at the College. Originally this group was made up entirely of volunteers who chose the Glee Club for the sheer joy of participation, and through a desire to further the musical objectives of the organization. In later years, the Stowe Singers took over as the chief performing choral organization of the school. When Stowe closed, Glee Club participation was required of all students taking the course Music for Teachers. Pictured above are members of the 1950 college Glee Club with their director Wirt Walton. (Photo courtesy of Geraldine Johnson.)

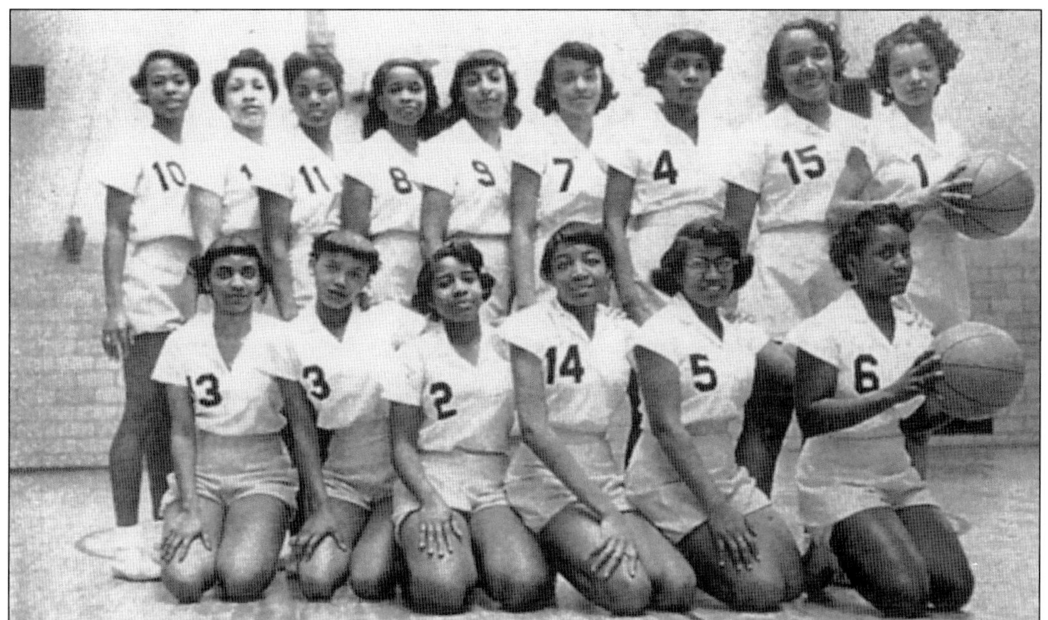

Members of the 1952 Stowe Teachers College Women's Basketball Team are pictured here. They are, from left to right: (first row) Vesta Noble, Mattie Griffin, Jesse Vaughns, Mattie Valentine, Marlene McGee, and Roberzene Crowder; (second row) Althea Ashford, Joyce Granberry, Clarice Butler, Delores Moses, Shirley Little, Margaret Manning, Earline Lee, Earline Golden, and Merlita Moore. The basketball team played games with Maryville, Principia, Webster, and Lindenwood Colleges. (Photo courtesy of Geraldine Johnson.)

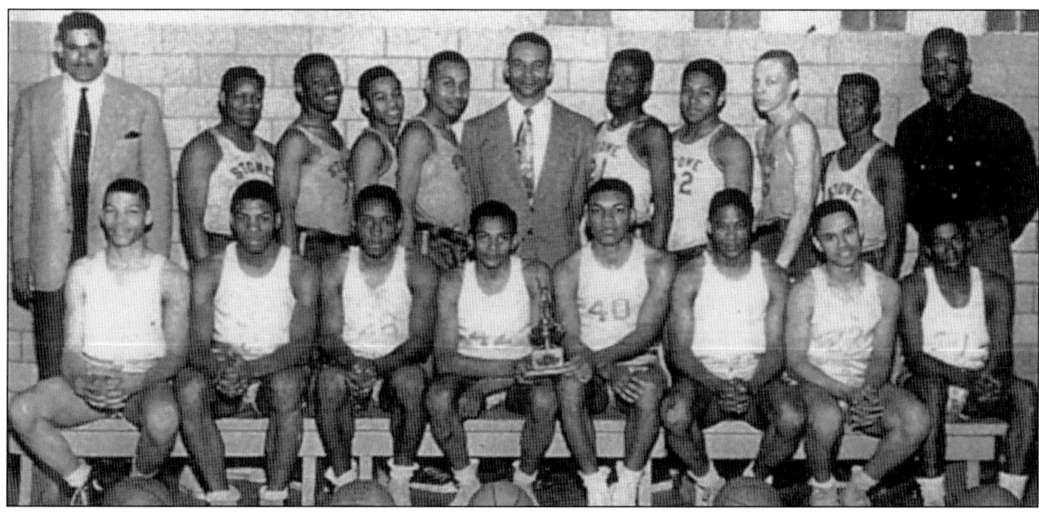

Coach George Elliott is pictured here with Stowe's 1952 men's basketball team. Members from left to right are: (first row) David Cunningham, Lloyd Kimbrough, James Jones, Joe White, Ernest Jones, Norval Cox, U.S. Falls, and Emanuel Buren; (second row) Mr. George Bynum, Elijah Crawford, Willie Sutherland, Orlando Wright, Clem Billingsley, Mr. George Elliot, Aaron Johnson, Ernest Jackson, Shannon Bennett, Arthur Givens, and George Beeks. The team under Coach Elliott won the Greater St. Louis Conference Championship in 1952. (Photo courtesy of Geraldine Johnson.)

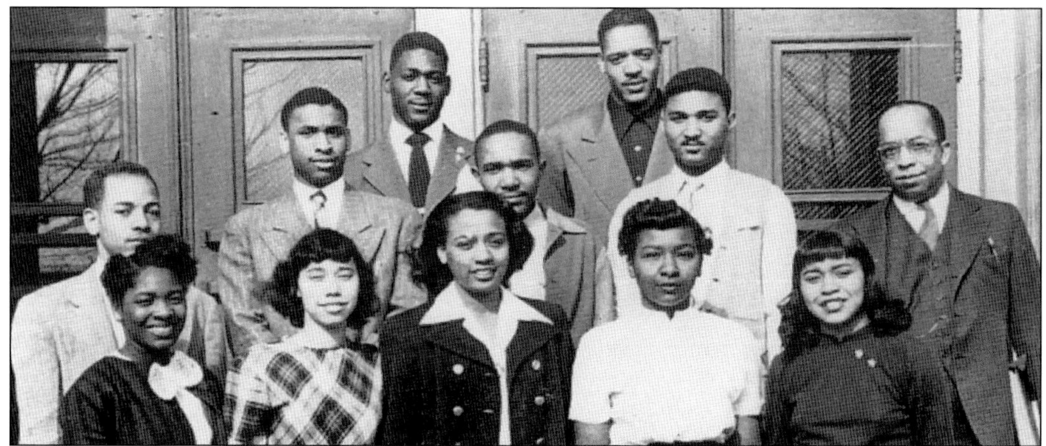

The Pan-Hellenic Council played a major role as the liaison organization for fraternities and sororities at Stowe. Its membership was composed of two Greeks from each group having a chapter. Members of the 1949 Pan-Hellenic Council, from left to right, with sponsor Dr. Harry S. Blackiston are: (first row) Barbara Attyberry, Betty J. O'Neal, Helen Beeks, Beatrice White, and Yvonne Lyons; (second row) Luther Conley, Earl Payne, Herman Prather, and Samuel Lee; (third row) William Moore, Walter P. Johnson, and Dr. Harry S. Blackiston. (Photo courtesy of Geraldine Johnson.)

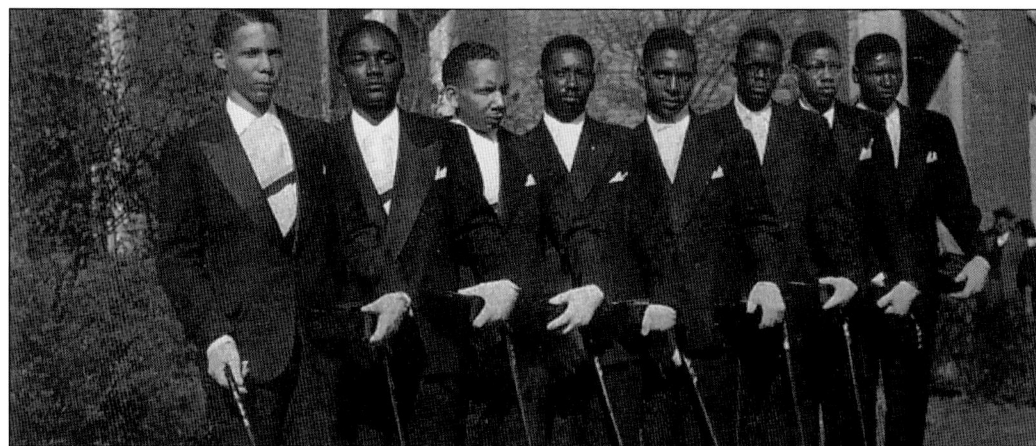

"Hell Week" was always an exciting time on Stowe's campus. This was a period when initiations took place for membership into the various fraternities and sororities. Pictured here are the pledges of Alpha Eta Chapter of Alpha Phi Alpha Fraternity. They are, from left to right: Bobby Wilks, James Brunson, Frank Wilson, George Rivers, Percy Laws, Henry L. Pearson, Stephen Dorn, and Commodore Jones. (Photo courtesy of Geraldine Johnson.)

Annie Turnbo Pope Malone (1869–1957), pictured here, was the founder of Poro College. In 1902, she moved from Illinois to 2223 Market Street in St. Louis to manufacture her product line. The business expanded after a few years and was moved to larger quarters at 3100 Pine, and in November 1918, to a new building at St. Ferdinand and Pendleton avenues (now Billups Avenue) in The Ville. (Photo courtesy of Odessa Farrell.)

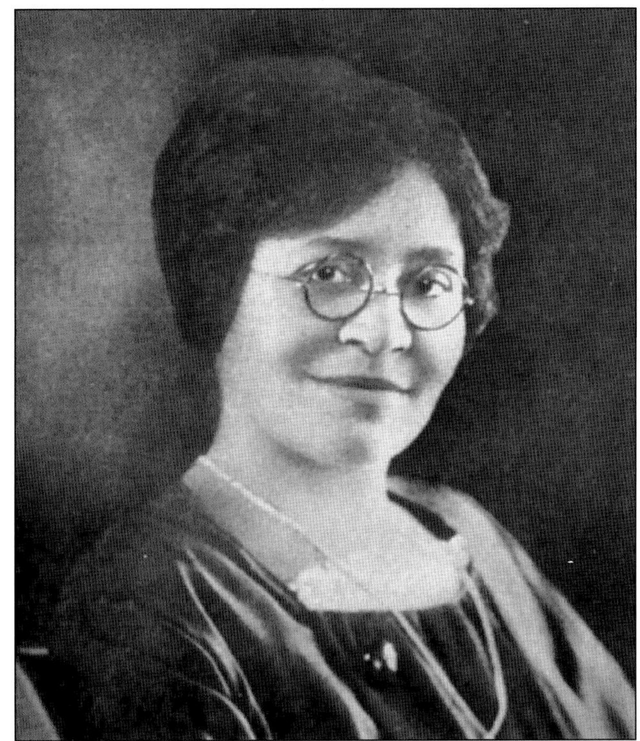

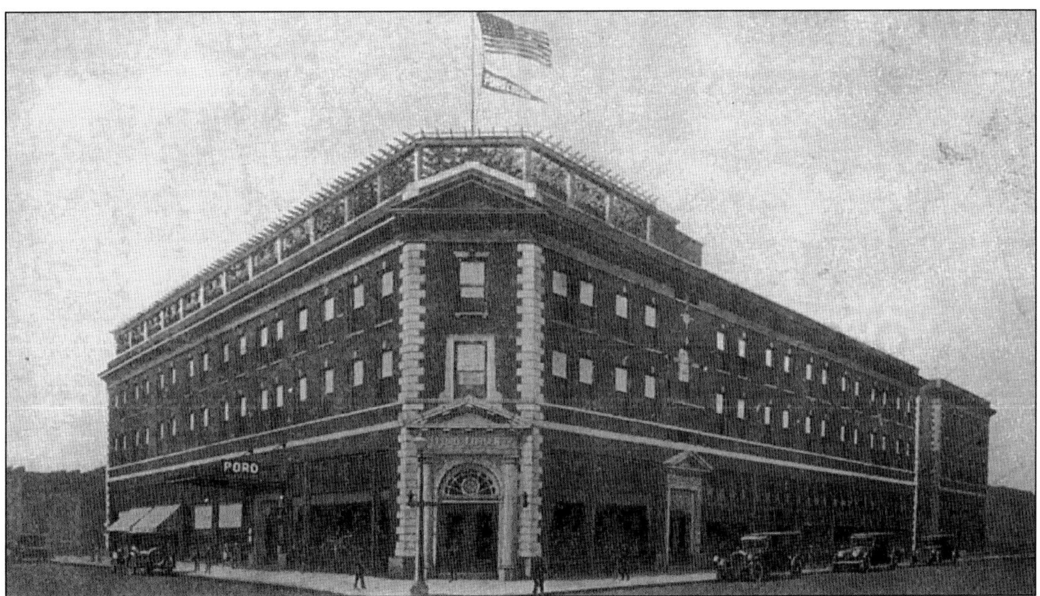

This is Poro College as it looked in 1918. The building occupied an entire city block. It included an instructional department in cosmetology, a beauty parlor, an auditorium, general offices, a cafeteria, a dining room, a sewing shop, guest rooms, a dormitory, and two emergency rooms for first-aid treatment. Following the 1927 tornado, thousands were sheltered, clothed, and fed through Poro College, which served as the principal relief unit for the American Red Cross. (Photo courtesy of John A. Wright.)

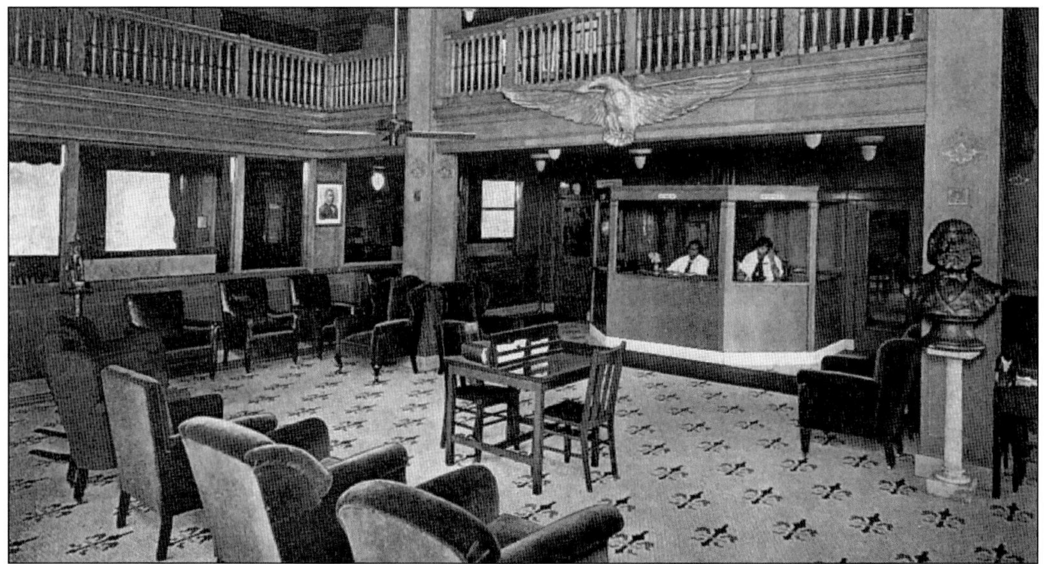

Shown here is a picture of Poro College's magnificent and spacious lobby with allegorical paintings on the walls, draperies of tan rep, artistic tile flooring, roomy mohair-covered overstuffed chairs, and mahogany writing desks. (Photo courtesy of Odessa Farrell.)

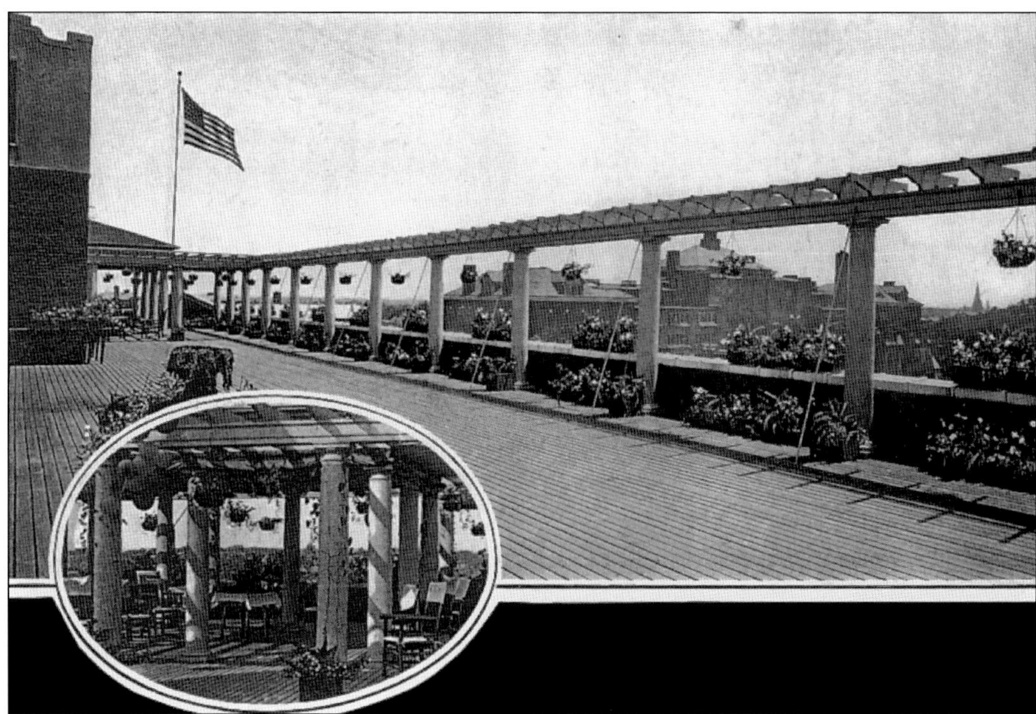

This is a photograph of Poro College's roof garden, with its profusion of flowering plants and vines. The garden was a beautiful and delightful place during the summer season and was available to the community for meetings, entertainment, and receptions. The Pergola at the north end of the Garden presented a fascinating picture. (Photo courtesy of Odessa Farrell.)

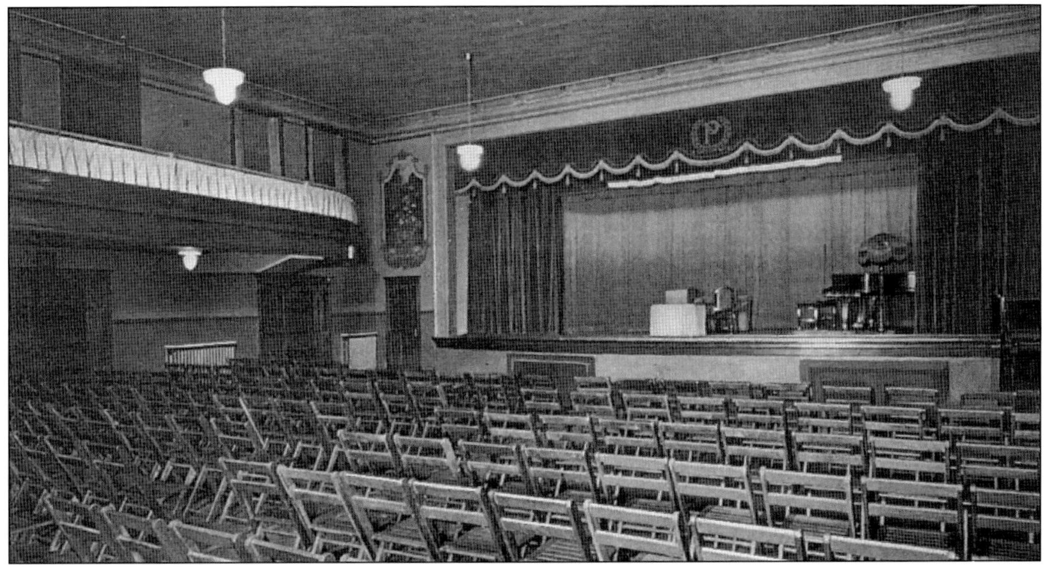

Each day the 800-seat Poro College auditorium was used for Devotional Exercises conducted by employees. The exercises immediately preceded the beginning of the day's work. The auditorium was equipped with movie facilities as well as a powerful radio receiver. This facility was available to religious, fraternal, civic, and social organizations for entertainment, lectures, conventions, and meetings. (Photo courtesy of Odessa Farrell.)

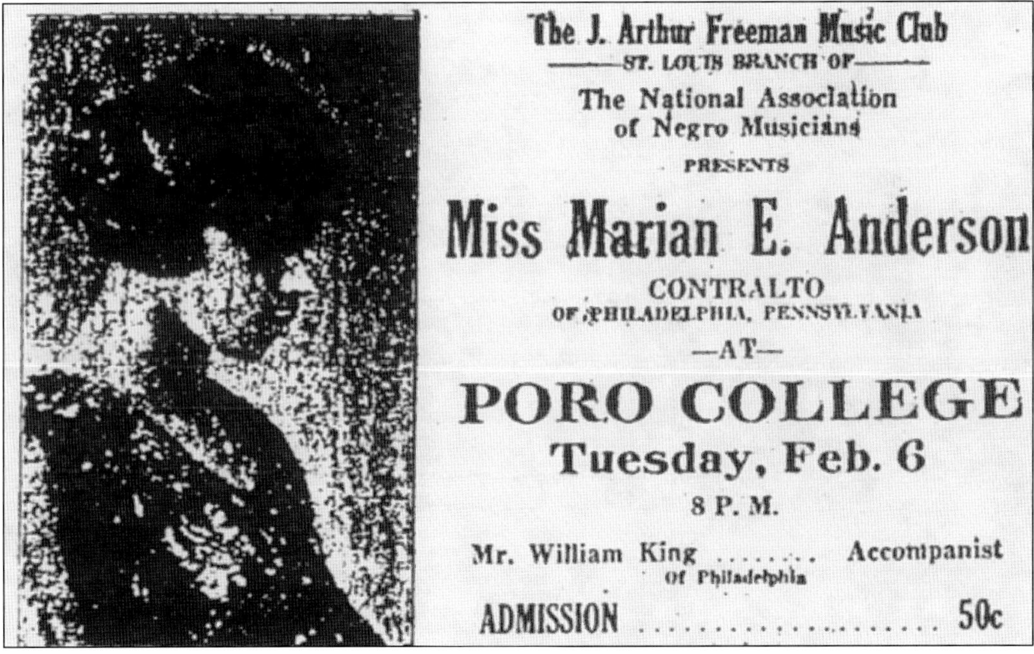

Many nationally known entertainers appeared in Poro College's Auditorium, such as Marian E. Anderson as seen in this 1923 newspaper advertisement. (Photo courtesy of the St. Louis Public Library.)

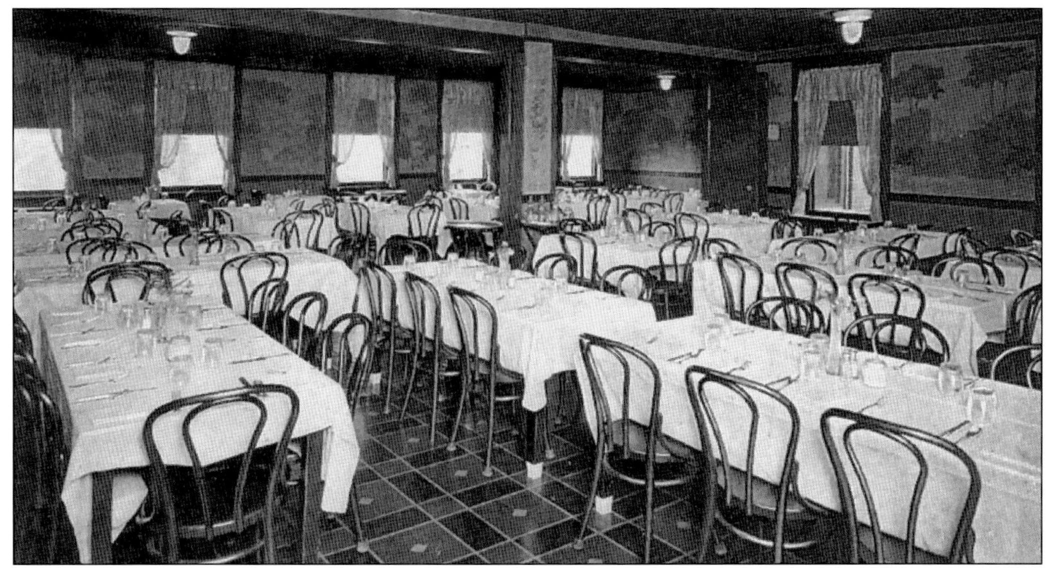

This Poro dining room was a very popular meeting place for many African-American organizations and its food was known to be outstanding. (Photo courtesy of Odessa Farrell.)

The Taste Of A

POR0 COLLEGE DINNER

Clings Like Ivy on the Wall

WHY GO HOME?

Um-m-m! A Delicious **BANANA SPLIT**, a **CRUSHED FRUIT SODA** or **SUNDAE** or a Dish of **GOOD ICE CREAM**, will give you just that "pep" to absorb the next services. Come on over. Frequent visits to the **BEAUTY DEPARTMENT of PORO COLLEGE** will mean to you what a live pastor does to a small congregation—an improvement in appearance, an appreciation of the best, and an increase in attendance, making more work for somebody. You are welcome.

(Please Bring This Ad With You)

Poro College Dinner ads, such as this one, appeared in church bulletins throughout the city. (Photo courtesy of St. James A.M.E. Church.)

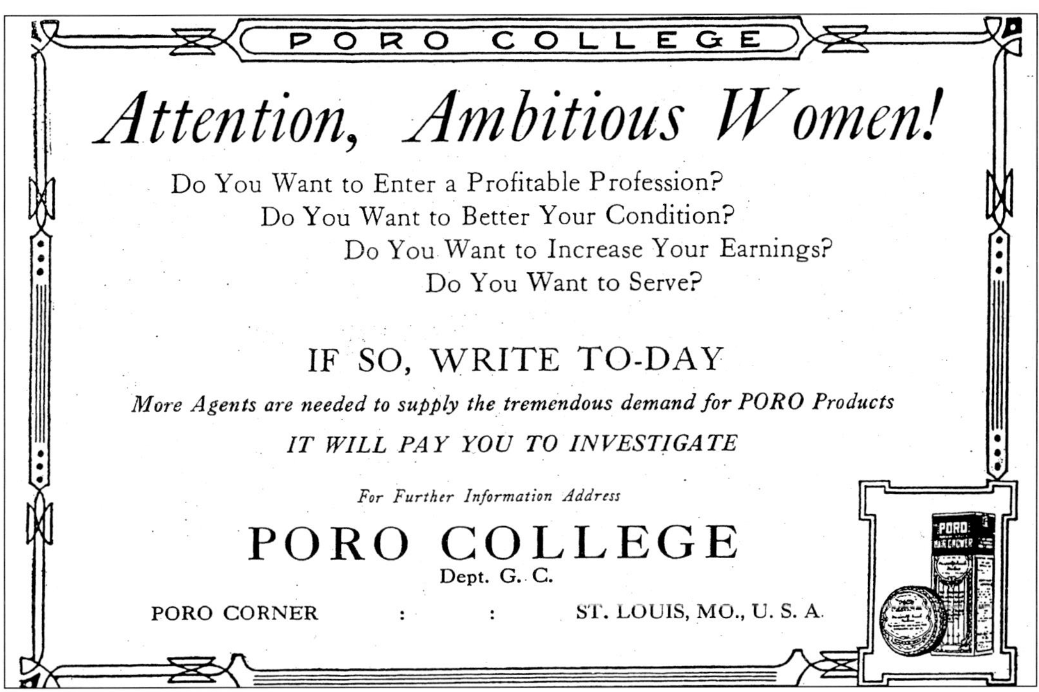

The Poro system achieved renown not only in the United States, but internationally in the Caribbean, Africa, and the Philippines. In the 1920s, Malone employed nearly 200 people in her business, including many Sumner High School students. Pictured here is a 1920s Poro advertisement. (Photo courtesy of Olivia Blackmore.)

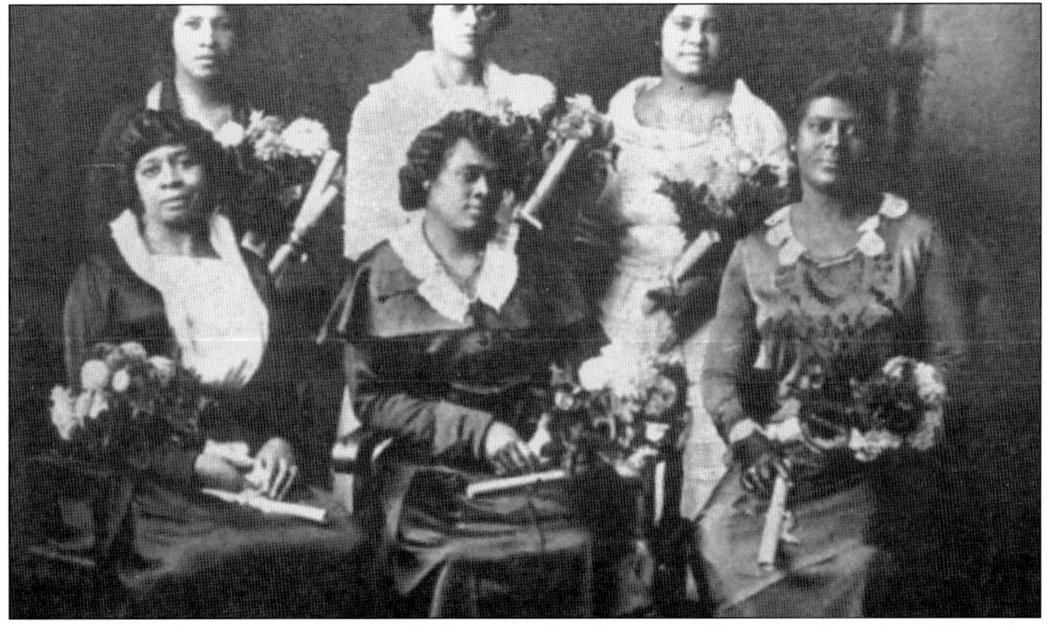

Six Poro graduates are pictured here with their certificates after the Thursday graduation exercise. (Photo courtesy of the University of Missouri-St. Louis, Western Manuscript Collection.)

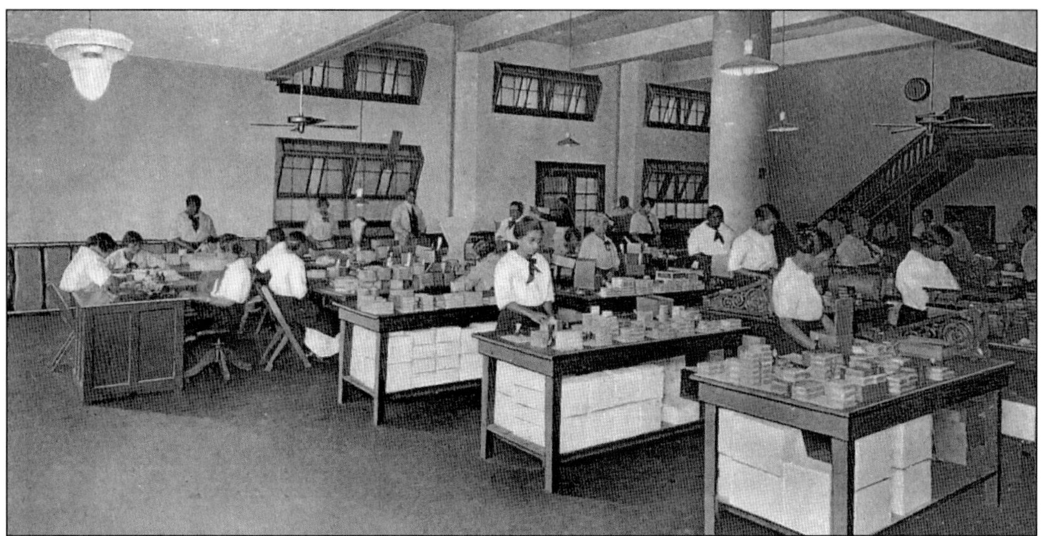

Thousands of shipments of Poro goods were sent to points throughout the world and to Poro College Branches and supply stations daily. The clerks in this picture are taking great care in packing the goods into the shipping cases to insure accuracy and safe transmission. (Photo courtesy of Odessa Farrell.)

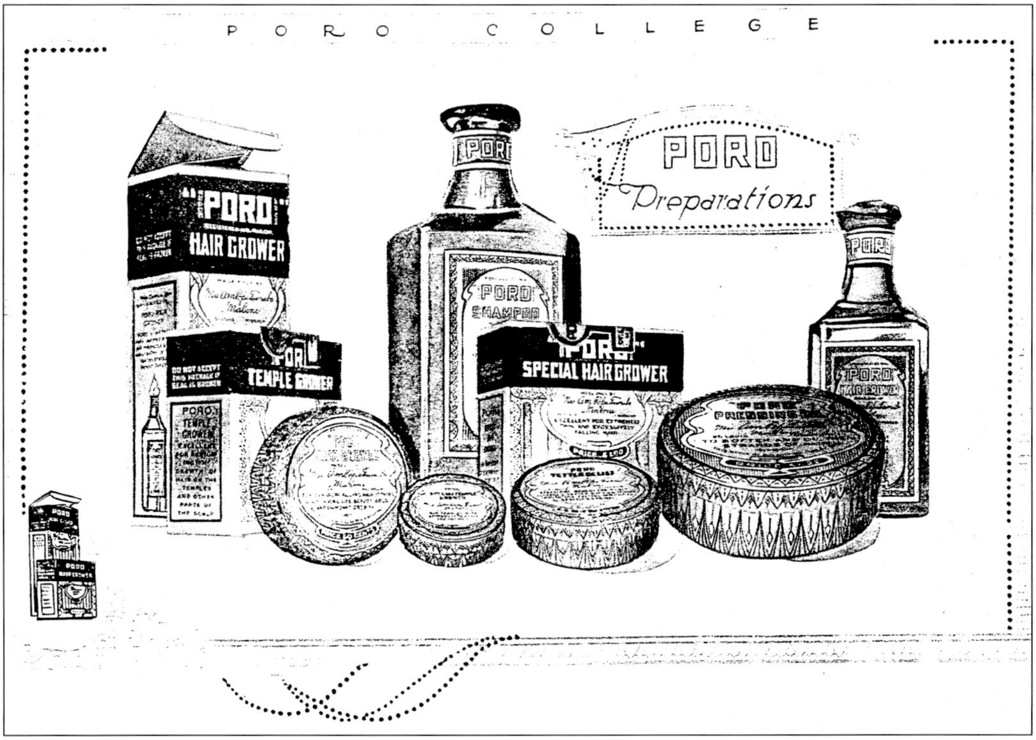

PORO COLLEGE

PORO
Preparations

PORO HAIR GROWER

PORO TEMPLE GROWER

PORO SHAMPOO

PORO SPECIAL HAIR GROWER

Pictured here are samples of the many products produced at Poro College. (Advertisement courtesy of Olivia Blackmore.)

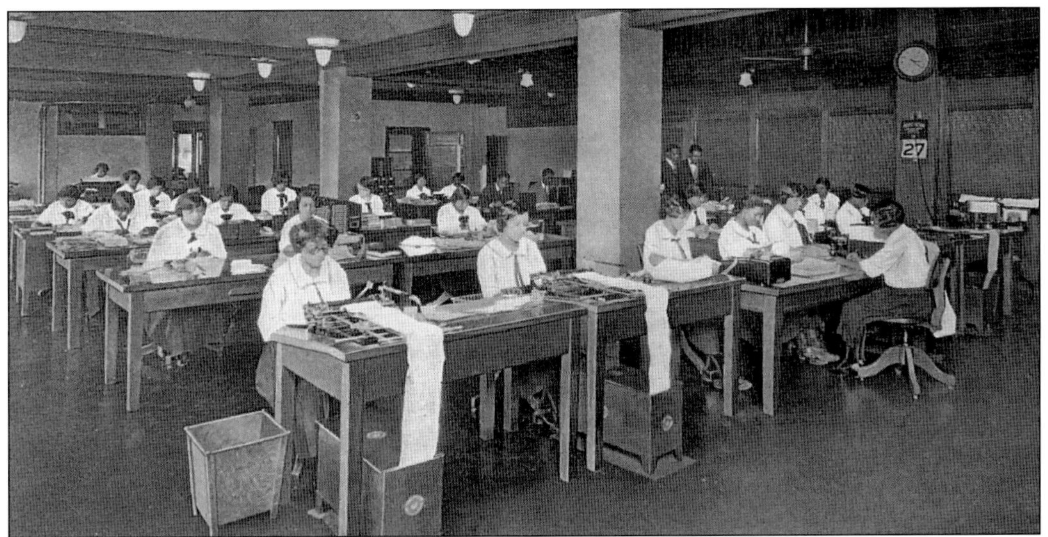

This order and receiving room was established at Poro College to handle the large volume of mail and orders coming to the college daily. (Photo courtesy of Odessa Farrell.)

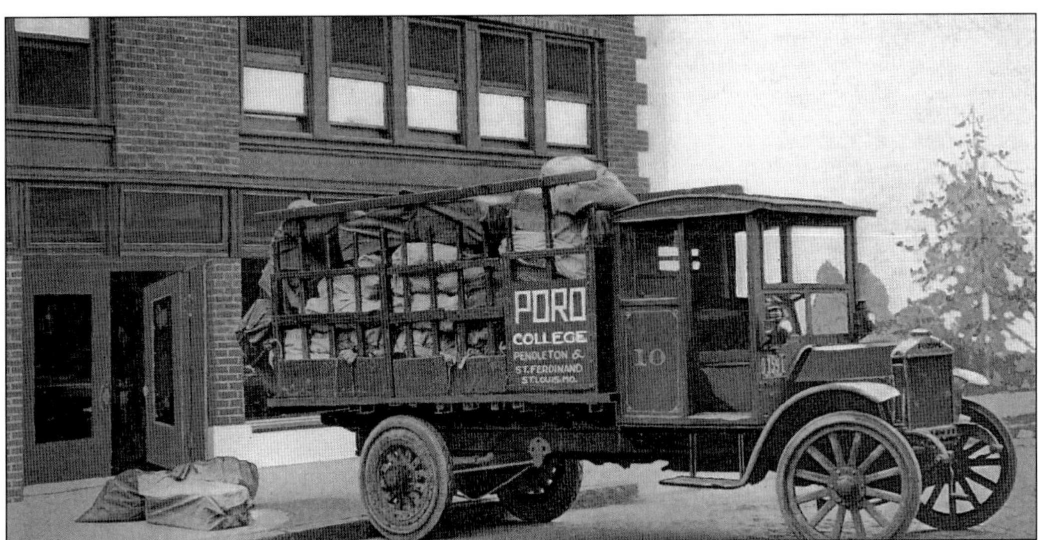

Pictured here is the Poro College mail and order delivery truck which transported mail and orders to the train station several times daily. (Photo courtesy of Odessa Farrell.)

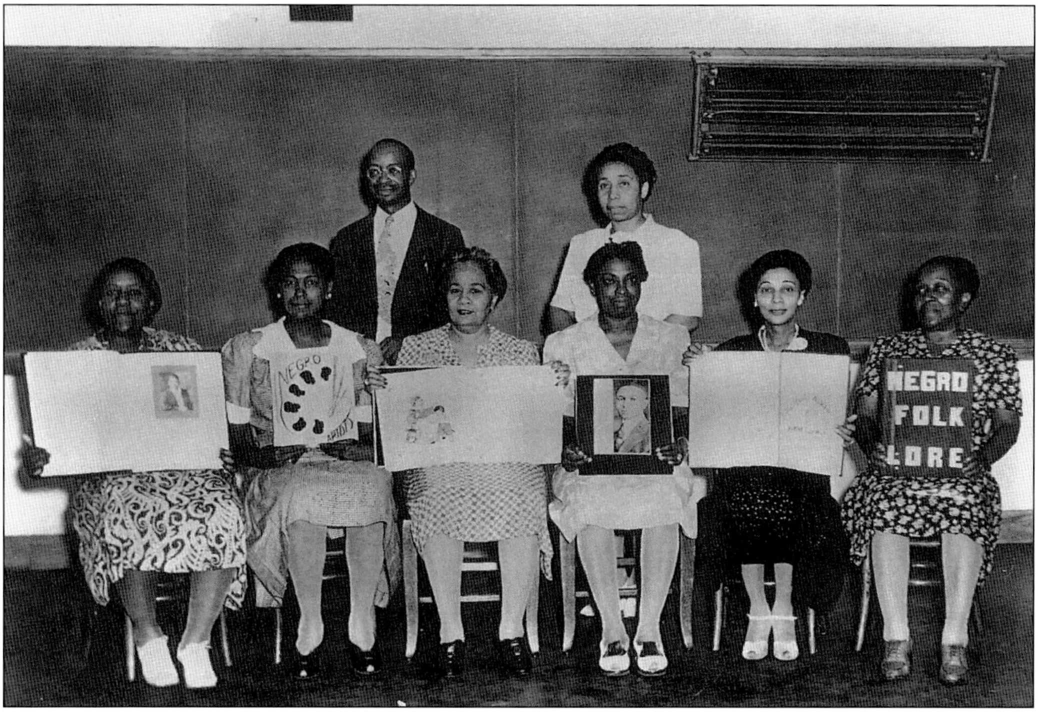

Poro College, during part of its history, served as the site for Saturday School established by Dr. Herman Dreer for teachers to assist them in the integration of African-American history into their curriculum. Pictured here is Dr. Dreer with Julia Davis and some of the Saturday School pupils. (Photo courtesy of Vivian Dreer.)

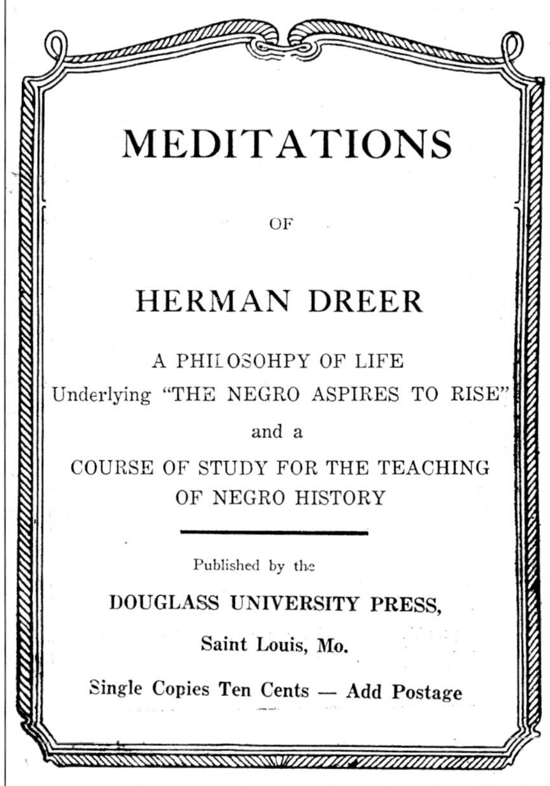

MEDITATIONS

OF

HERMAN DREER

A PHILOSOHPY OF LIFE
Underlying "THE NEGRO ASPIRES TO RISE"
and a
COURSE OF STUDY FOR THE TEACHING
OF NEGRO HISTORY

Published by the
DOUGLASS UNIVERSITY PRESS,
Saint Louis, Mo.
Single Copies Ten Cents — Add Postage

Dr. Herman Dreer wrote this booklet published by the Douglass University Press to promote the teaching of Negro history. Dreer was a strong believer that African-American history should be a part of every teacher's and school's curriculum offerings. (Photo courtesy of Vivian Dreer.)

Three

INSTITUTIONS
THE SOUL OF THE COMMUNITY

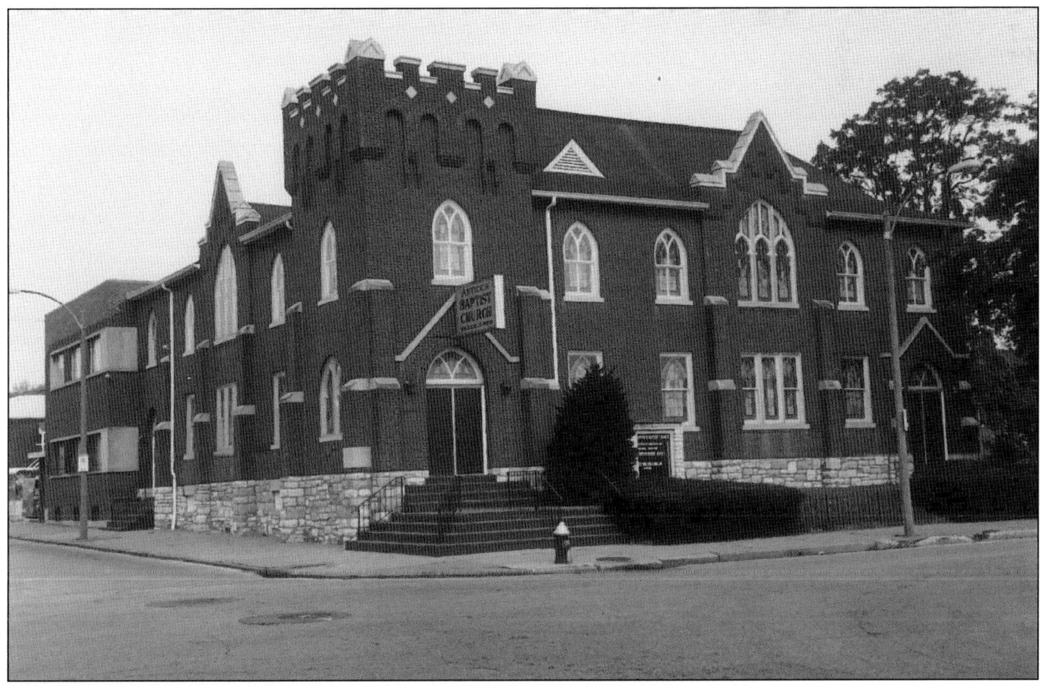

Throughout The Ville's history, institutions have played a vital role in the community's life. Antioch Baptist Church, pictured here, is the oldest Protestant church and institution in The Ville. It was organized in March 1878 in a member's home on Wash Avenue (now Whittier Street). In 1880, the congregation moved to a frame building on Lambdin Avenue near Kennerly. Antioch was incorporated on May 6, 1884, and the congregation purchased a second building on Kennerly Avenue from the Baptist Home Mission Board of New York. In 1909, the Antioch congregation bought the Goode Avenue Methodist Episcopal Church at Goode Avenue (now Annie Malone Drive) and West North Market Street. Eleven years later, the growing membership erected the building in this picture. (Photo by John A. Wright.)

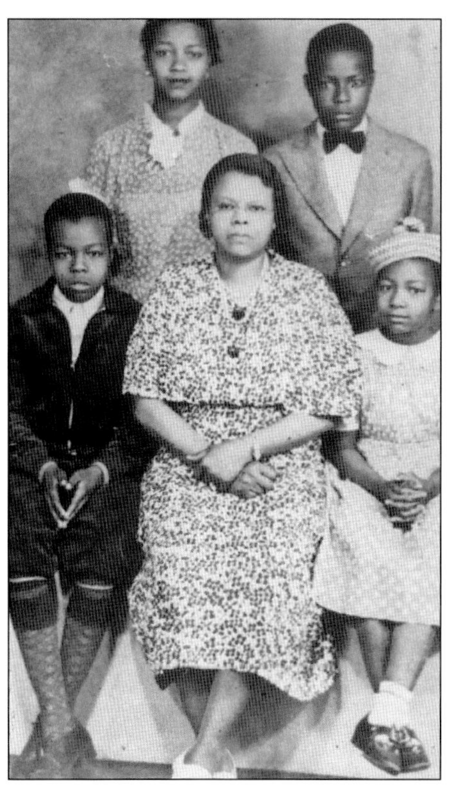

Antioch has always been a home for many community residents in and out of The Ville. These church members are members of the Madison family. At the time of this picture, they were four of the six living great-grandchildren of Dred Scott, with the wife of the grandson James Madison. Madison was the son of Eliza Scott, daughter of Dred, who married Wilson Madison. Pictured here, seated, are Alexander, Mrs. Grace Madison, and Pauline. Standing are Rose and Joseph Henry. (Photo by Nathan Young. Courtesy of University of Missouri-St. Louis, Western Manuscript Collection.)

Antioch has maintained many of its traditions over the years. Pictured here is the "Harvest Home—Bringing in the Sheaves" celebration that started many years ago and is still celebrated each year around Thanksgiving. Each member of the church is asked to bring items to share with needy residents of the community. (Photo courtesy of Antioch Baptist Church.)

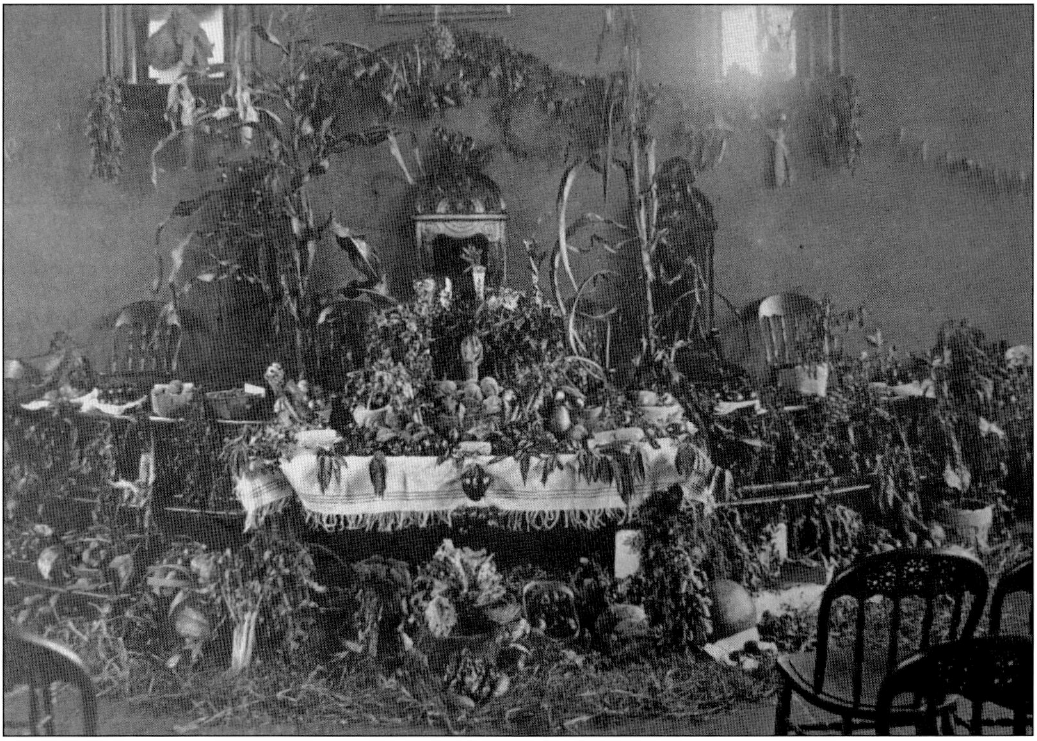

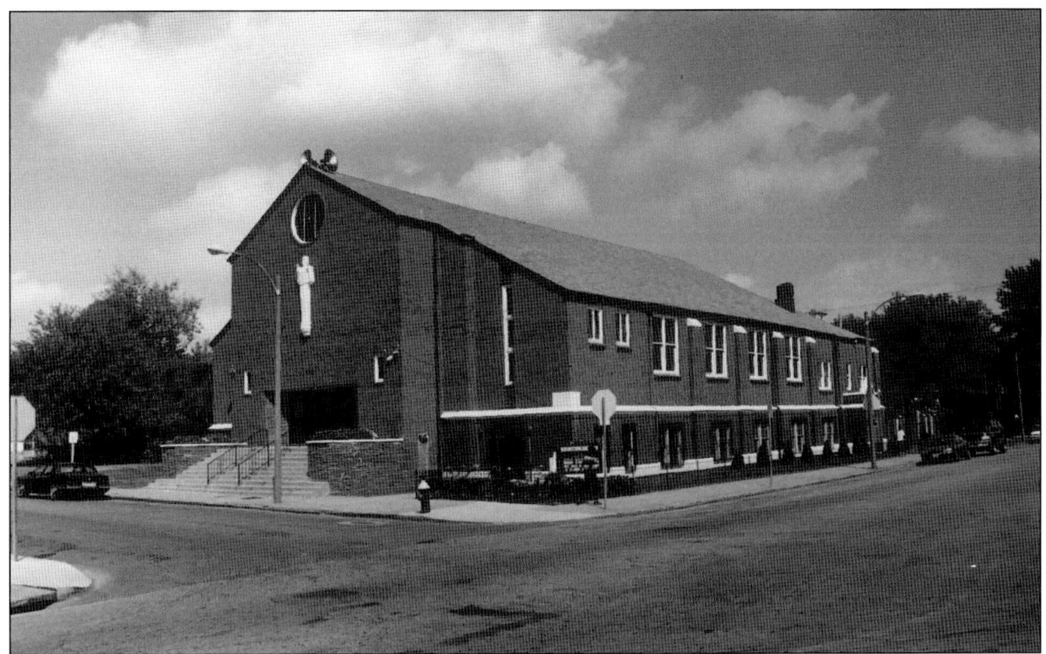

St. James African Methodist Episcopal Church is the second oldest Protestant church in The Ville. It was organized in 1884 to serve the African Americans who were moving into the community. The first church, a frame structure, was built at St. Ferdinand and Pendleton. The present sanctuary in this picture was completed in 1950–51. (Photo by John A. Wright.)

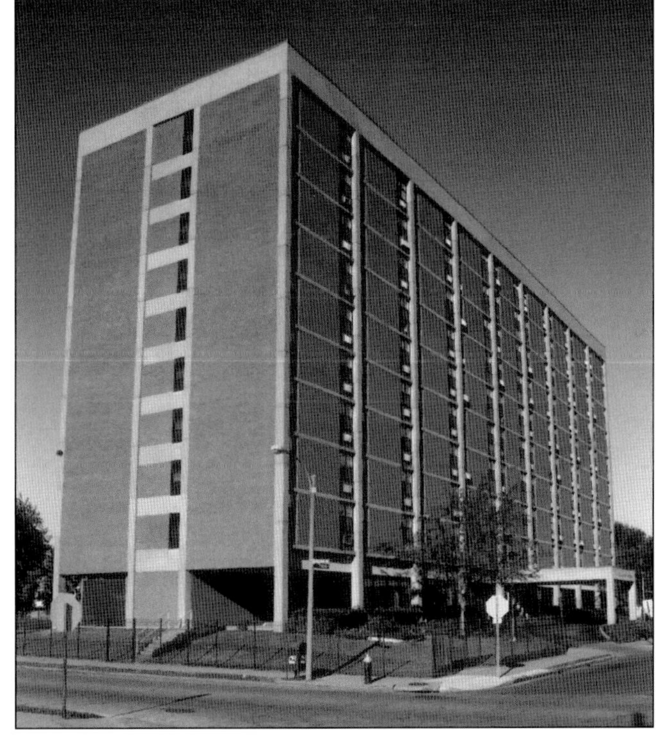

St. James African Methodist Episcopal Church purchased the Poro Building in 1965 and razed it, replacing it with the James House, a residential facility for senior citizens. This ten-story apartment building at Billups and St. Ferdinand avenues is part of a "turnkey" project sponsored by the Office of Housing and Urban Development. St. James A.M.E. raised $45,000 toward the construction of the project which now houses over 200 self-sufficient senior citizens. James House was the first church-developed housing project in St. Louis. (Photo by John A. Wright.)

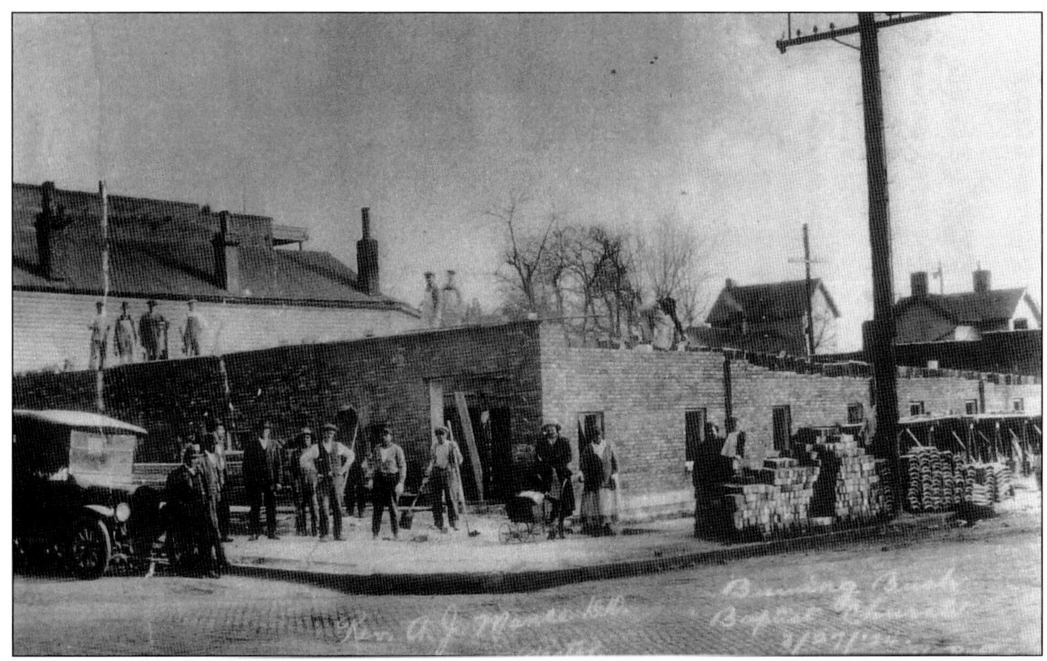

Burning Bush Baptist Church was founded in 1906. In this 1924 photo, construction is taking place on a new facility at the southeast corner of North Market and Newstead avenues. This church was later turned over to Newstead Baptist Church. (Photo courtesy of Newstead Baptist Church.)

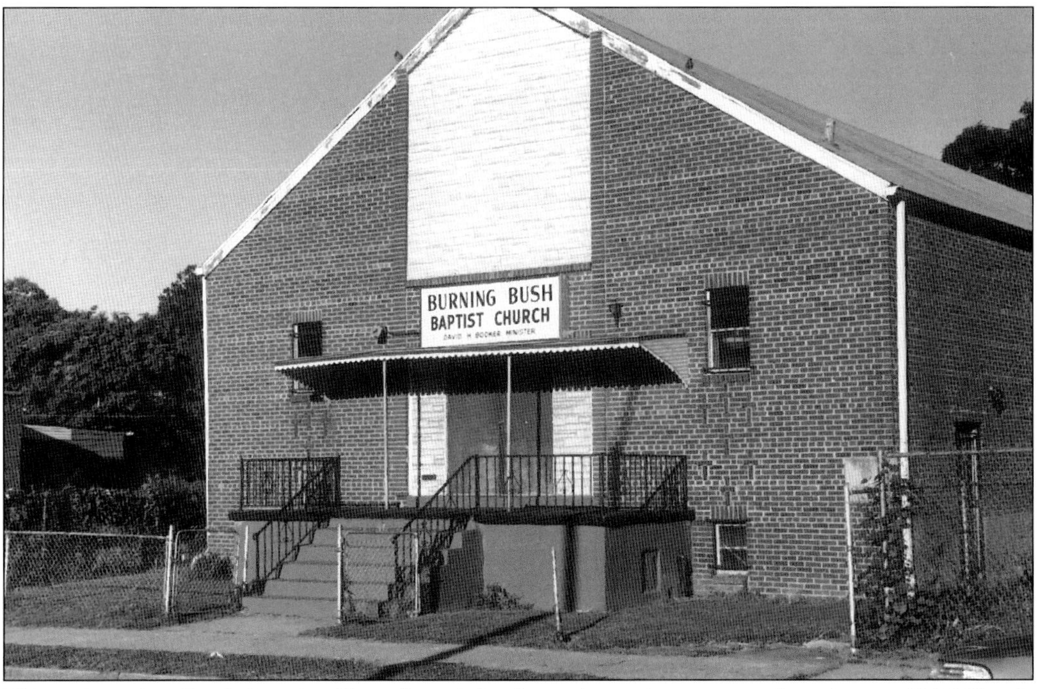

This is Burning Bush Baptist Church as it looks today at its present location at 1925 North Sarah Avenue. (Photo by John A. Wright.)

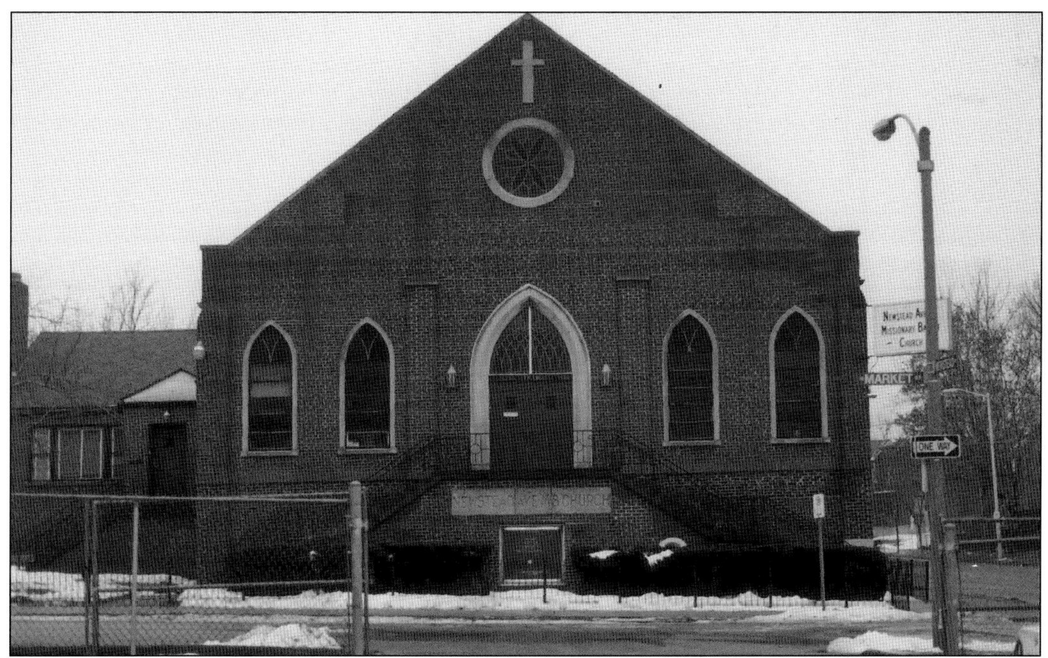

Newstead Baptist Church, known as the "Friendly Church on the Corner," was organized December 31, 1930, by the Rev. William Harris Sr., moderator of the Antioch District Baptist Association and pastor of Calvary Baptist Church, the Rev. W.L. Perry, pastor of Antioch Baptist Church, and other Christians who had attended the Burning Bush Baptist Church. The Revered Macon Bell was elected as be church's first pastor. (Photo by John A. Wright.)

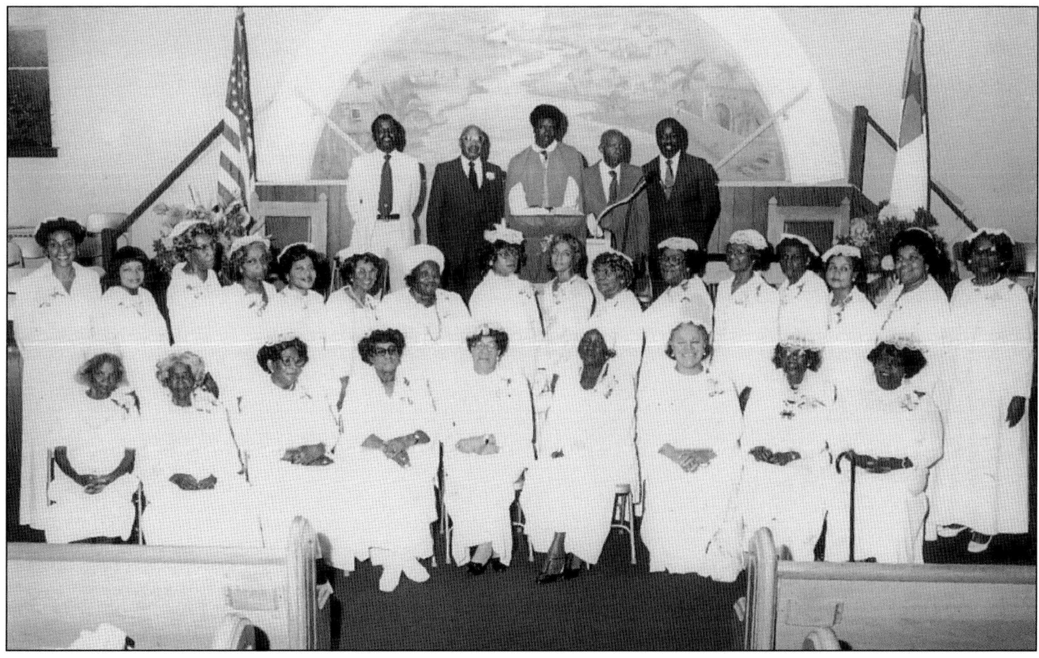

Pictured here are some of the early members of the Newstead Avenue Baptist Church Mother's Board. (Photo courtesy of Mable George.)

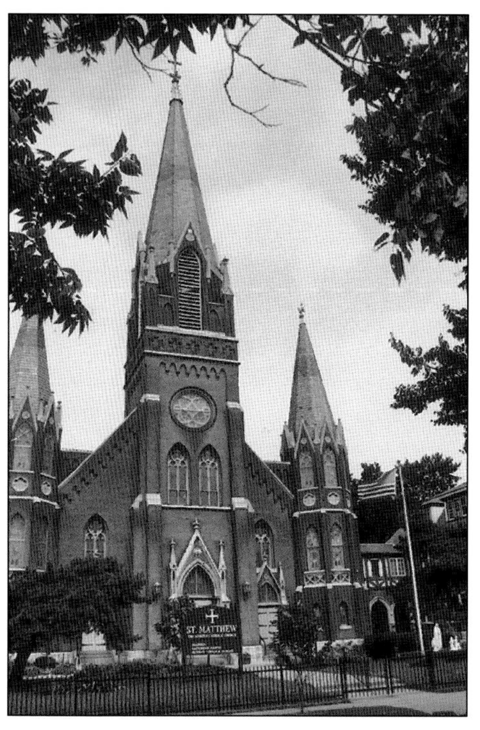

St. Matthew the Apostle Parish was established in 1893 by the Rev. Joseph Terrance Shields, a young immigrant from County Tyrone, Ireland, to serve the expanding city population west of Grand Avenue. The parish began with 150 families in a small frame building. Before the frame church was completed, religious services were held at Turner Hall on Whittier and North Market streets. The cornerstone for the church in the photograph above was laid August 12, 1906. (Photo by John A. Wright.)

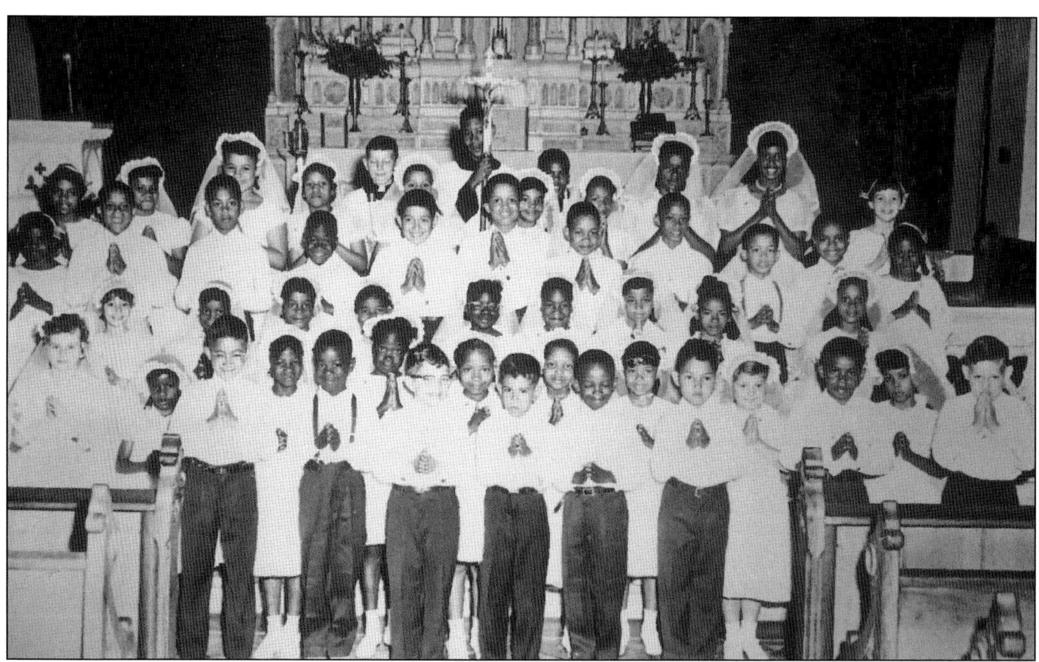

Pictured here is an integrated group of young parishioners after their first communion at St. Matthews Catholic Church. During the 1950s, black parishioners were assigned the last seats in the church, and were asked to pay 10¢ rent for their use. Today black parishioners now make up the majority of the church's membership, and are fully welcome in the church and assume leadership roles. (Photo courtesy of the Midwest Jesuit Archives.)

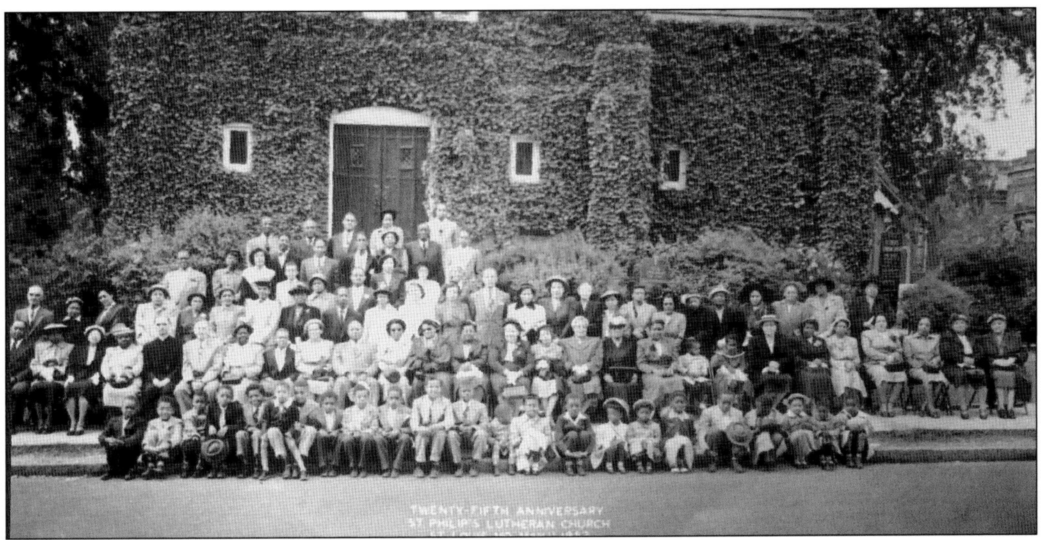

St. Phillips Lutheran Church, pictured here, is a descendant of the Carr Street Mission. It was organized in 1926 on Goode Avenue (now Annie Malone Drive). In 1966, the congregation discussed leaving the area, but chose instead to reaffirm its commitment to the community by constructing a new building on the same site. This photograph, taken outside of the church on May 11, 1952, was of church members who had gathered to celebrate the church's 25th anniversary. (Photo courtesy of St. Phillips Lutheran Church.)

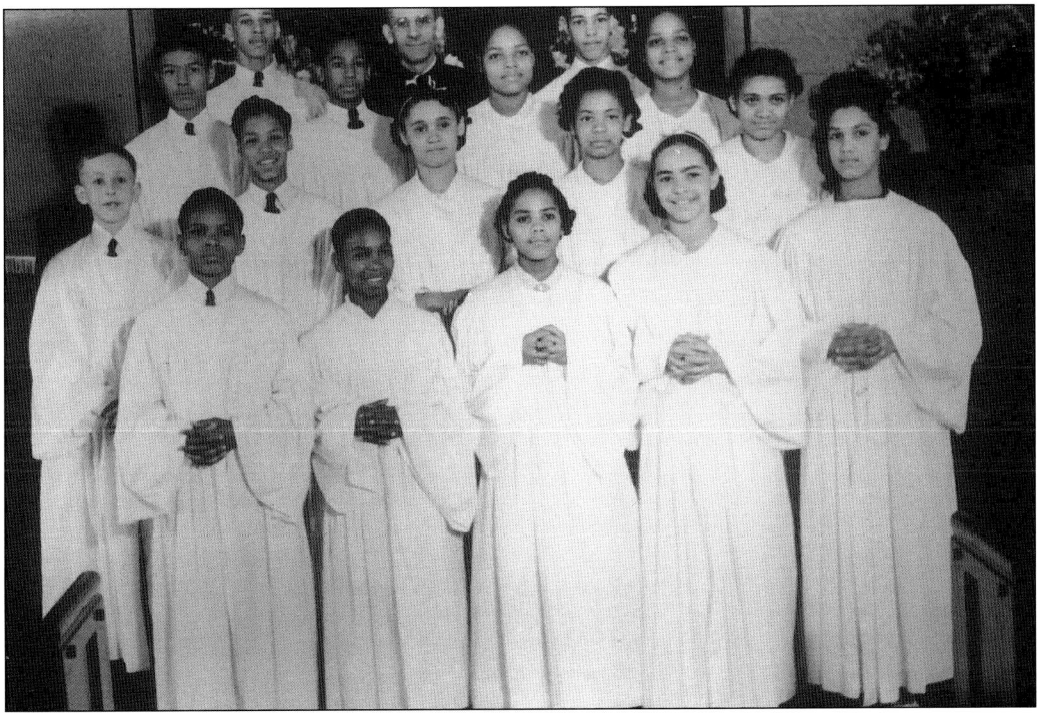

These students are members of the May 5, 1947 confirmation class. St. Phillips has the largest Lutheran congregation in the St. Louis black community.(Photo courtesy of St. Phillips Lutheran Church.)

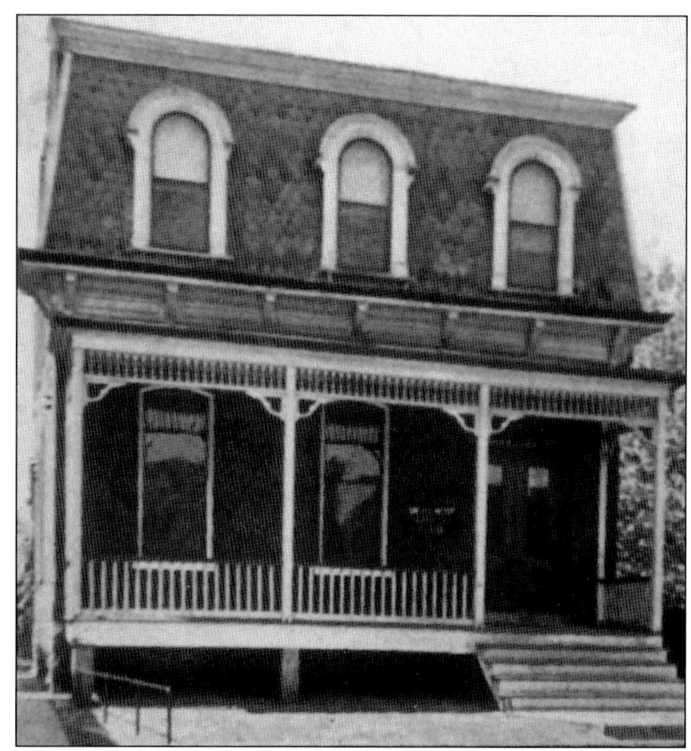

Pictured here is the Sacred Heart Center at 4406 Garfield Avenue after its move from 1924 North Taylor in 1940. Beginning in 1939, students were released from near by schools an hour early to come to the center and other churches for religious instruction classes. The center sponsored a wide range of activities for boys and girls, and a Mother's Club for adults on nutrition, home nursing, and sewing. (Photo courtesy of the Midwest Jesuit Archives.)

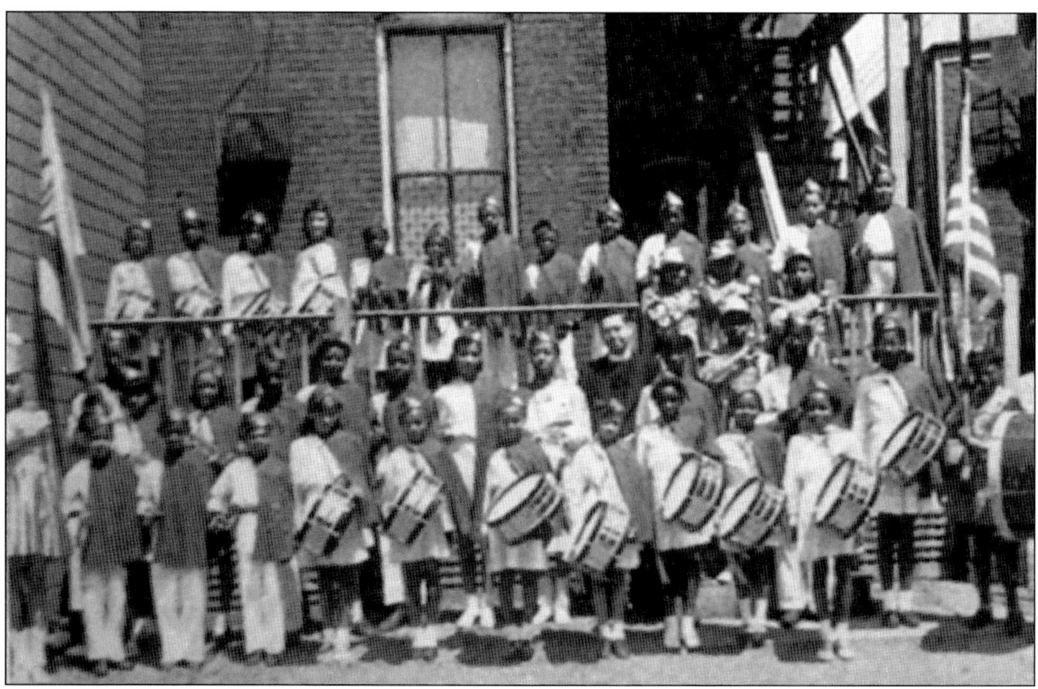

Activities at the Sacred Heart Center for children included scouting for boys and girls as well as Brownies and Cubs. Pictured here are members of the Sacred Heart Center's Drum and Bugle Corp. (Photo courtesy of the Midwest Jesuit Archives.)

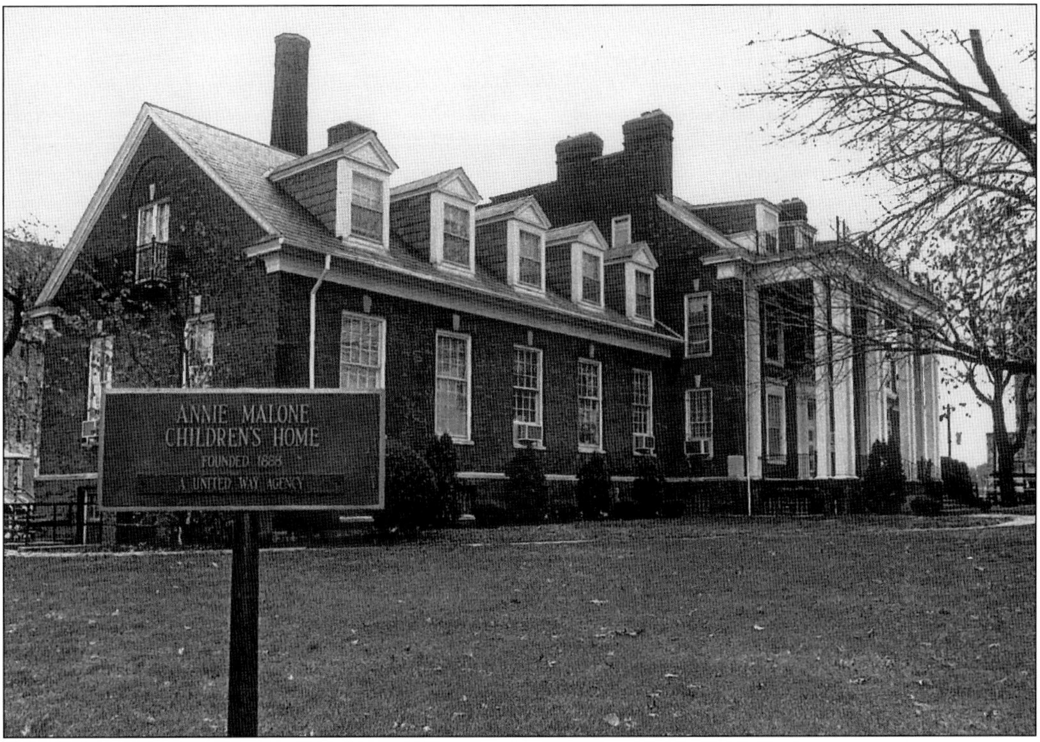

Annie Malone's Children's Home, pictured here, has been an important part of The Ville community for many years. Its history began in 1888 when a group of caring women established the St. Louis Colored Orphans' Home in a building at 1427 N. 12th Street. In 1905, the home was moved to a site on Natural Bridge, and in 1922, through the vision and generosity of Annie M. Malone, the agency relocated to its present location at 2612 Annie Malone Drive (formerly Goode Avenue). (Photo courtesy of Annie Malone Children's Home.)

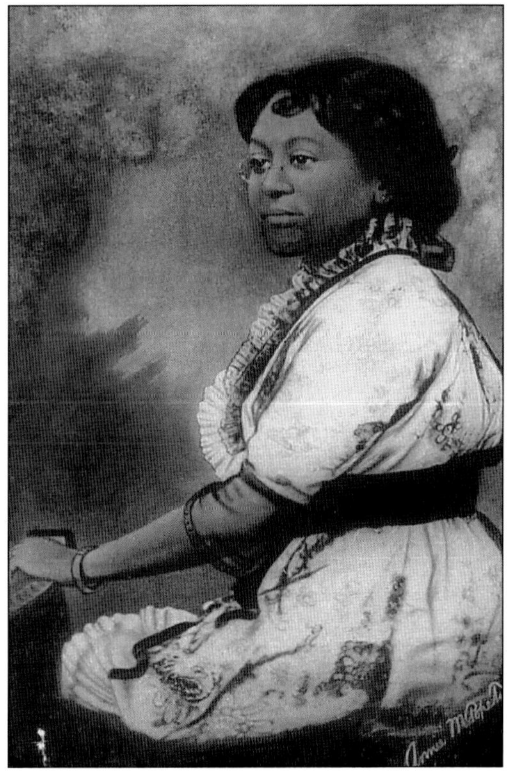

This portrait of Annie M. Malone hangs in the hall of the Annie Malone Children's Home. Ms. Malone donated the first $10,000 for the St. Louis Colored Orphan's Home site, and in 1946, the home was renamed Annie Malone Children's Home in her honor. Malone was the founder of Poro College and a pioneer manufacturer of cosmetic products for African-Americans. She served as president of the home's board from 1919 to 1943. (Photo courtesy of Annie Malone Children's Home.)

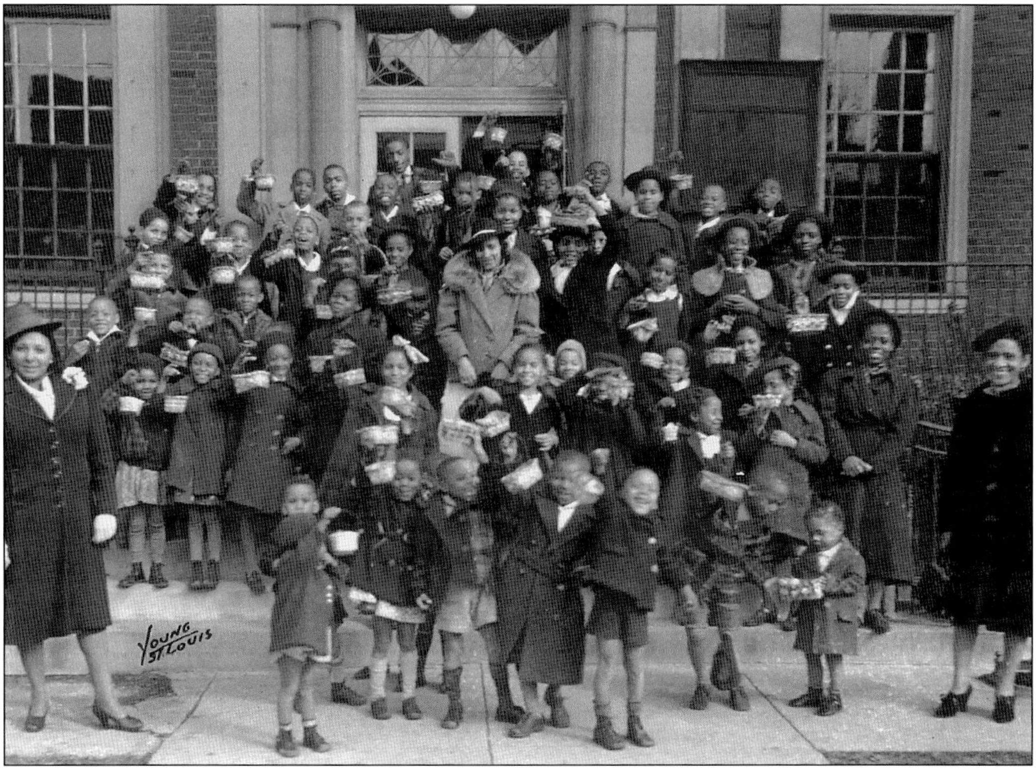

The Annie Malone Children's Home has always tried to make children feel at home and special by observing traditional community celebrations and holidays. As seen in this photograph, youngsters are enjoying an Easter celebration and showing off their baskets. The home presently serves more than 130 children annually in residential care, 200 families in the crisis center, and more than 1,000 teenagers through their community based programs. (Photo courtesy of Annie Malone Children's Home.)

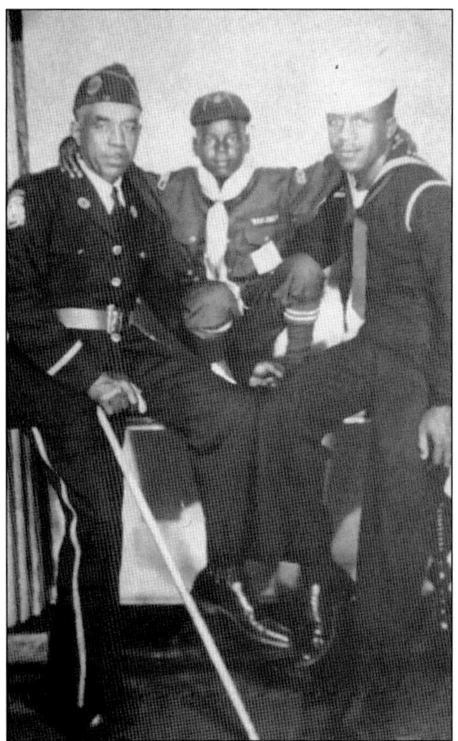

Each year hundreds of people and groups come together to participate in the May Day Parade. Pictured here after the 1943 May Day Parade is Abe Davis, a World War I veteran and one of the founders of the Jake Linder American Legion Post 107 in The Ville. Linder was reported to be the first African-American from St. Louis killed in World War I. Seated on Davis' right is his grandson Clarence H. Vincent, a Cub Scout with Pack 124, and his nephew Benjamin F. Davis in the sailor's uniform on the left. (Photo courtesy of James Vincent.)

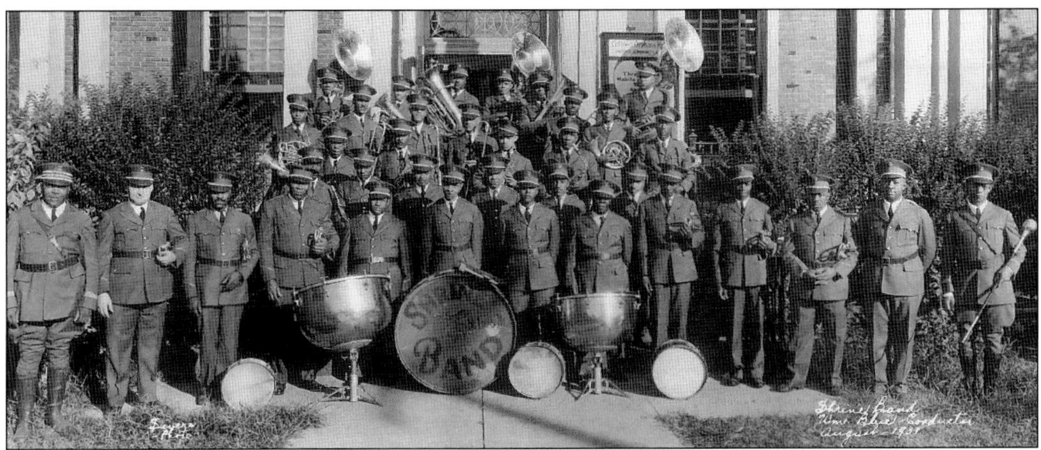

Since 1909 the May Day Parade has been a major community event bringing groups and bands together to aid Annie Malone Children's Home in its most significant fund raising efforts. The Shriner's Band in this picture formed by William Blue has been an active participant annually in the May Day Parades. (Photo courtesy of Odessa Farrell.)

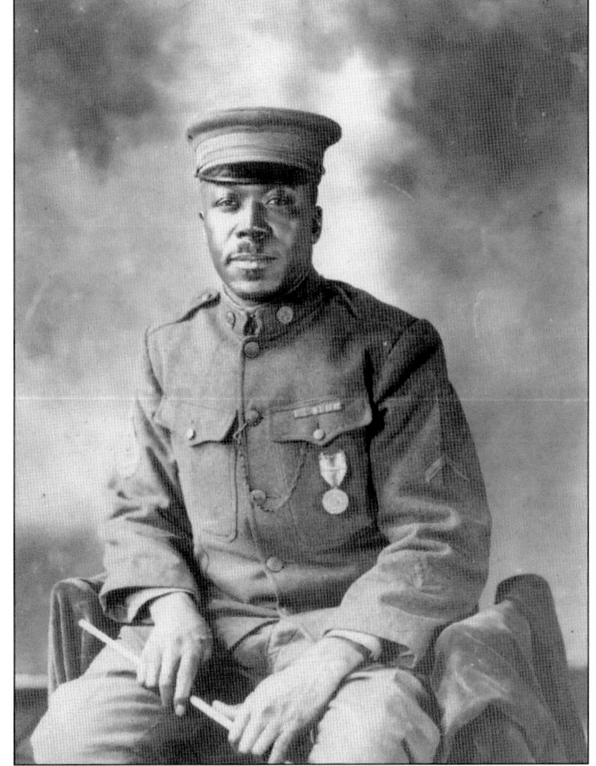

William Blue, pictured here, was founder of the Shriner's and American Woodmens Bands. Both bands were active participants in the May Day Parade. In the early 1920s, Blue was the head of the Haskell and Blues School of Music in St. Louis. He also wrote the Tuskegee Cadets March in 1906. (Photo courtesy of Odessa Farrell.)

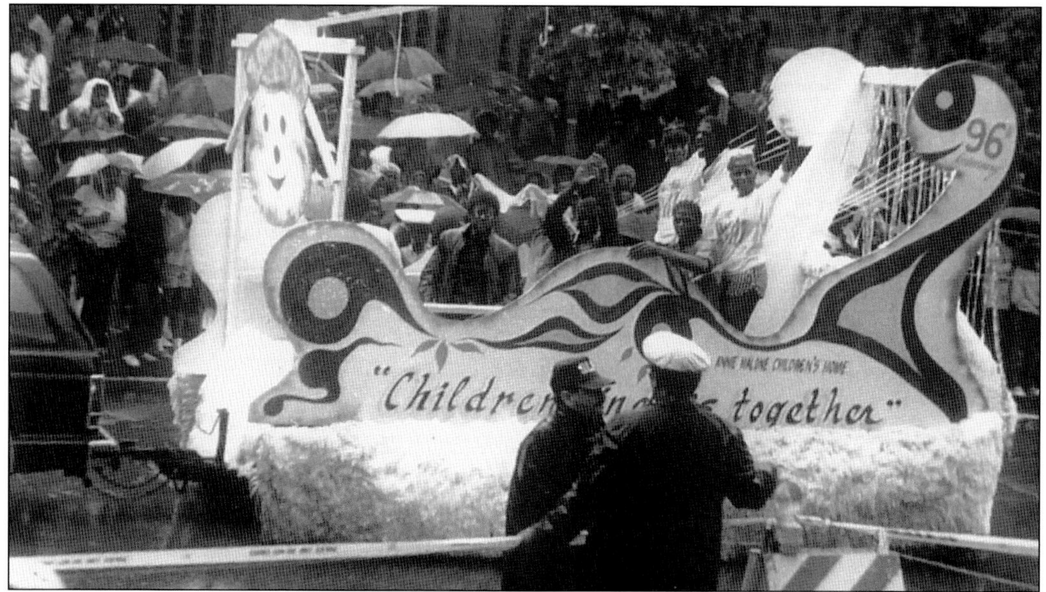

One of the thrills of the early May Day Parades was watching the marching precision of the various groups, and admiring floats like the one photographed as it was going through the streets of The Ville. Residents would sit in windows and on porches all afternoon and call out to their friends as they would go by. Because of safety concerns, the parade now goes down Natural Bridge Road a few blocks north of The Ville community. (Photo courtesy of the Annie Malone Children's Home.)

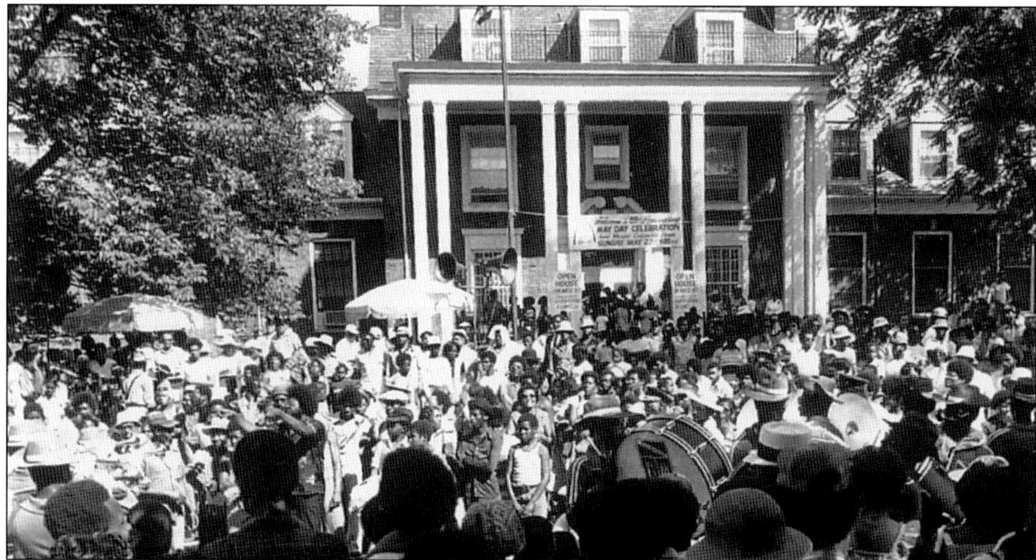

At the end of each May Day Parade, participants would pass a viewing stand in front of the children's home. Spectators like these are awed by the intricate dance routines of marching bands, the wail and throb of drum and bugle corps, and the difficult steps of majorettes and drum majors. Viewers are also treated as they watch the rhythmic cadence of the Greek step shows and the elegance of the Eastern Stars and Daughters of Isis. (Photo courtesy of Annie Malone Children's Home.)

Homer G. Phillips (1880–1931) was the prime mover in the battle to include funding for a hospital for African Americans in a 1923 bond issue. Phillips did not live to see the hospital's completion because he was shot to death while waiting for a bus in a never-solved murder. The incident took place at Aubert Avenue and Delmar Boulevard on June 18, 1931. (Photo by Nathan Young. Courtesy of the University of Missouri-St. Louis, Western Manuscript Collection.)

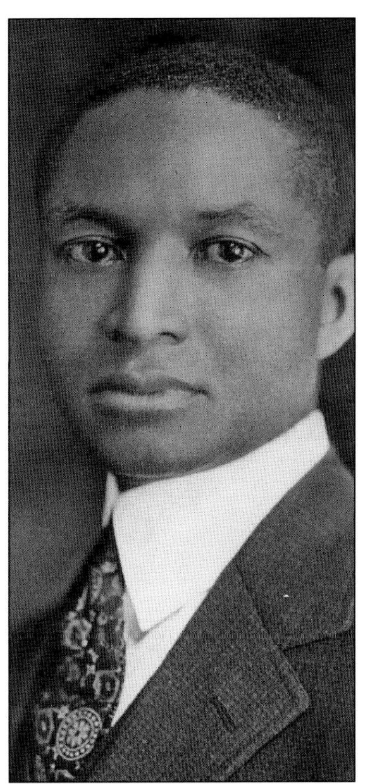

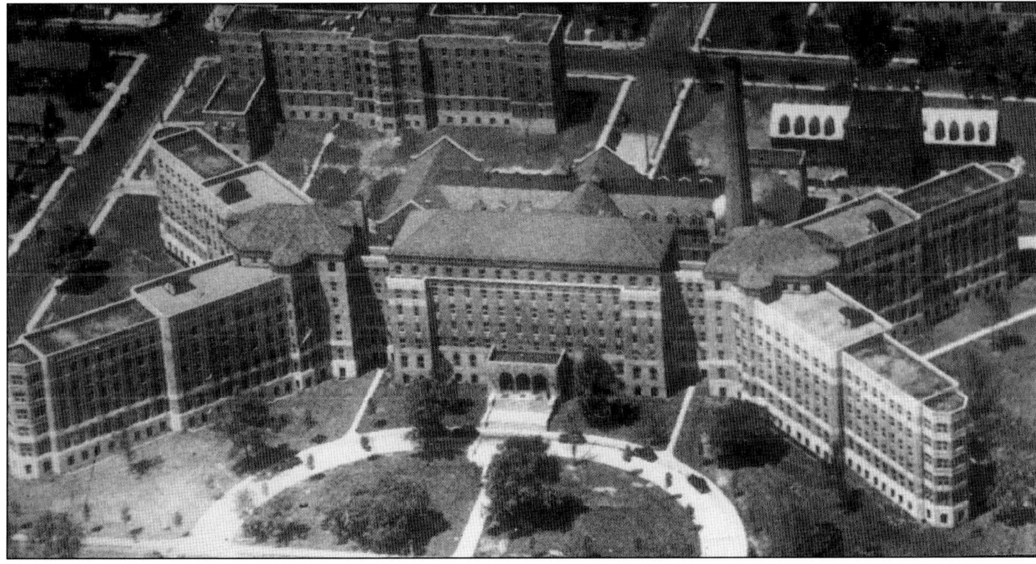

This is the way Homer G. Phillips Hospital looked at its dedication in 1937. The hospital was comprised of five buildings, namely the central or administration building, north and south ward buildings, service building, the nurses' home with an annex for apartments of the superintendent and medical director, and quarters for interns and resident physicians. Resident physicians and interns were also housed on the sixth floor of the administration building. (Photo courtesy of the University of Missouri-St. Louis, Western Manuscript Collection.)

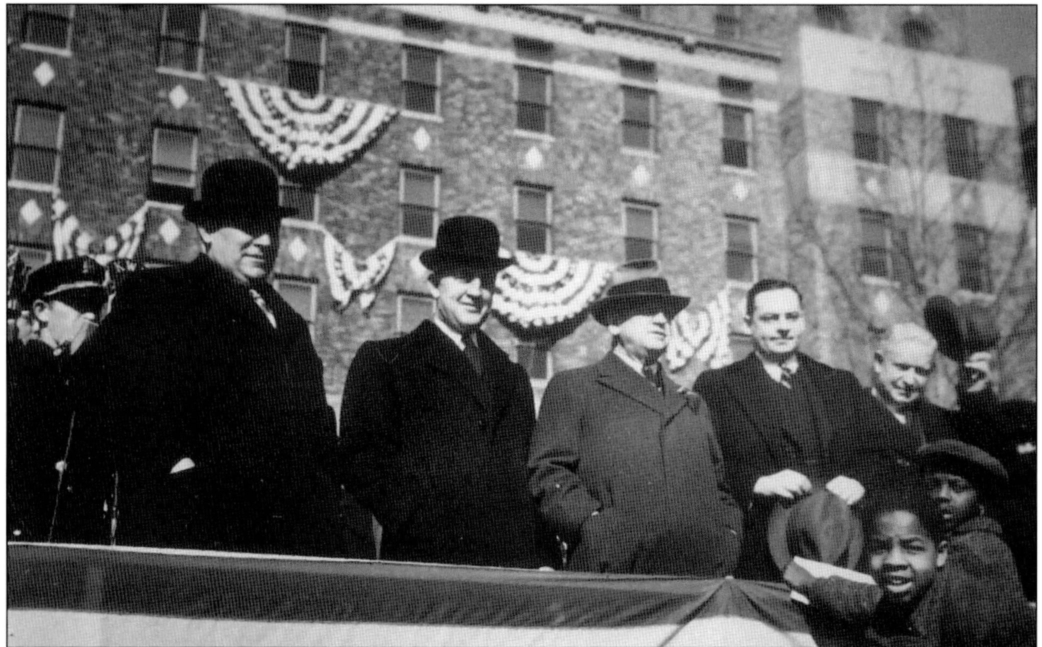

Among the guests of honor present at the dedication of Homer G. Phillips Hospital were, from left to right: Gov. Lloyd C. Stark of Missouri; Honorable Harold L. Ickes, Secretary of the Interior; Congressman Thomas Hennings Jr.; and Comptroller, Louis Holte. (Photo courtesy of the University of Missouri-St. Louis, Western Manuscript Collection.)

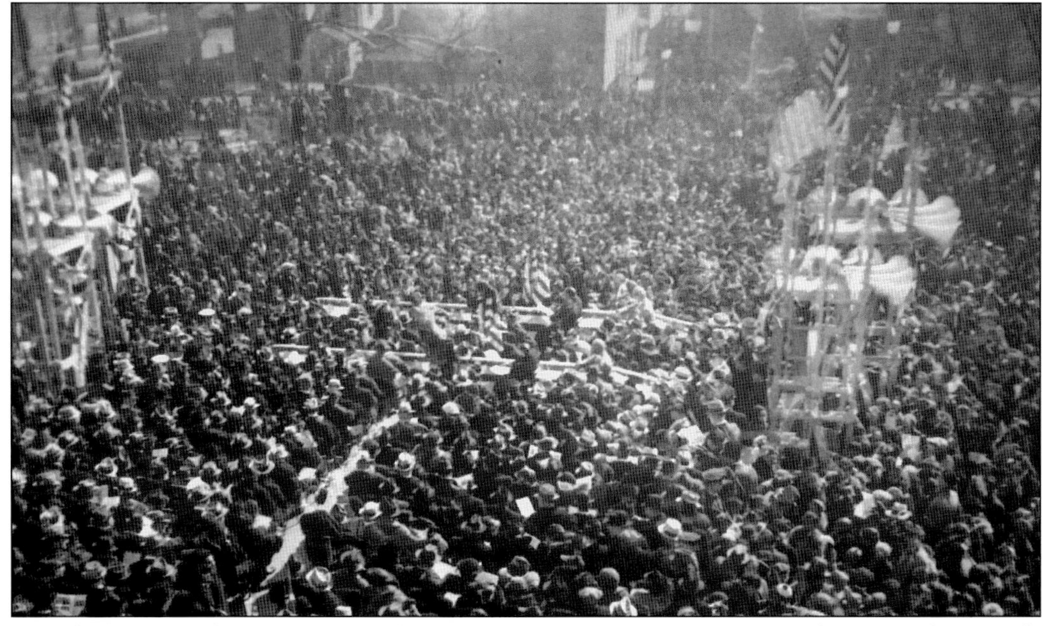

The dedication of Homer G. Phillips Hospital was a major event in the city. Thousands of people jammed the streets around the hospital for blocks, as it can be seen in this photo. (Photo courtesy of University of Missouri of Missouri-St. Louis, Western Manuscript Collection.)

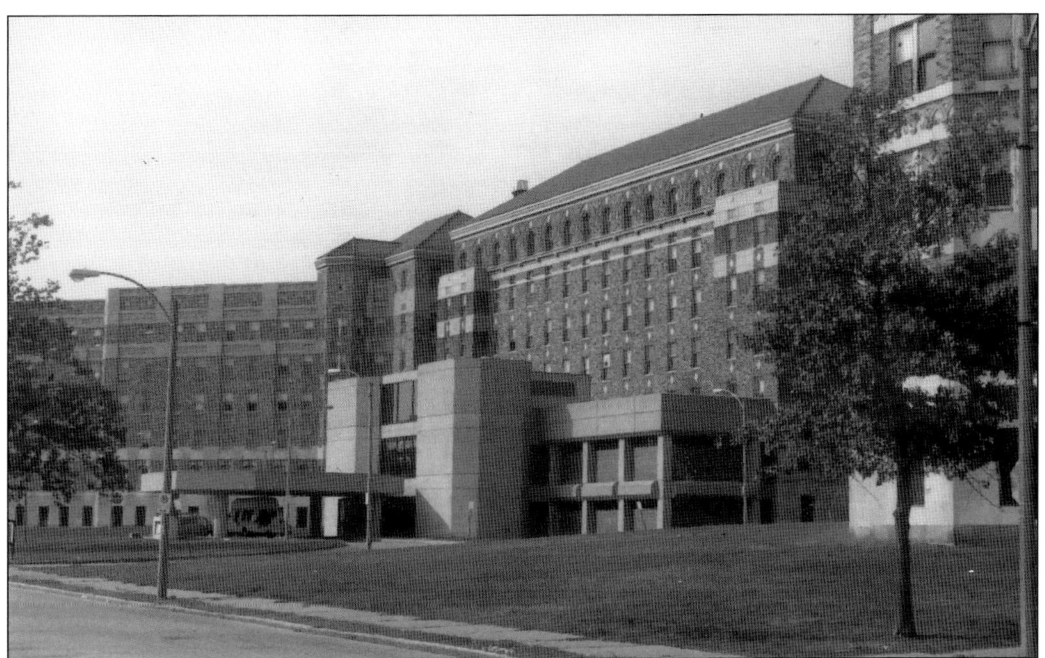

From the outset, Homer G. Phillips Hospital, pictured here, was an extremely busy place. During fiscal year 1938–39, 10,571 patients were admitted, for a total of 210,940 days of hospital care given. The average daily patient census was 575. During 1939–40, there were 1,277 live births, 660 major operations, and 702 minor operations. (Photo by John A. Wright.)

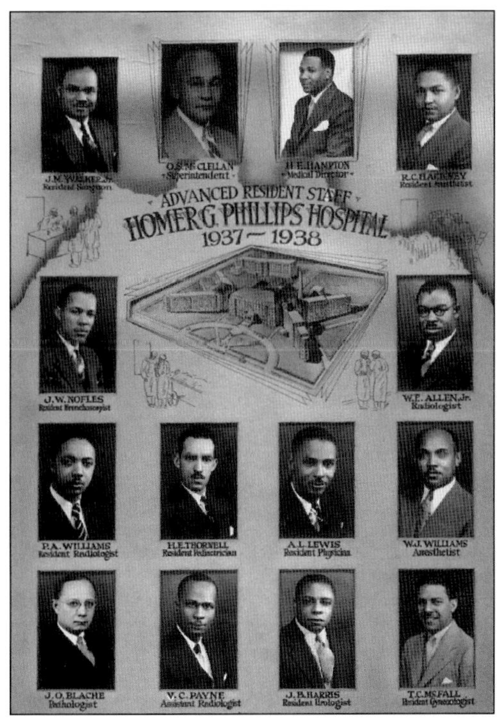

Pictured here is the first class of advanced residents at Homer G. Phillips. From its first year of operation (1937), Homer G. Phillips Hospital was a training institution. By 1939, the house staff consisted of 52 black physicians, and the hospital accepted approximately 50 percent of the black graduates of United States medical schools annually. (Photo courtesy of the University of Missouri-St. Louis, Western Manuscript Collection.)

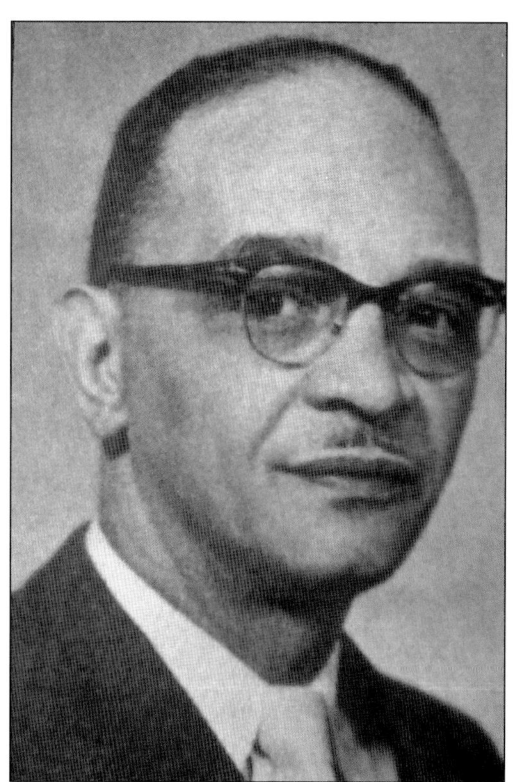

Homer G. Phillips' first medical director was Dr. Henry E. Hampton, who was succeeded in 1941 by Dr. William Sinkler, pictured here. In 1956, he became the chief of surgery. It was Sinkler's opinion that the hospital should train African-Americans so that in the future they would be able to stand on their own. Sinkler lived to see the fulfillment of his efforts. At the time of his untimely death in September 1960, every department at Homer G. Phillips had an African-American as director or associated director. (Photo courtesy of Dr. Frank Richards.)

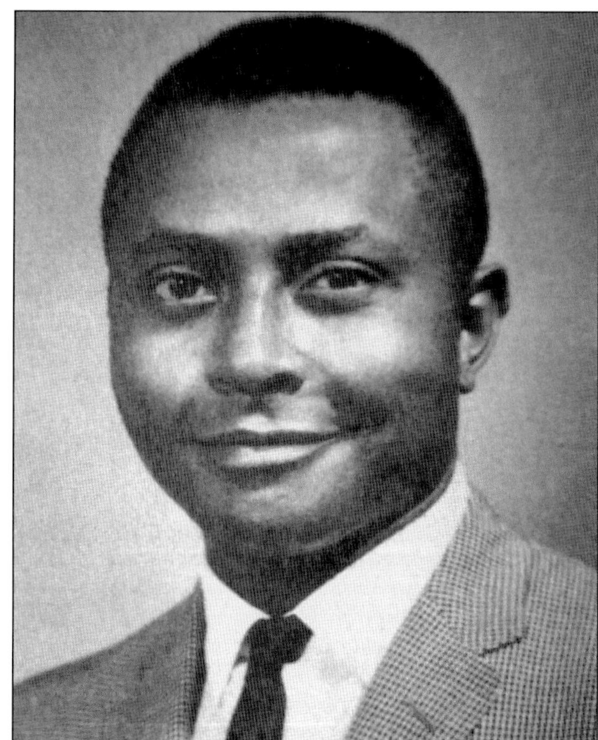

This photograph is of Dr. Andrew Spencer, who followed Dr. Sinkler as the chief of surgery. He continued as chief until the hospital closed in the late 1970s. (Photo courtesy of Frank Richards.)

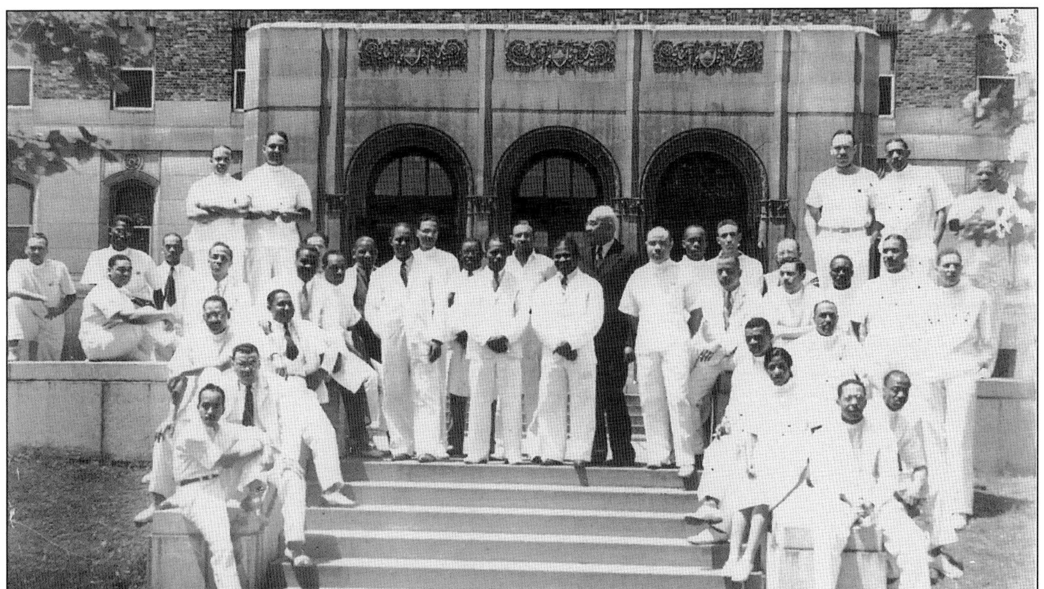

Homer G. Phillips was a Class "A" General Hospital approved for junior internships, assistant residencies, and residencies by the American Council on Medical Education and the American College of Surgeons. Pictured here in front of the hospital is a class of interns taken in the late 1930s or early 1940s. Although there were small numbers of blacks graduating from predominantly white medical schools, they were not considered for hospital training in those institutions after the M.D. degree had been awarded. (Photo courtesy of Vivian Dreer.)

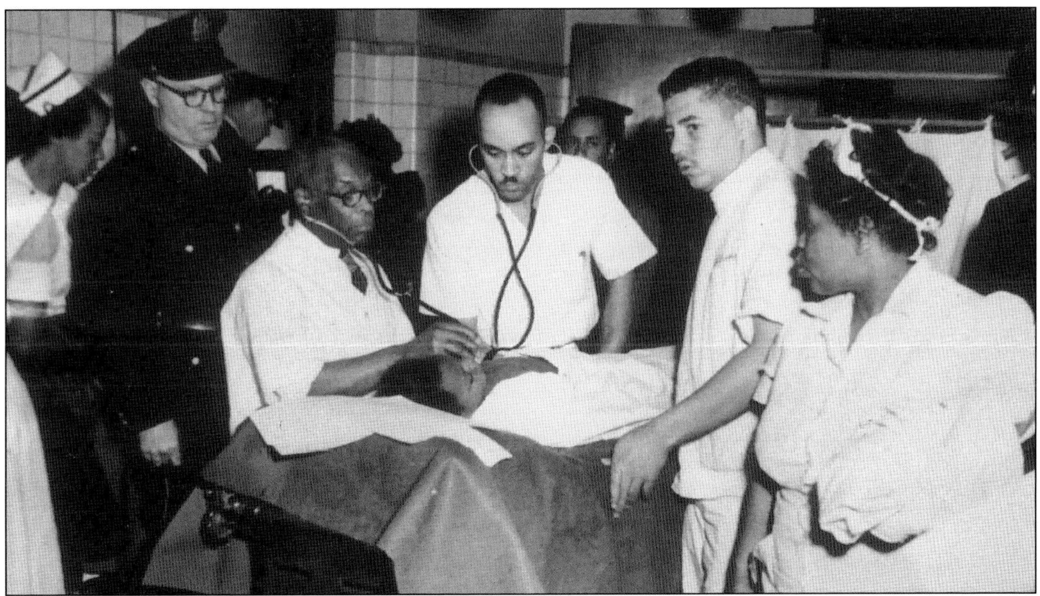

The Homer G. Phillips Hospital emergency room was always a busy place. Dr. Roscoe Haskell is shown examining a young boy. Haskell was the first superintendent of City Hospital No. 2 and served from 1918 to 1925. (Photo courtesy of the University of Missouri-St. Louis, Western Manuscript Collection.)

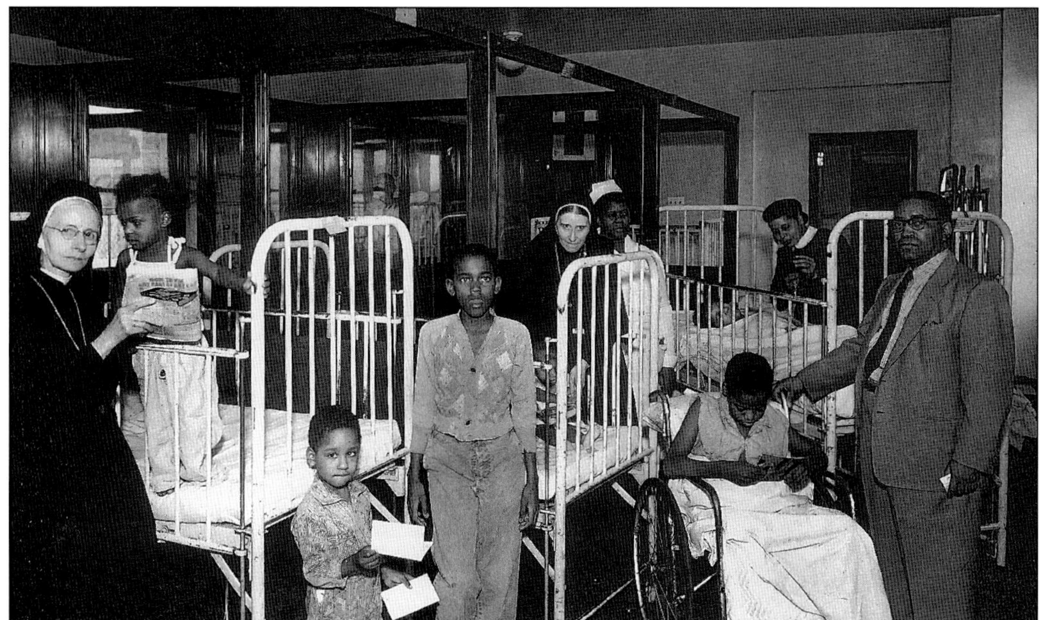

Sister Colette de Galzain and Mother Flora Sapart, from the Society of Helpers of the Holy Souls (Now Called Society of Helpers), are pictured here with Mr. Virgil McKnight on the ward at Homer G. Phillips Hospital. The society donated a great deal of their time and energy serving the African-American community. (Photo courtesy of Sister Patricia Hottinger.)

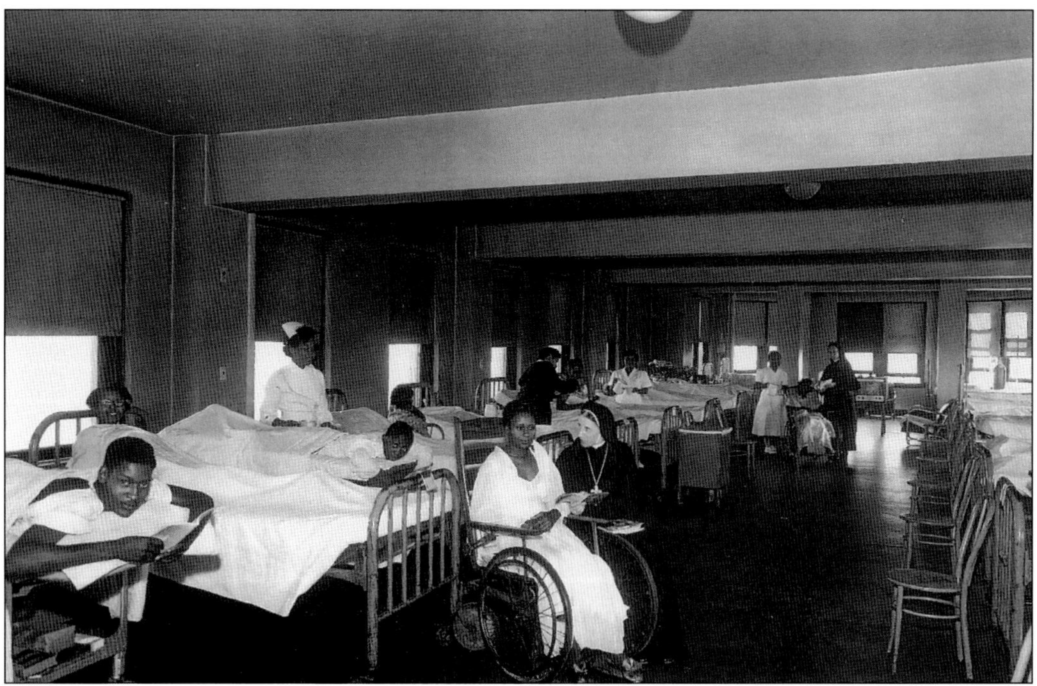

Nuns from the Society of Helpers are shown here on the ward ministering to the sick. As seen in this picture, patients did not have private rooms. A curtain wall was rolled over to the beds when privacy was needed. (Photo courtesy of Sister Patricia Hottinger.)

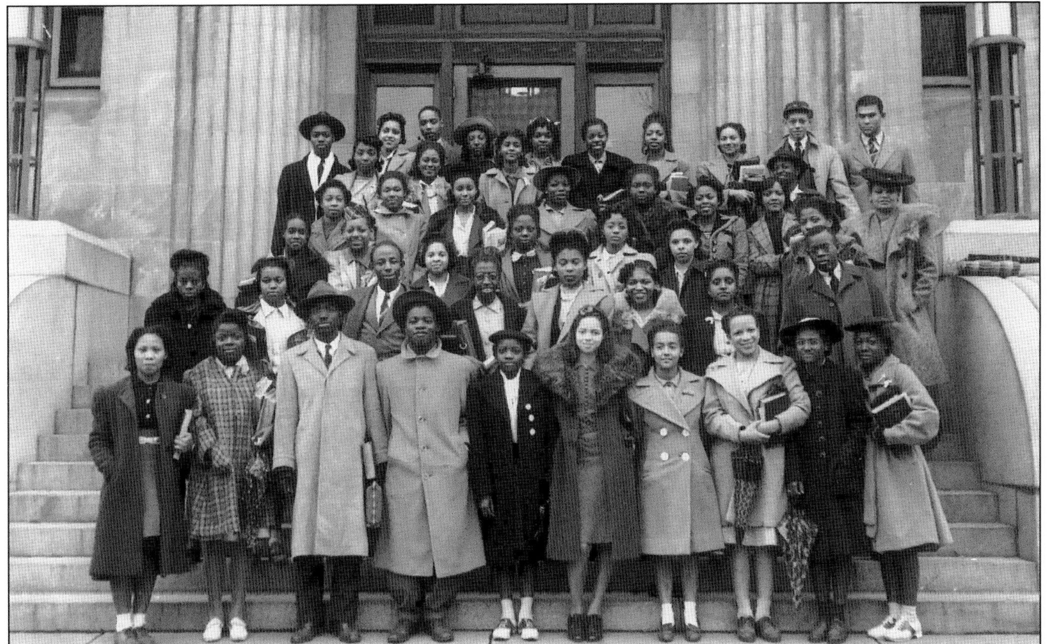

Homer G. Phillips was not only a training center for doctors and nurses, it also provided learning opportunities for students in the community. This group of students from Sumner High School are participating in a field trip to the hospital. (Photo courtesy of the St. Louis Public Schools Archives.)

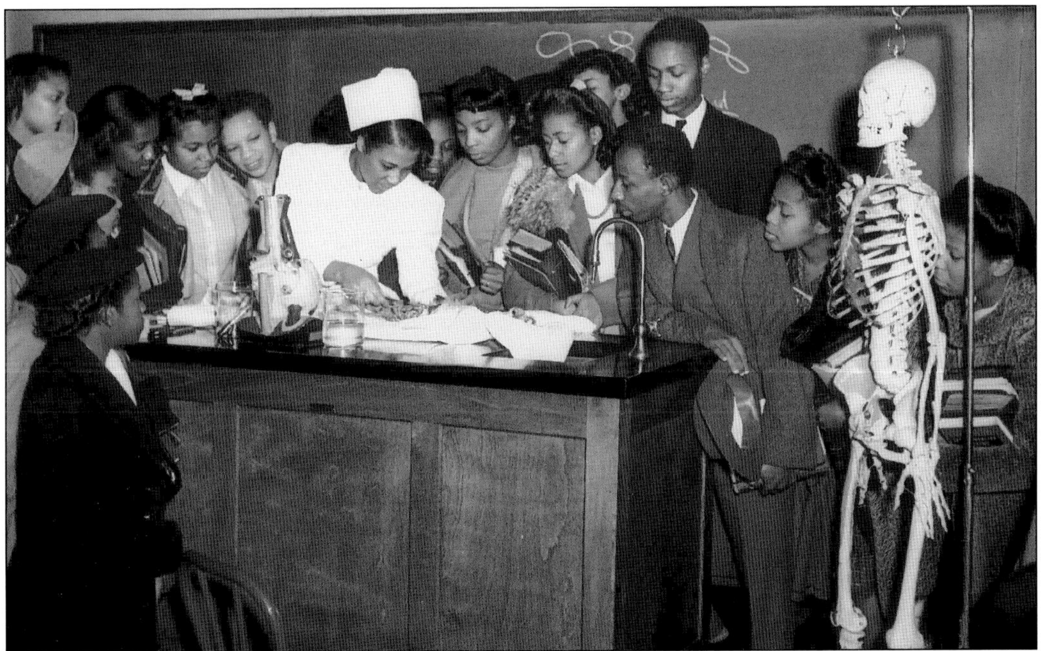

While on field trips at Homer G. Phillips Hospital, students were able to gain first hand experiences in nursing education. These students are giving full attention to a nurse performing a dissection. (Photo courtesy of the St. Louis Public Schools Archives.)

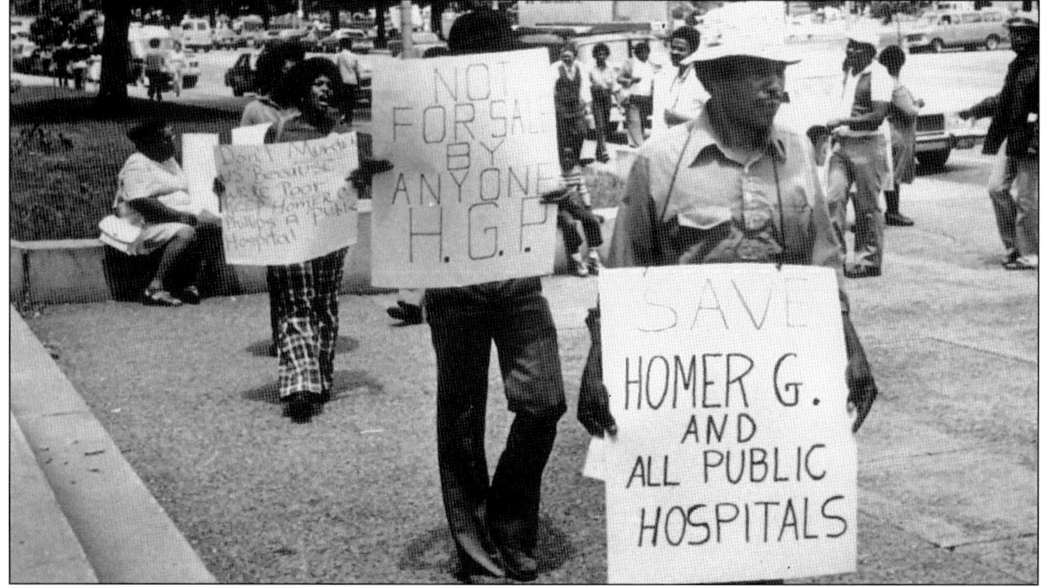

As the city began to reduce its budget for health care facilities it also began discussions to close or merge Homer G. Phillips with the Max C. Starkloff Memorial Hospital. These proposals brought strong protest, which led to pickets and sit-ins from citizens like the ones pictured here. At that time, the hospital employed approximately 800–900 people and was the major source of employment in The Ville. (Photo courtesy of the Mercantile Library.)

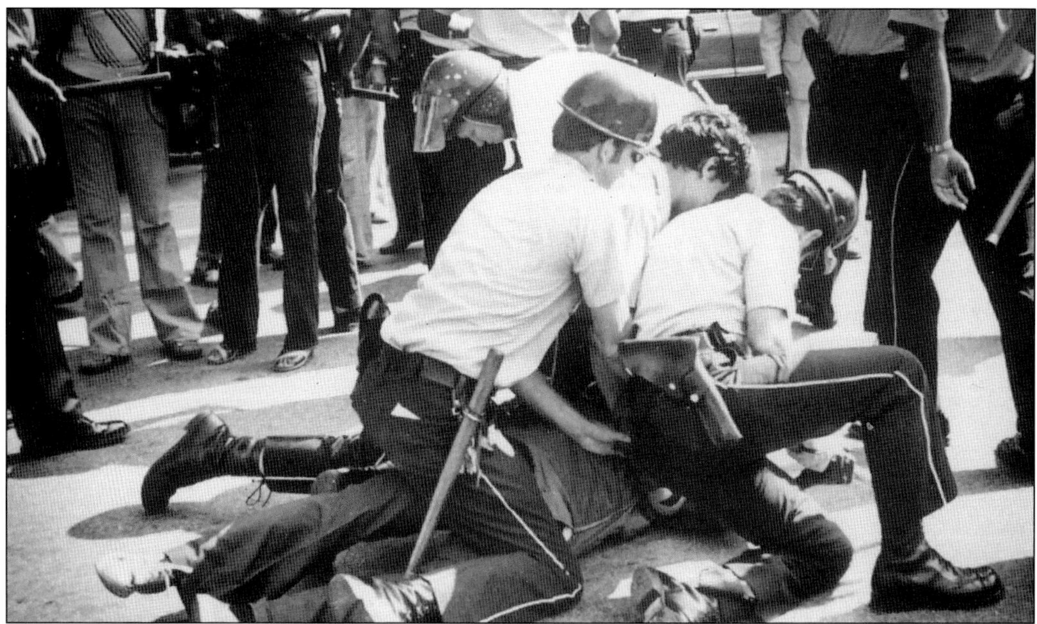

In 1973, St. Louis commissioned two separate audits of the city hospital. Both recommended closing City Hospital No. 1 and retaining Homer G. Phillips. However, in 1979, Homer G. Phillips closed its doors. As it can be seen from this picture the closing did not go down easily in the community. Several hundred police officers were needed to keep the peace as the last patients were removed. (Photo courtesy of the Mercantile Library.)

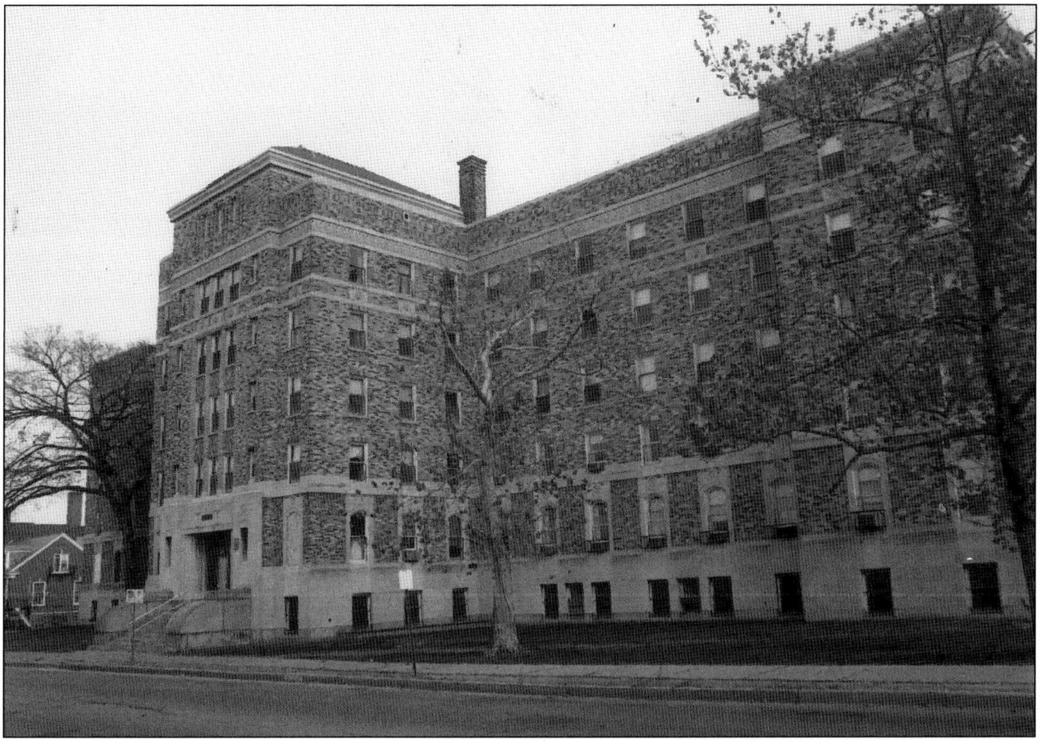

This five story building was the nurses' residence. It provided living quarters for 147 students and 14 faculty members adjacent to the hospital with a connecting tunnel. (Photo by John A. Wright.)

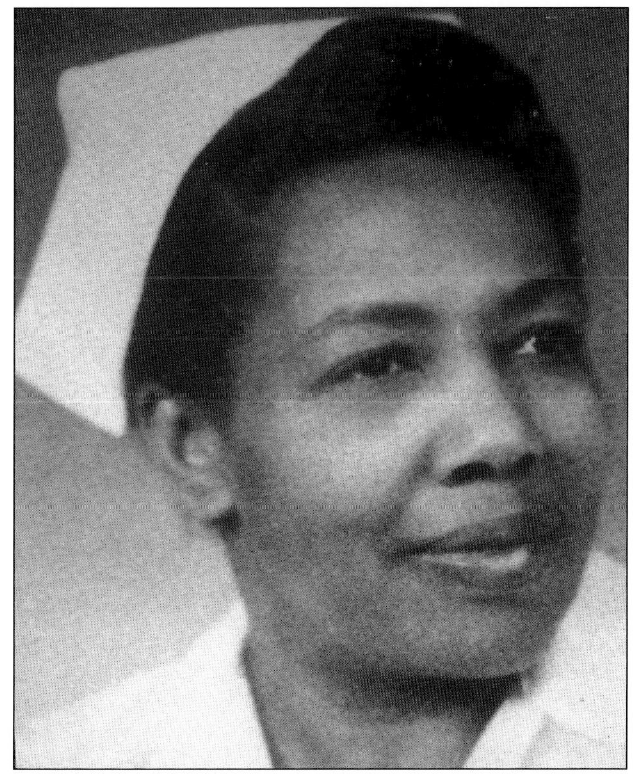

Minnie Edyth T. Gore, pictured here, was the former director of nursing at Homer G. Phillips Hospital. During her directorship, she graduated 600 of the total number of 1,036 nurses who received their training at Homer G. Phillips Hospital School of Nursing. It was also under her leadership that the hospital received national accreditation for its diploma program from the National League for Nursing Accreditation Service. (Photo courtesy of Geraldine Johnson.)

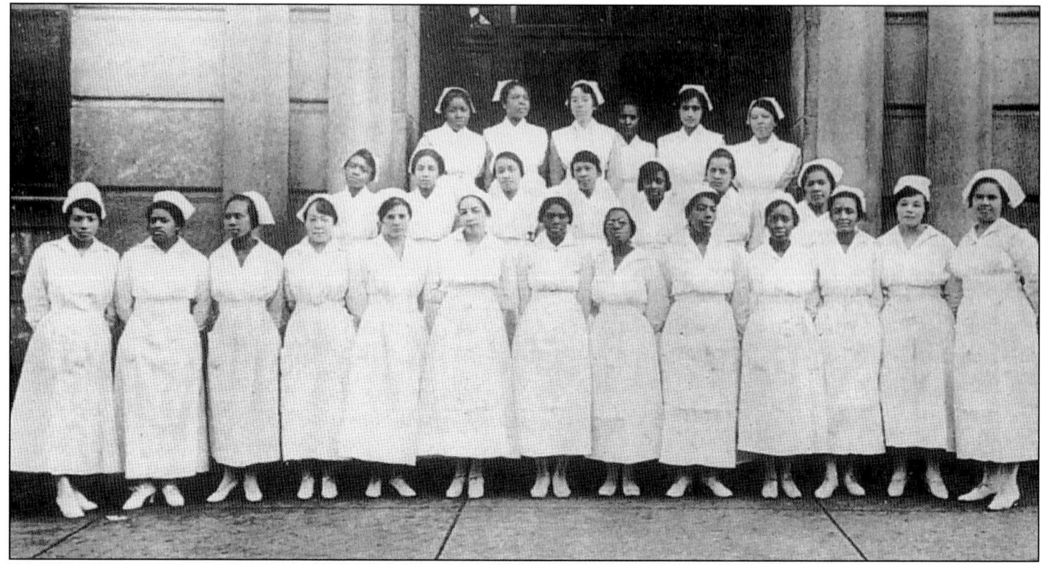

City Hospital No. 2 School of Nursing (now known as Homer G. Phillips School of Nursing) was accredited in 1920. Pictured here are members of the 1922 student body and staff. Bessie Newsome Cole, a member of the first graduating class, worked for the Visiting Nurses' Association in St. Louis. Estelle Massey Riddle Osborne96, a member of the second class, went on to become superintendent of the Homer G. Phillips Hospital School of Nursing, a teacher at New York University, and president of the National Association of Colored Graduate Nurses. (Photo courtesy of Jacqueline Ervin Creighton and Ella Brown.)

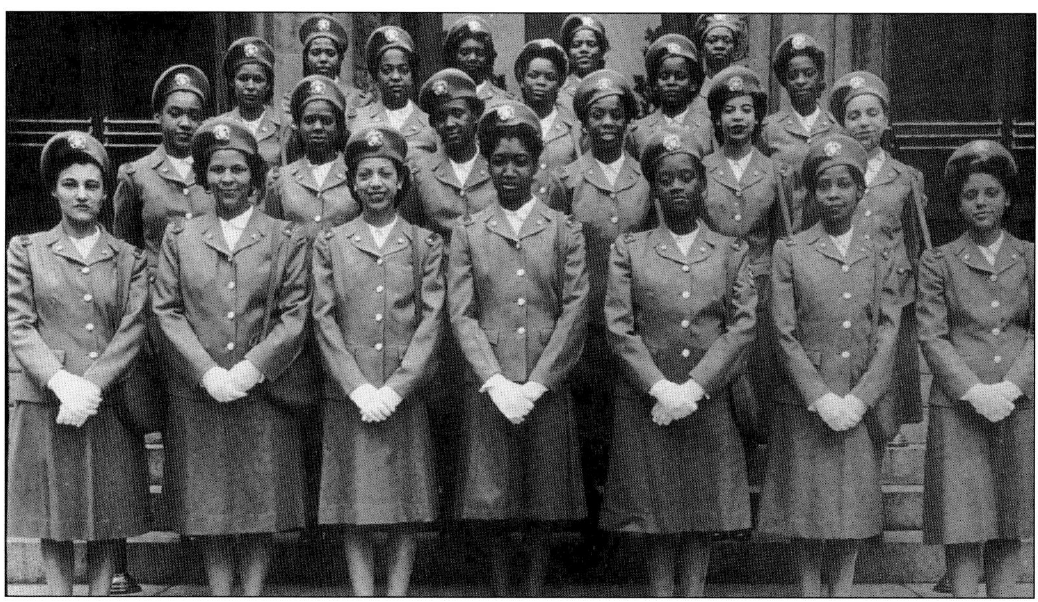

These young ladies are members of the Cadet Nurses' Corps. The United States Public Health Service approved the federal Cadet Nursing Training Program for Homer G. Phillips in July 1943. Under this program, the students were provided uniforms, tuition, board, registration fees, and books, as well as a monthly allowance. (Photo courtesy of Jacqueline Ervin Creighton and Ella Brown.)

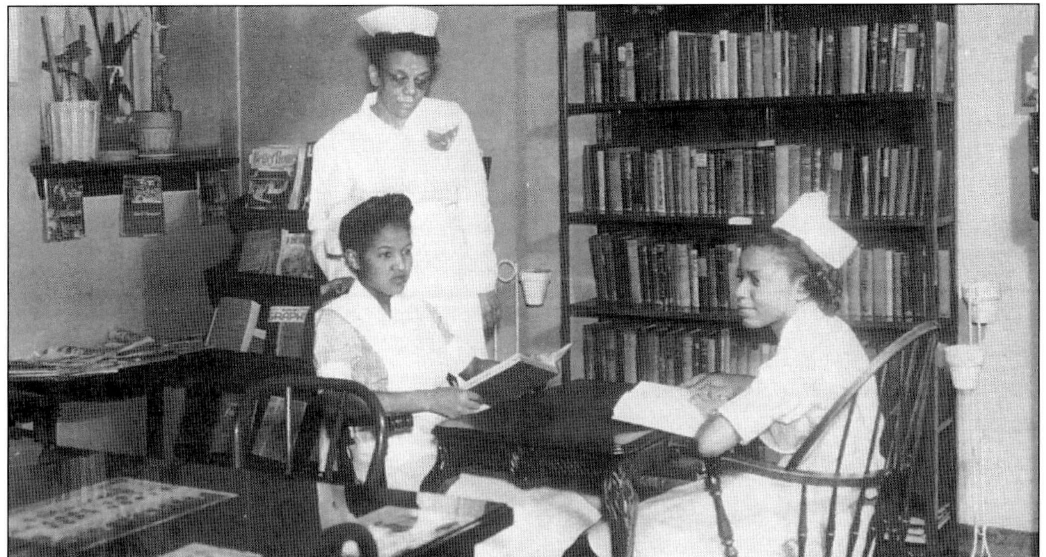

The Homer G. Phillips Hospital School of Nursing offered courses in biological and physical sciences, social and medical sciences, nursing, and the allied arts such as nutrition, gynecological nursing, surgical techniques, etc. These young students are reviewing their class material. (Photo courtesy of Jacqueline Ervin Creighton and Ella Brown.)

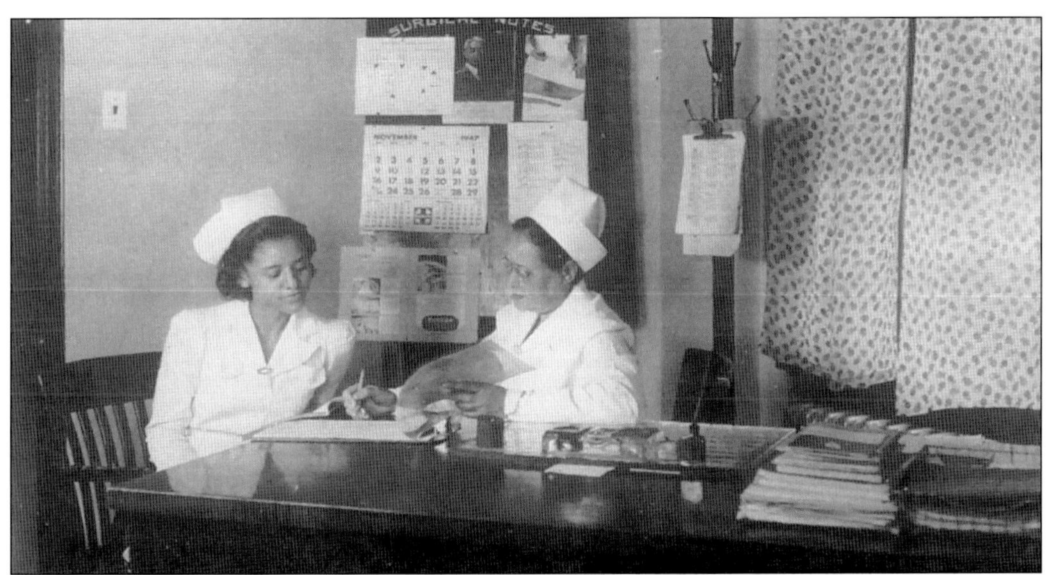

Members of the house and visiting staff at the hospital aided in the teaching program at the nursing school. These faculty members are reviewing the program and assignments for the day. (Photo courtesy of Jacqueline Ervin Creighton and Ella Brown.)

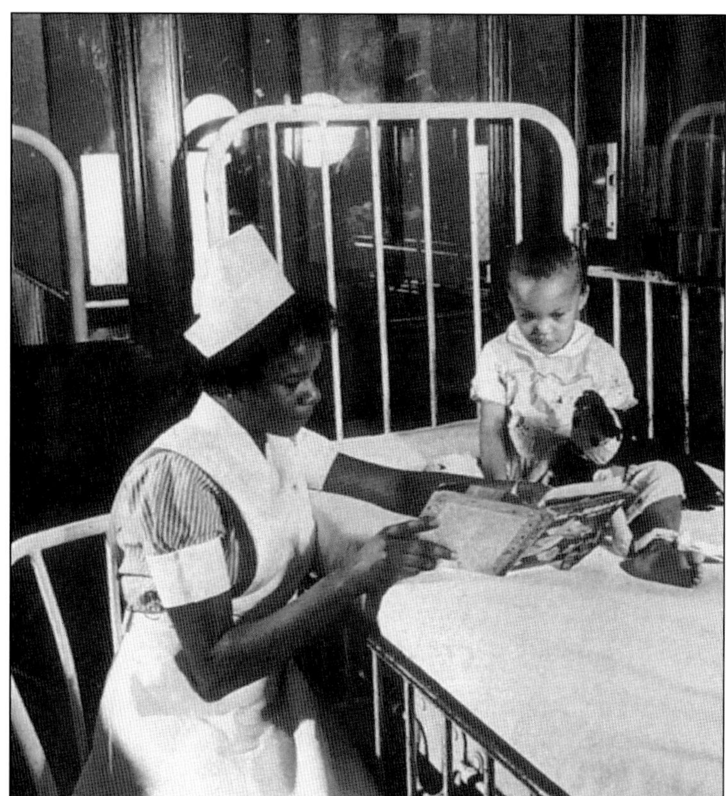

As part of the nurse's training program, students, like the one in this picture reading to a young child, were taught how to personalize their patient care. (Photo courtesy of Jacqueline Ervin Creighton and Ella Brown.)

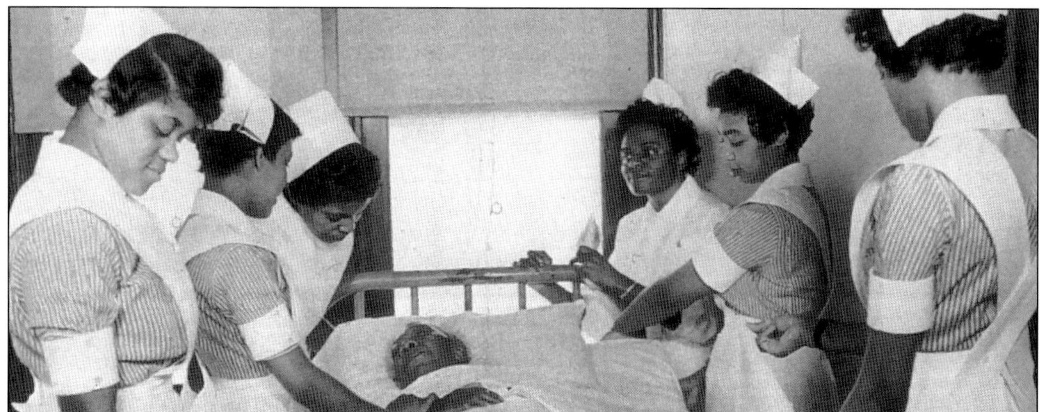

These students are accompanying staff nurses on their daily rounds to become acquainted with bedside patient care. (Photo courtesy of Jacqueline Ervin Creighton and Ella Brown.)

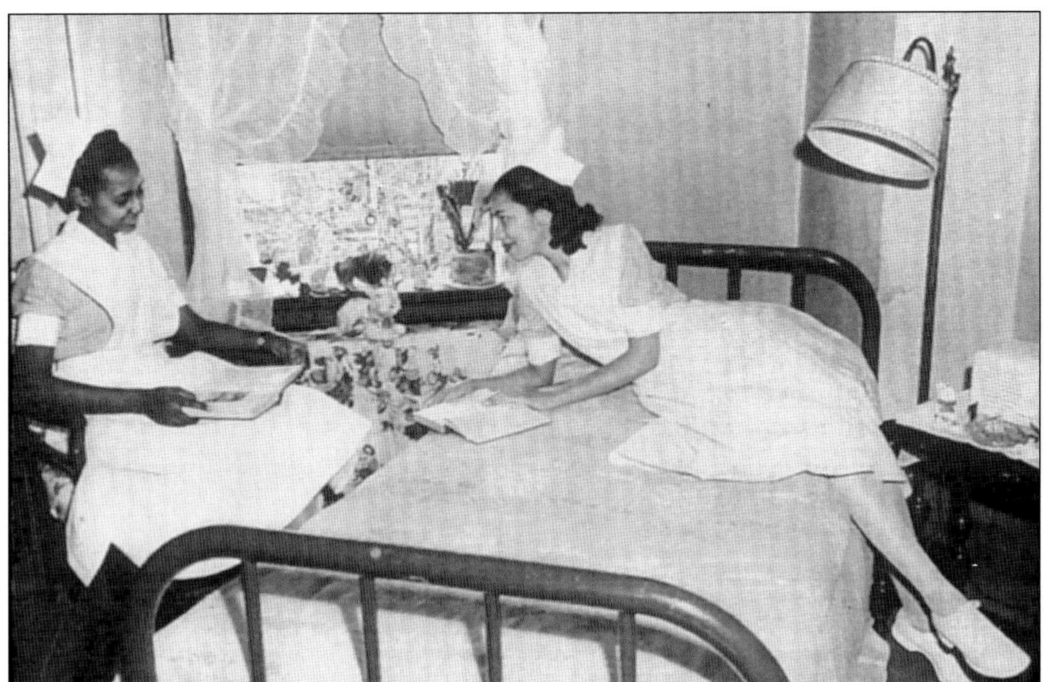

Students needing a quiet place for study could always find haven in their rooms as the students pictured here. (Photo courtesy of Jacqueline Ervin Creighton and Ella Brown.)

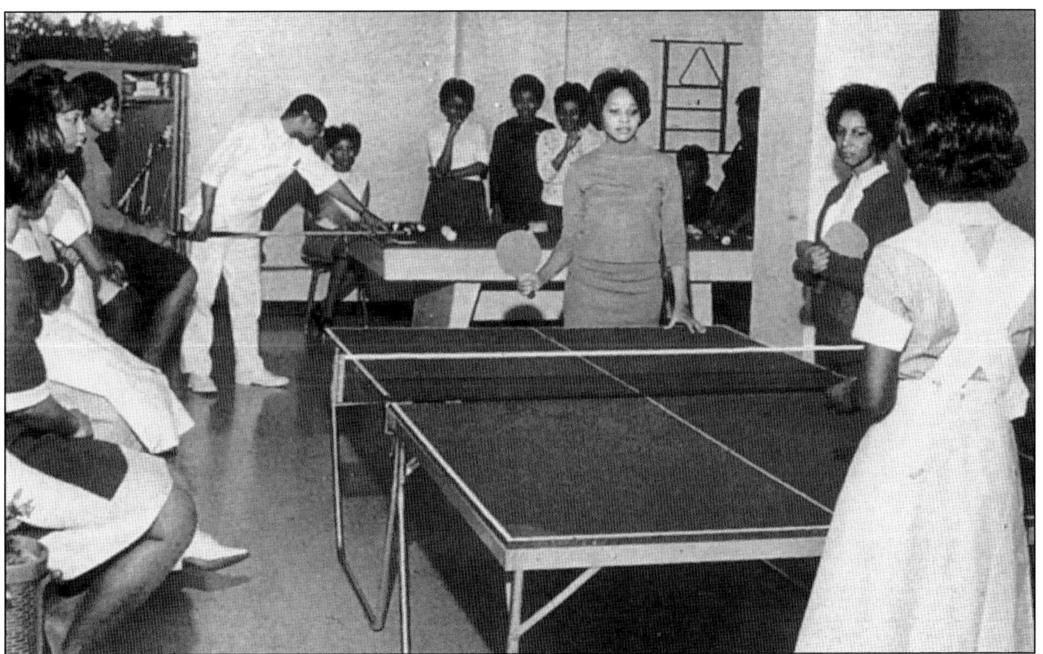

These students are taking time out to watch television and play games in the student lounge. (Photo courtesy of Jacqueline Ervin Creighton and Ella Brown.)

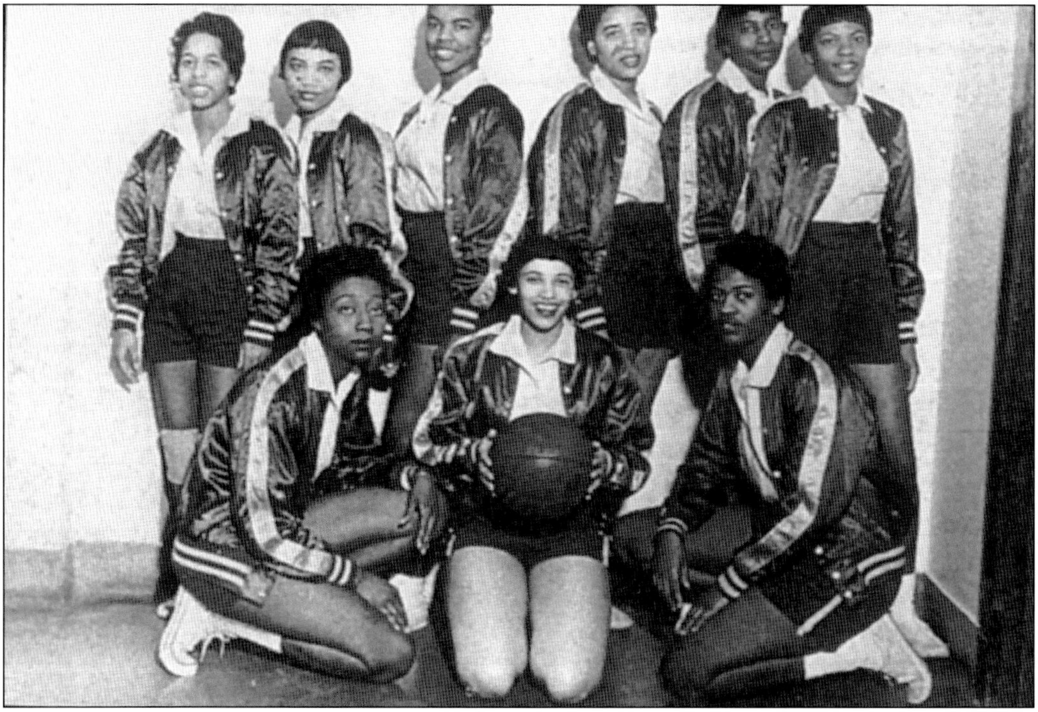

Homer G. Phillips Hospital School of Nursing provided many extra-curricular activities for its students. Pictured here are members of the school's basketball team. (Photo courtesy of Jacqueline Ervin Creighton and Ella Brown.)

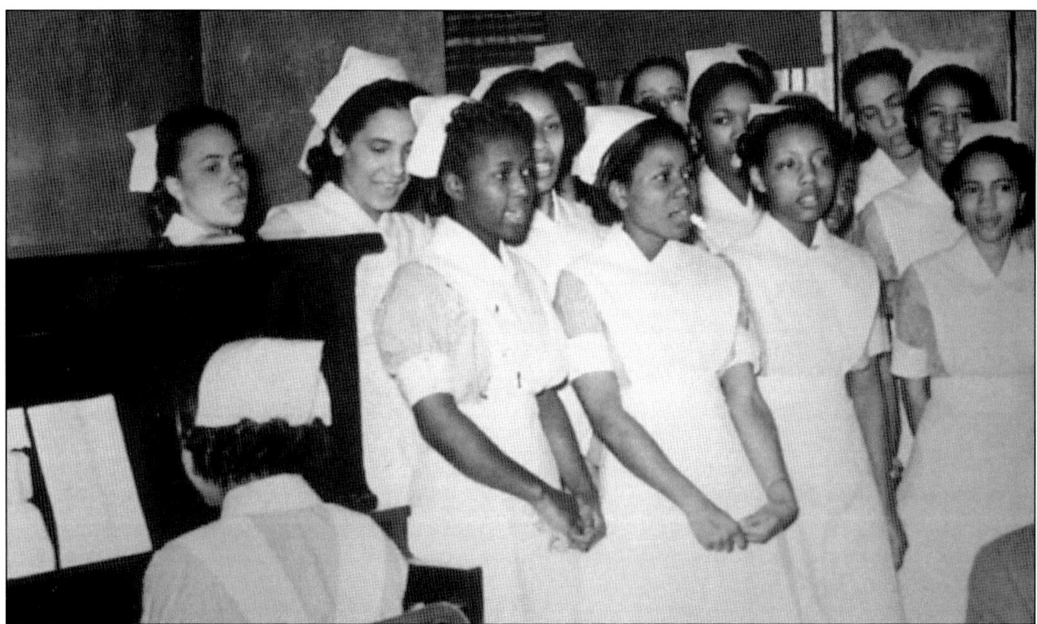

Members of the Homer G. Phillips Hospital School of Nursing's choir are shown here during their performance at the dedication of the school's library in 1941. (Photo Courtesy of the University of Missouri, Western Manuscript Collection.)

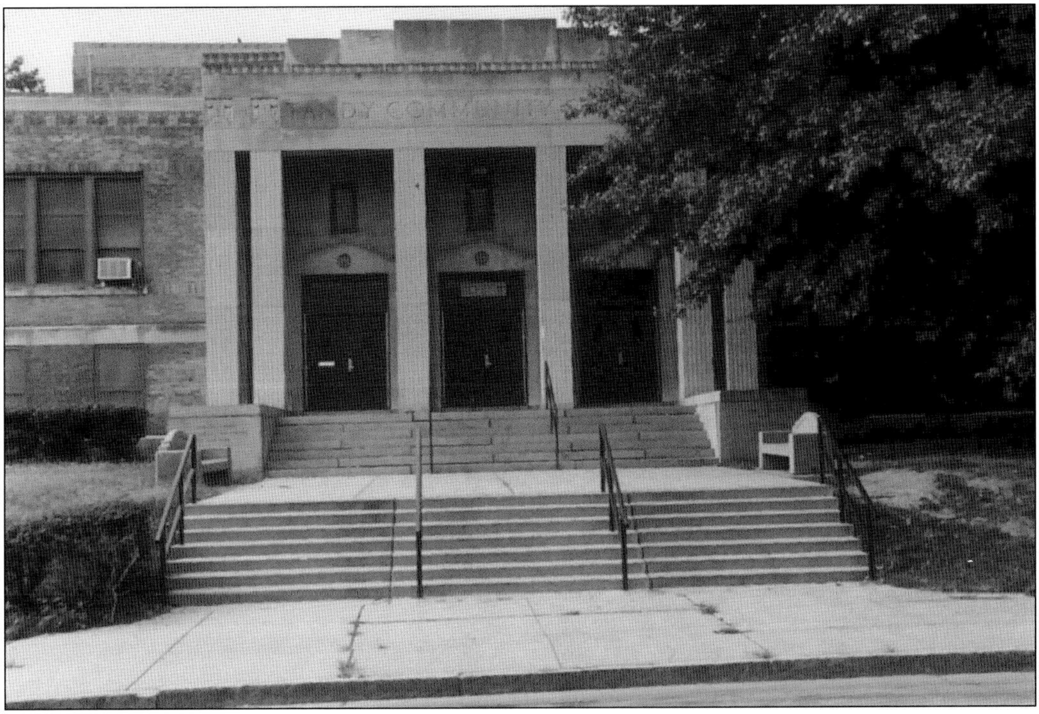

The building in this photograph is Tandy Community Center which opened in 1938. The Center had reading rooms, a swimming pool, a basketball court, boxing, and an industrial arts program. The committee that pressed for this recreational facility for African-Americans included Messrs. James Cook, David Grant, C.M. Evans, C.B. Broussard, W.H.J. Beckett Vashon, and Dr. O.S. McLellan. (Photo by John A. Wright.)

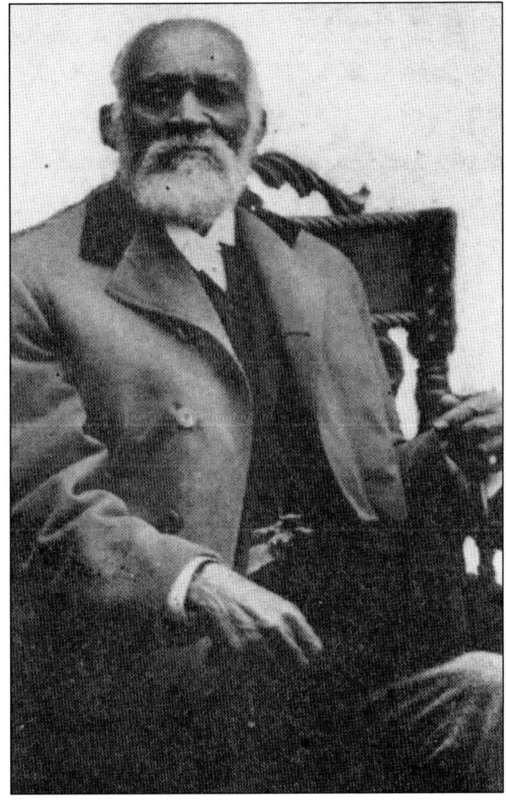

This distinguished gentleman is Charlton H. Tandy, for whom Tandy Community Cener is named. Tandy was a military hero in the Civil War, and a leader in the movement for public education for blacks in Missouri, and one of the founders of Lincoln University. During the 1880s, he worked to enforce an 1867 court order allowing blacks to ride inside public transportation vehicles. To prevent drivers from passing up black passengers, he grabbed the reins and held the horse until passengers, black and white alike, were allowed to board. (Photo by Nathan Young. Courtesy of University of Missouri-St. Louis, Western Manuscript Collection.)

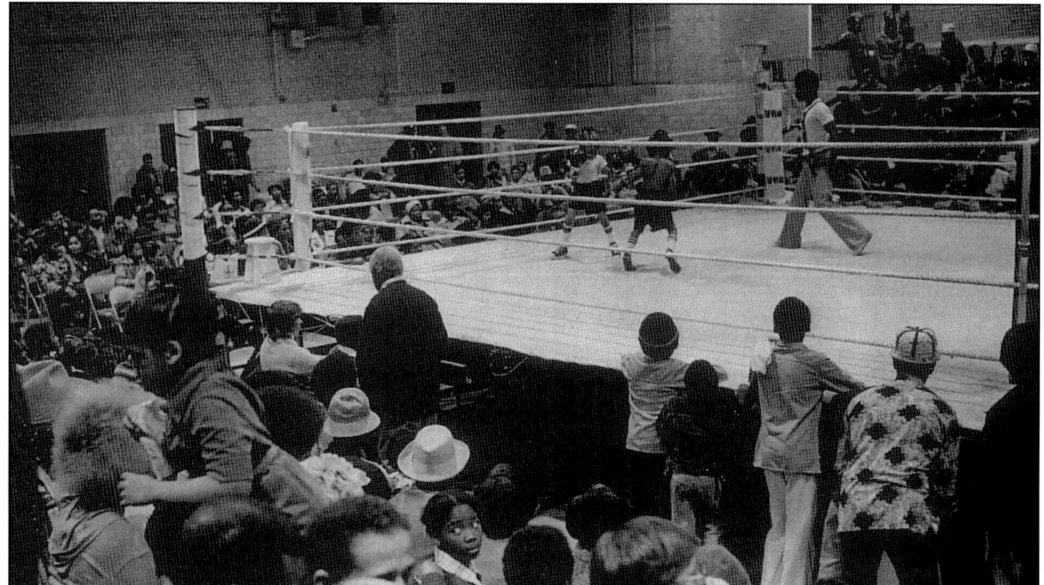

Tandy Center serves as headquarters for the Silver Gloves Boxing Tournament, an annual event sponsored by the Department of Parks, Recreation, and Forestry. It is felt that through participation in the center's activities, youngsters develop carry-over values such as courage, aggressiveness, self-confidence, discipline, and faith in one's ability to meet crises—all great assets needed to adjust in society. (Photo courtesy of Helen Baily.)

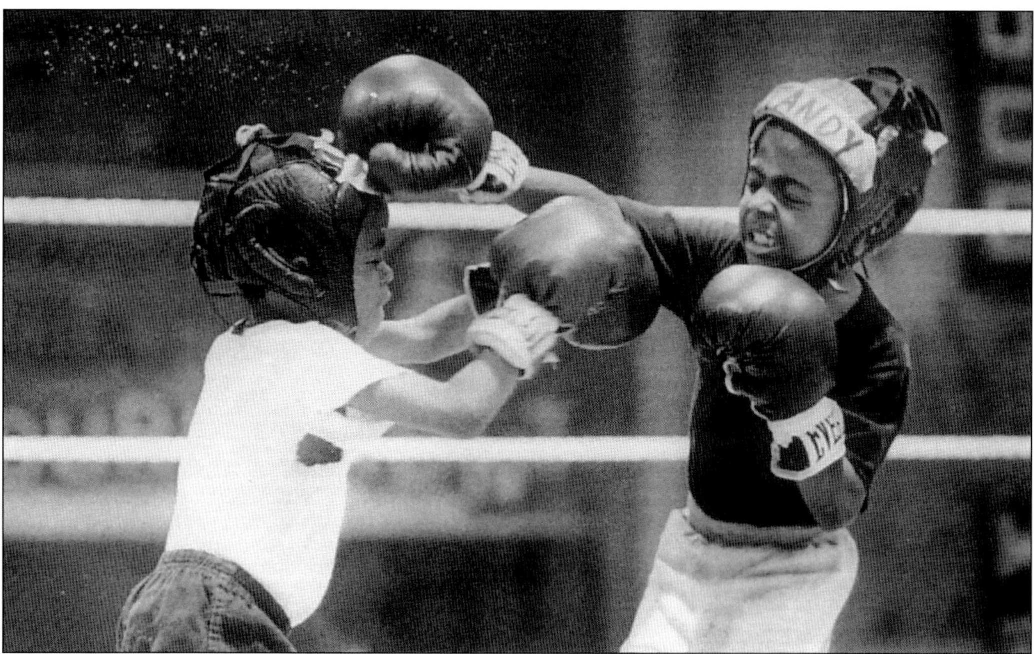

These young boxers are learning the physical qualities of speed, agility, endurance, rhythm, and the coordination of body movements. The managers believe there is no other sport activity that develops as well "the ability to lose courteously and to win meekly." (Photo courtesy of Helen Baily.)

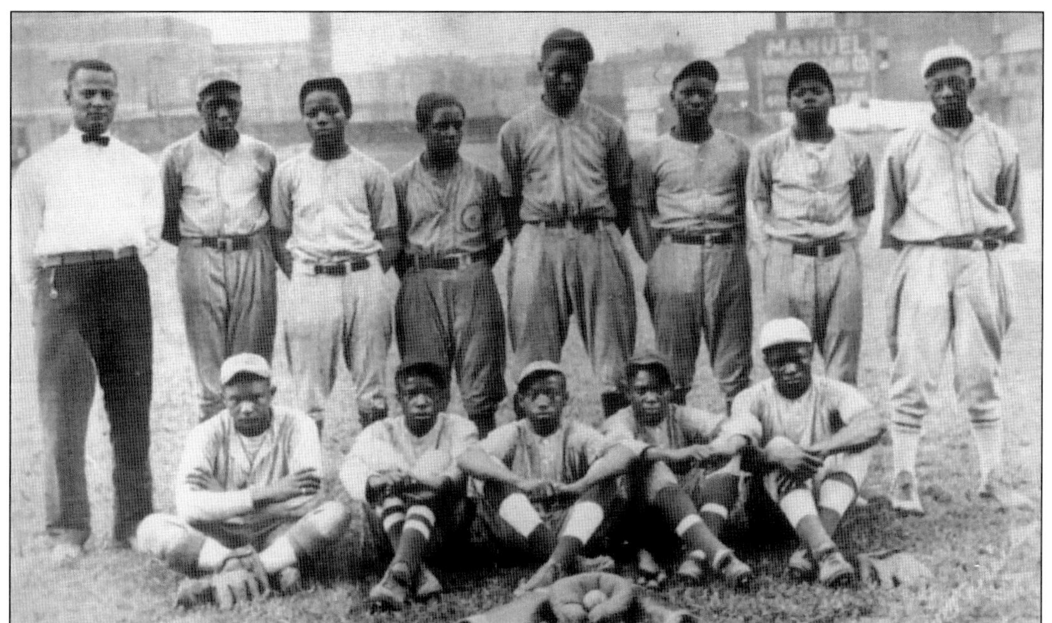

Pictured here are some early members of the Tandy Baseball League after a game on Vashon Field. The 5.6 acres of Tandy Field, where the team played and practiced, was purchased by the city in 1915 for $102,380. The Sunday afternoon's AAA baseball games provided a valuable enjoyment to a community that was restricted from attending the city's major league ballpark because of race. (Photo courtesy of the University of Missouri-St. Louis, Western Manuscript Collection.)

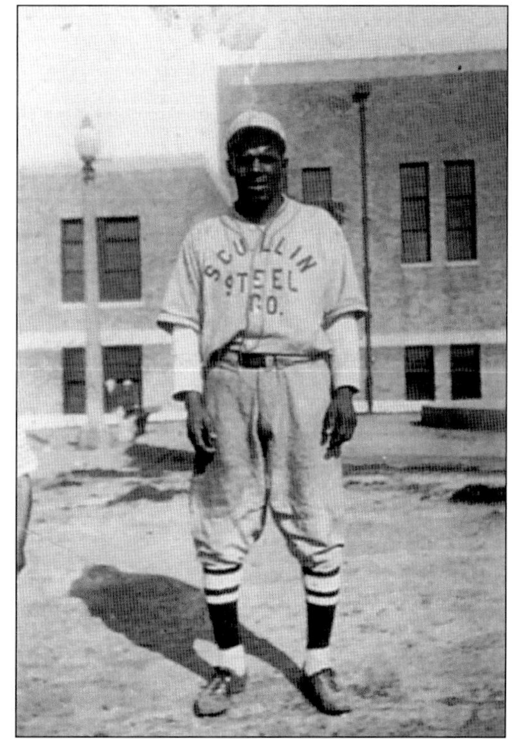

Luther Pollard, seen in this picture, was a member of the Scullin Steel Co. baseball team. Many of the companies with black employees sponsored teams that played in the Tandy League. (Photo courtesy of Edmond and Dorothy Squires.)

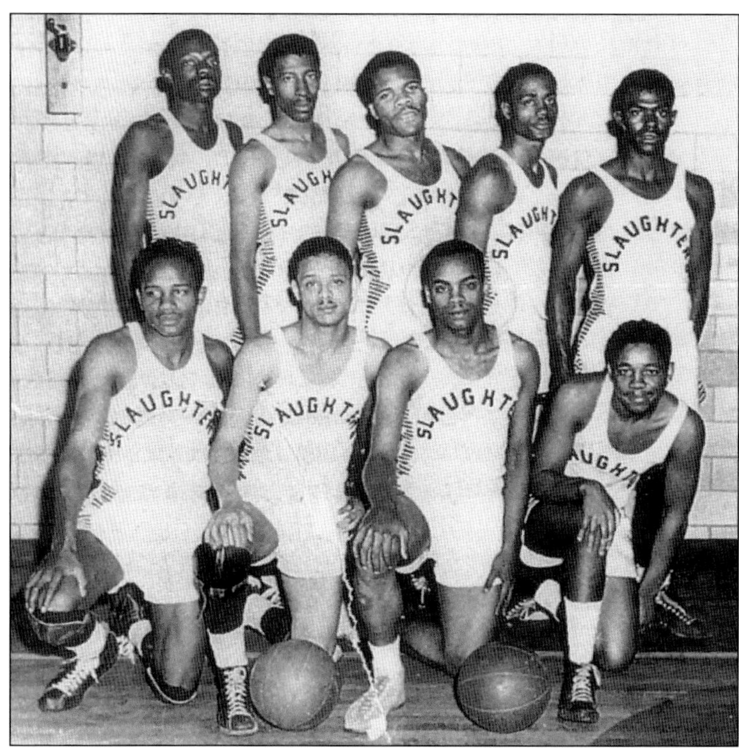

The Tandy Basketball League provided many young men an opportunity for recreation. The team in this photograph was sponsored by Eugene Slaughter, owner of Slaughter Cleaners established in 1946 at 4585 Easton Avenue. Members of the team were, from left to right: (first row) Jerall Harris, Laqresa Hodges, Demosthenes DuBose, and (?) Thrope; (second row) Sherman Hawkins, Floyd Hart, Gilbert Gerdine, Luther Jones, and Sam Jones. (Photo courtesy of Demosthenes DuBose.)

In Poro Building 4300 St. Ferdinand

JEfferson 1400

The Amytis

Our Own Theatre De Luxe

For the not so active Ville resident, or those wanting a relaxing evening or afternoon, the Amytis movie theater was always available. As this advertisement stated it was home of the finest entertainment on both stage and screen. Where else could one see two movies, a cartoon, a chapter play, a newsreel, and start a collection of dishes—all for 35¢? (Advertisement courtesy of Jackie Dace.)

The safety of The Ville neighborhood was charged to the officers of the 10th District. Their headquarters was located at Deer Street and Easton Avenue (now Dr. Martin Luther King, Dr.). When officers like Sergeant Oliver Lee Middlebrooks, pictured here, said to clear the corner, he meant clear the corner immediately, and it was done. Middlebrook joined the police department in the early 1920s, and worked The Ville neighborhood in the late 1940s and early 50s. (Photo courtesy of the NBC Lounge.)

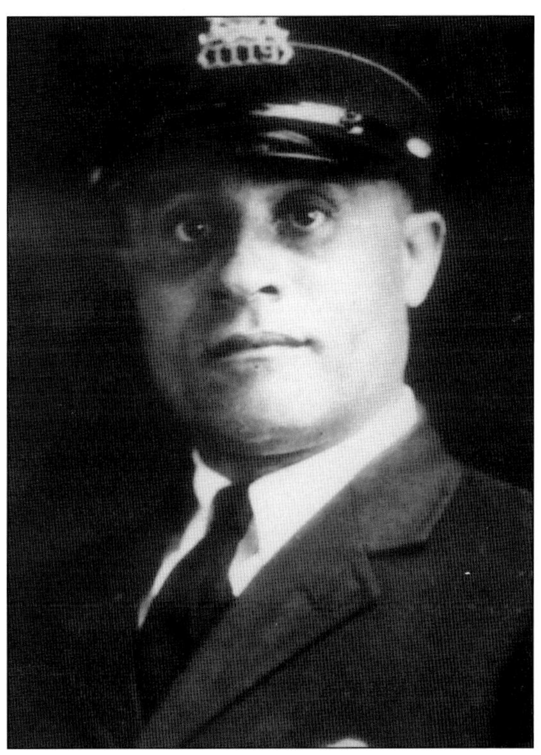

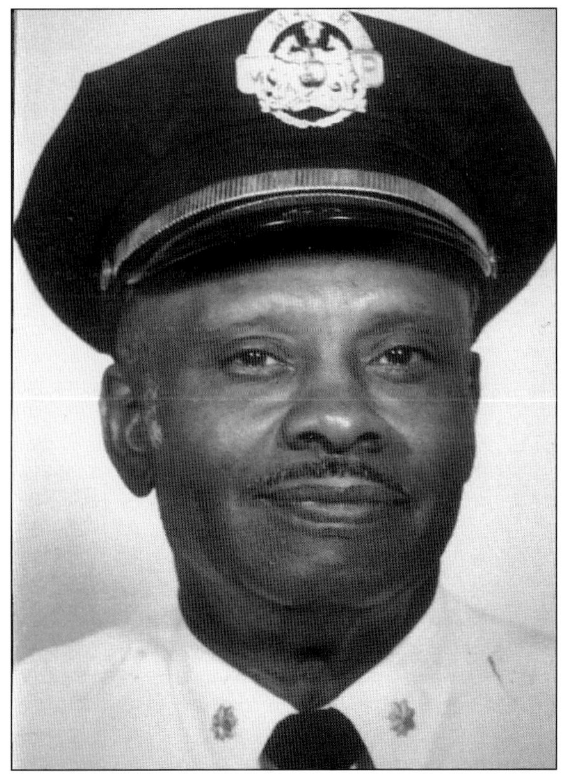

There was no question that Captain Tom Brooks, pictured here, had the respect of the community. He was the commander of the Deer Street Station for six years. Brooks joined the police department in 1933 and was promoted to corporal in 1947, sergeant in 1950, and captain in 1960. He was the second African-American major in the St. Louis Police Department. His name can also be found as a member of the Missouri-Baseball Hall of Fame because of his years playing with the Pullman Porters. (Photo courtesy of the NBC Lounge.)

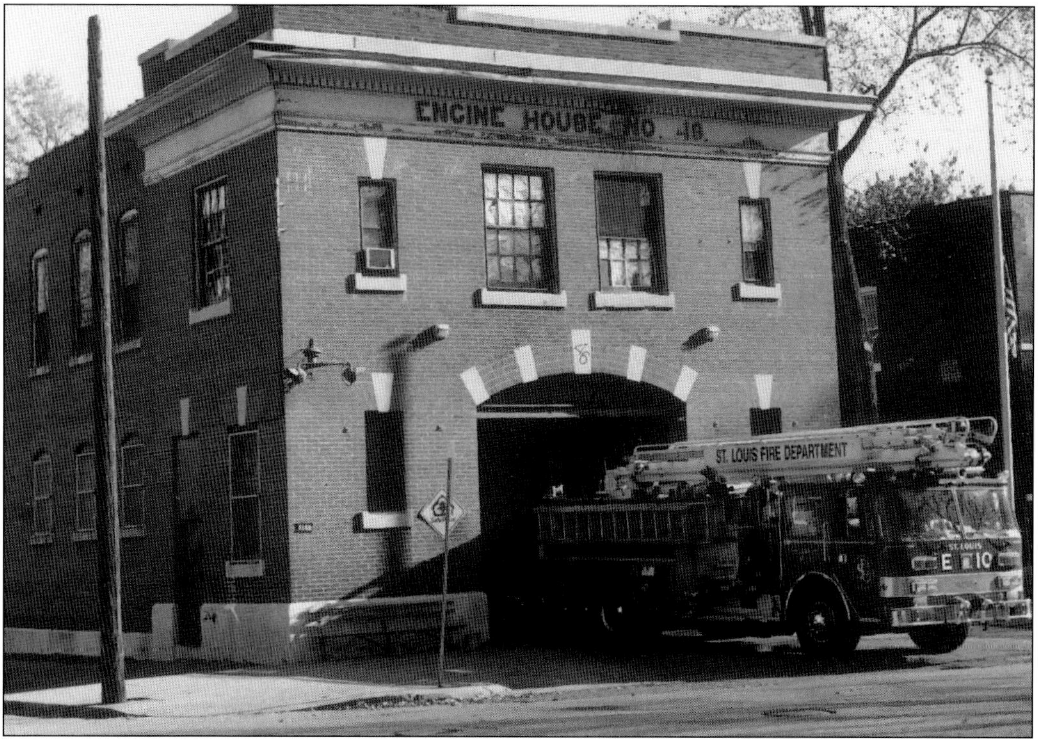

Engine House No. 18, pictured here, has served the community for years, but it was once a segregated facility. African-American firemen who filled in at the house had to sleep in certain beds and were not allowed to be a part of the dinner club. Through the efforts of the black firefighters, working conditions have changed throughout the city. (Photo by John A. Wright.)

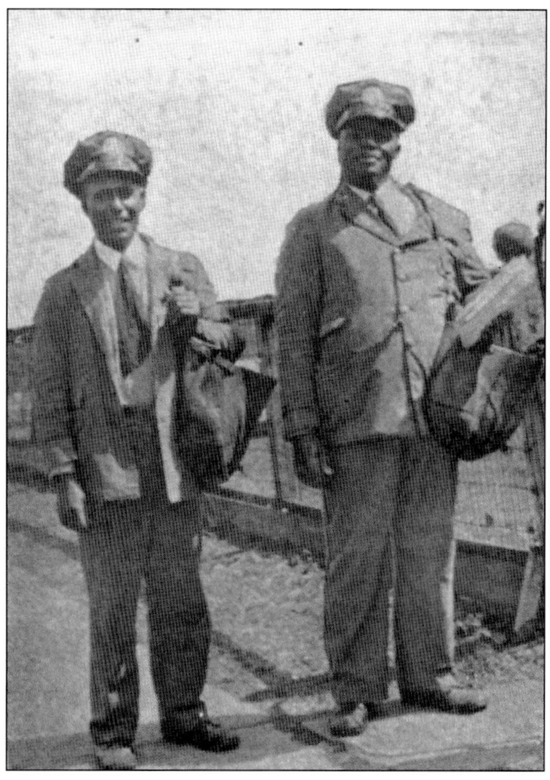

These men were part of the postal staff at the Frederick Douglass Branch of the U.S. Post Office located in the Poro Hotel that served The Ville Community. (Photo by Nathan Young. Courtesy of the University of Missouri-St. Louis, Western Manuscript Collection.)

Four

Justice Delayed But Not Denied

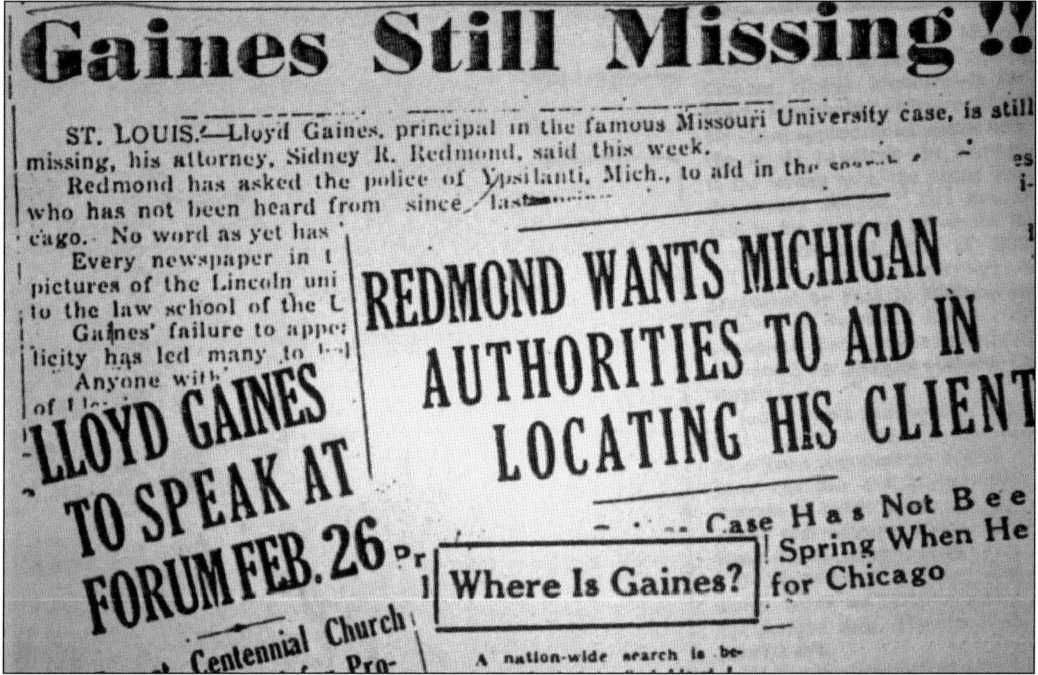

Gaines Still Missing!!

ST. LOUIS.—Lloyd Gaines, principal in the famous Missouri University case, is still missing, his attorney, Sidney R. Redmond, said this week.

Redmond has asked the police of Ypsilanti, Mich., to aid in the

who has not been heard from since

cago. No word as yet has

Every newspaper in

pictures of the Lincoln uni

to the law school of the

Gaines' failure to appe

licity has led many to

Anyone with

REDMOND WANTS MICHIGAN AUTHORITIES TO AID IN LOCATING HIS CLIENT

LLOYD GAINES TO SPEAK AT FORUM FEB. 26

Centennial Church

Case Has Not Bee

Spring When He

for Chicago

Where Is Gaines?

A nation-wide search is be-

In 1938, as Lloyd Gaines was poised to become a major figure in the desegregation of America, he vanished. On December 12, 1938, he won a monumental civil rights victory. The U.S. Supreme Court ruled 6 to 2 that Gaines could not be barred from the University of Missouri's segregated law school unless the state could provide a facility of equal stature within its borders.

News articles like those above reported that a few months after Gaines Supreme Court victory, he left a Chicago fraternity house, telling the housekeeper he was going to purchase some stamps. Taking only the clothes he wore, he disappeared into the night and has never been seen or heard from again. The reasons for his disappearance have remained a mystery to his family, friends, and scholars for decades. (Photo courtesy of Lincoln University.)

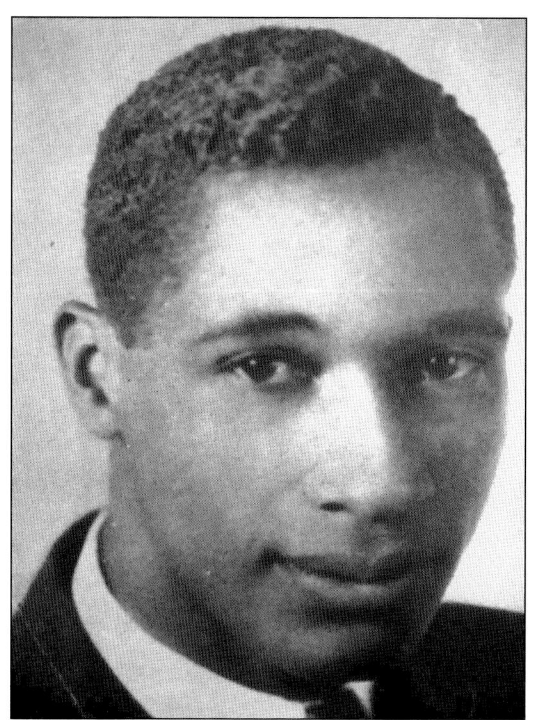

Lloyd Gaines, pictured here, was born in 1911. He graduated first in a class of 50 from Vashon High School in 1931. He then enrolled in Stowe Teachers College where he earned 26 credits and transferred to Lincoln University in Jefferson City on a scholarship. After graduating from Lincoln, Gaines applied for admission to the University of Missouri's Law School. He was advised by the university to apply for an out of state scholarship. (Photo courtesy of Lincoln University.)

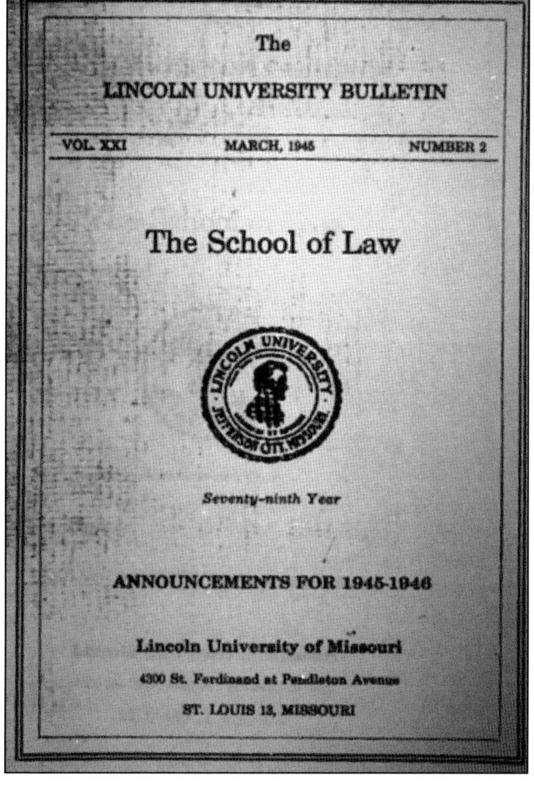

The

LINCOLN UNIVERSITY BULLETIN

VOL. XXI MARCH, 1945 NUMBER 2

The School of Law

Seventy-ninth Year

ANNOUNCEMENTS FOR 1945-1946

Lincoln University of Missouri

4300 St. Ferdinand at Pendleton Avenue

ST. LOUIS 13, MISSOURI

With the assistance of the National Association for the Advancement of Colored People, a legal team was assembled to represent Gaines to enable him to enroll in the University of Missouri's Law School. The team took the case to the United States Supreme Court and won. But, instead of admitting Gaines, the state passed a bill providing $275,000 for the establishment of Lincoln Law School. Pictured here is the school's 1945–46 bulletin. (Photo courtesy of Lincoln University.)

Lincoln University officials decided to establish its law school in St. Louis rather than on its Jefferson City campus. By August of 1939, space had been secured in the Poro College. The law school opened for the fall semester of 1939, with 30 students. Freshman Julian Rogers Jr. of Detroit, Michigan, is pictured here leaving the school. (Photo courtesy of Lincoln University.)

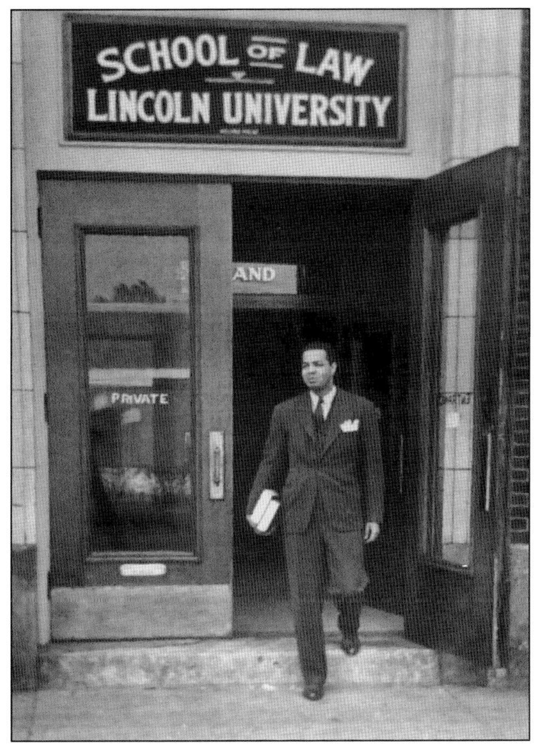

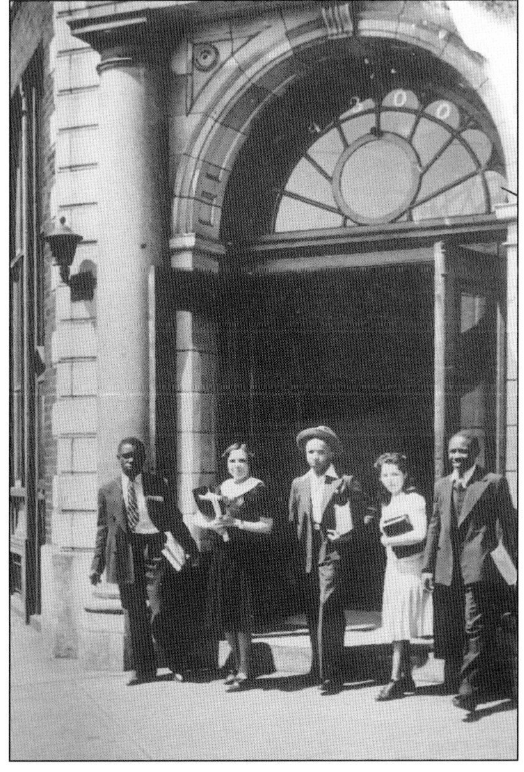

Most of Lincoln's Law School graduates went on to excel in their fields. Dorothy Freeman, second from the right, was the first woman of color admitted to the Missouri Bar. She did not let the fact that she was a polio victim hold her back. Aquinoldo Lemor, the tall gentleman in the hat, went on to become dean of the law school at Southern University. (Photo courtesy of Lincoln University.)

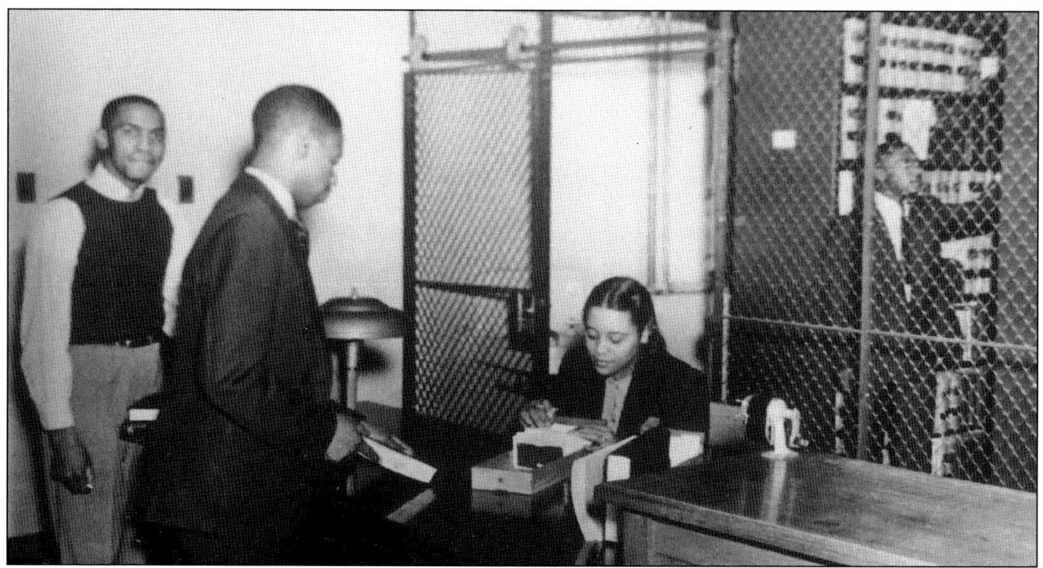

The Lincoln Law School Library opened with 10,000 volumes. These 1940–41 law students are waiting to check out books. While the bill approved by the state provided Lincoln University with $275,000 to "elevate" it to "equal status," it provided $3 million to the University of Missouri for its programs. (Photo courtesy of Lincoln University.)

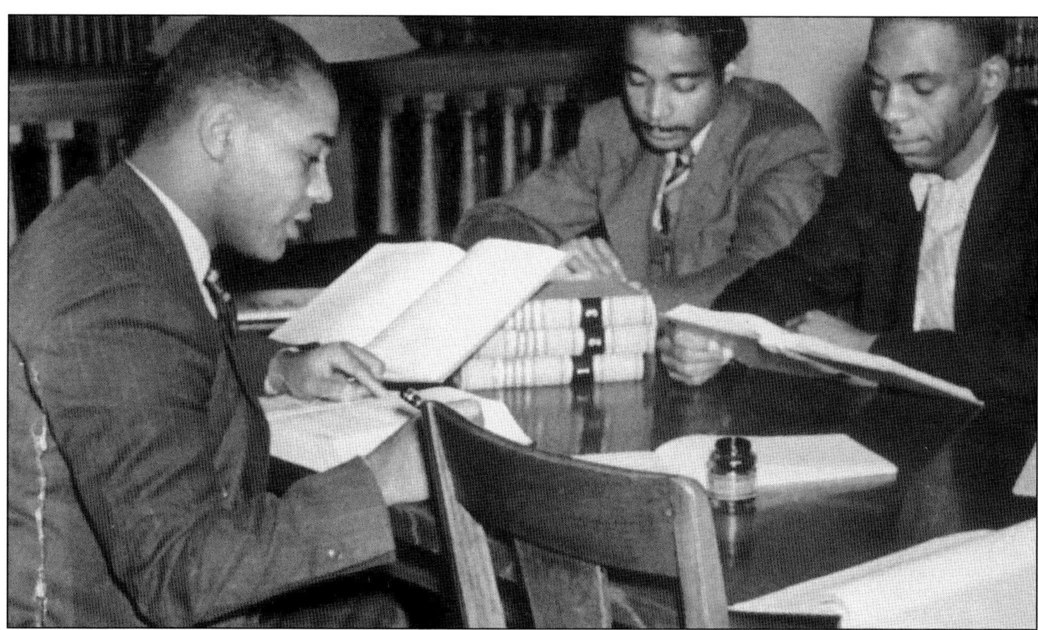

In spite of the large volume of books made available to these students, the NAACP contended that the hastily organized segregated law school was in no way equal to the University of Missouri's program. Although a number of groups, such as the Colored Clerks Circle, picketed the school and named it the "The Jim Crow School," the school opened and the case filed by the NAACP to determine whether the new law school was, in fact, equal to the University of Missouri's was thrown out because the plaintiff, Lloyd Gaines, could not be found. (Photo courtesy of Lincoln University.)

Many students enrolled in Lincoln University's Law School to study law with an emphasis on civil rights. It was felt they would not have had that opportunity at the University of Missouri-Columbia where emphasis was on corporate law, tax law, and the like. (Photo courtesy of Lincoln University.)

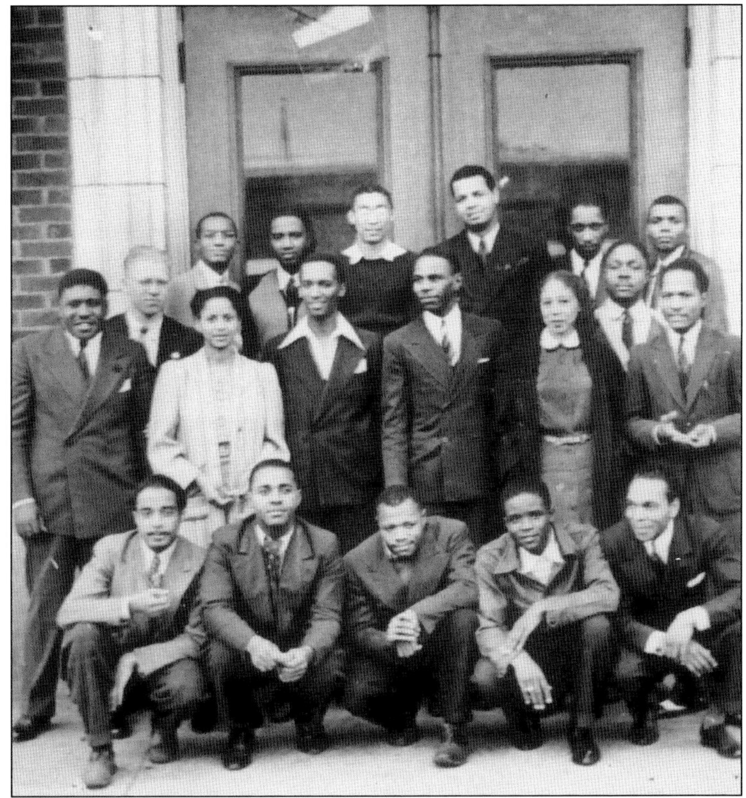

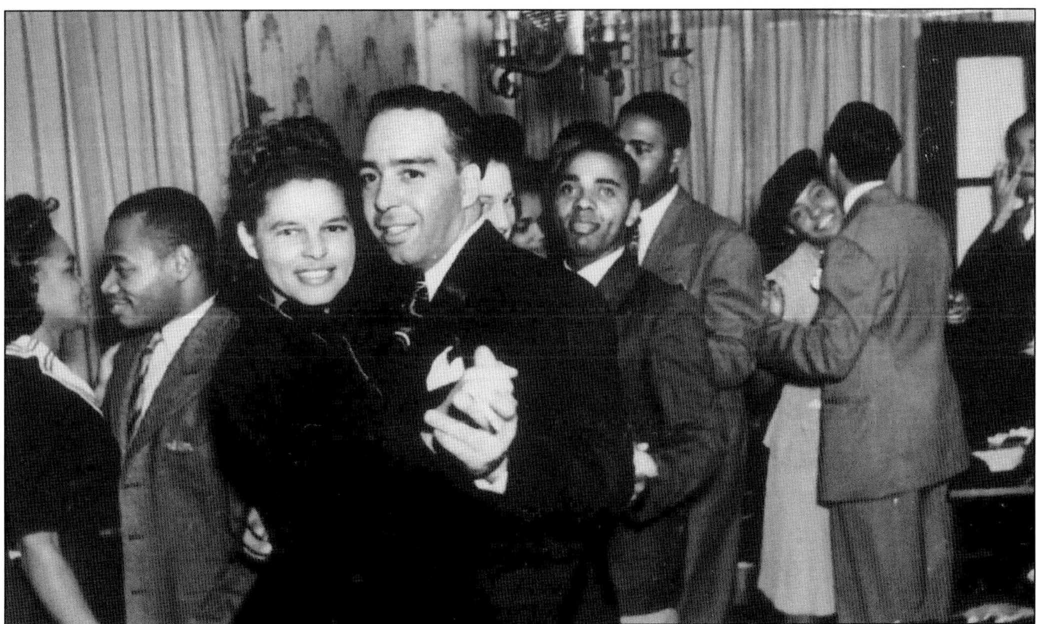

Law school was not all study. These 1940–41 Lincoln Law School students are taking time out for some socializing. (Photo courtesy of Lincoln University.)

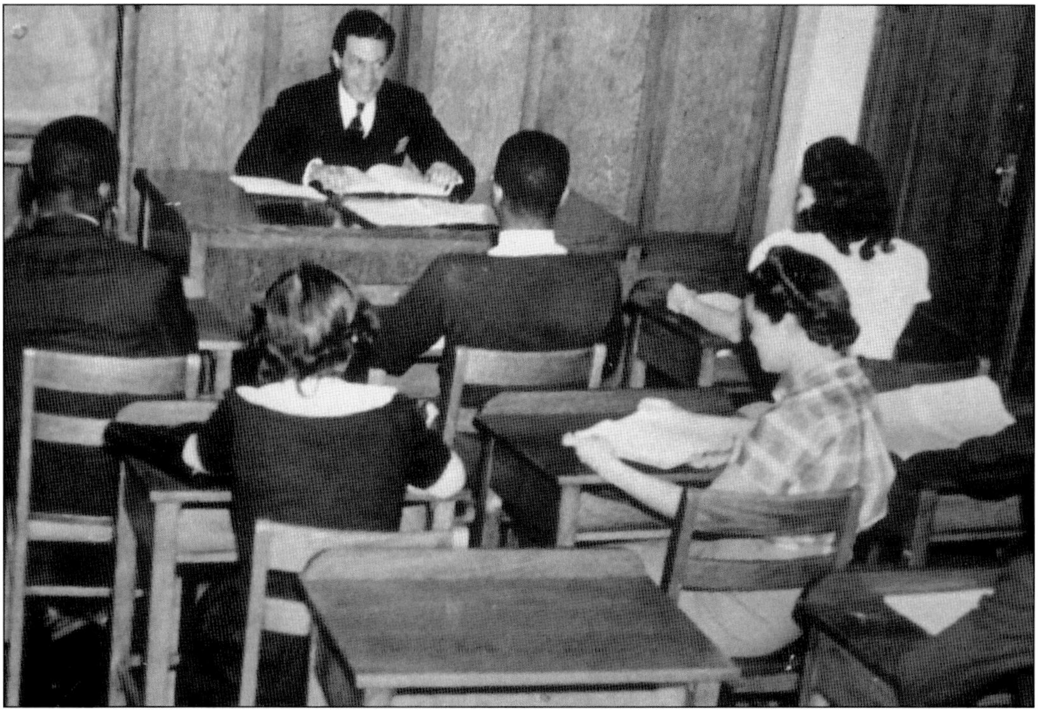

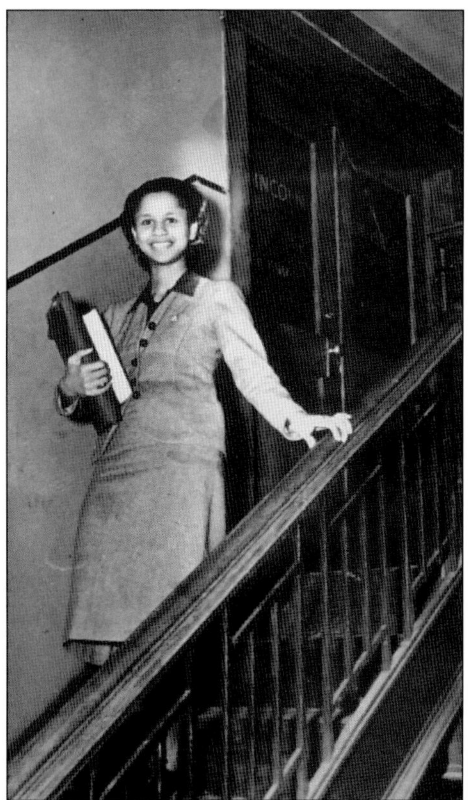

Sitting at the desk is Scovel Richardson, a member of the faculty and dean of the Lincoln University Law School. Richardson launched a civil rights case on his own when he purchased a home at 4635 N. Market Street that was under a restriction. A suit was immediately filed against him but through a series of demurrers he delayed the ruling until the restriction had expired. At that point the case was thrown out. Richardson was later appointed to the United States Board of Parole by President Dwight Eisenhower, and later to a judgeship in the United States Customs Court in New York. (Photo courtesy of Lincoln University.)

Margaret Bush Wilson, pictured on the steps in the Lincoln Law School after graduation, went on to become the Assistant Attorney General of Missouri, Acting Deputy Director of the St. Louis Model City Agency, instructor of Civil Procedure, C.L.E.O., and Legal Services Specialist for the Missouri Technical Assistance Office, War on Poverty. In 1975, she became the first black woman to chair the NAACP National Board of Directors (a position she held until 1984). (Photo courtesy of Lincoln University.)

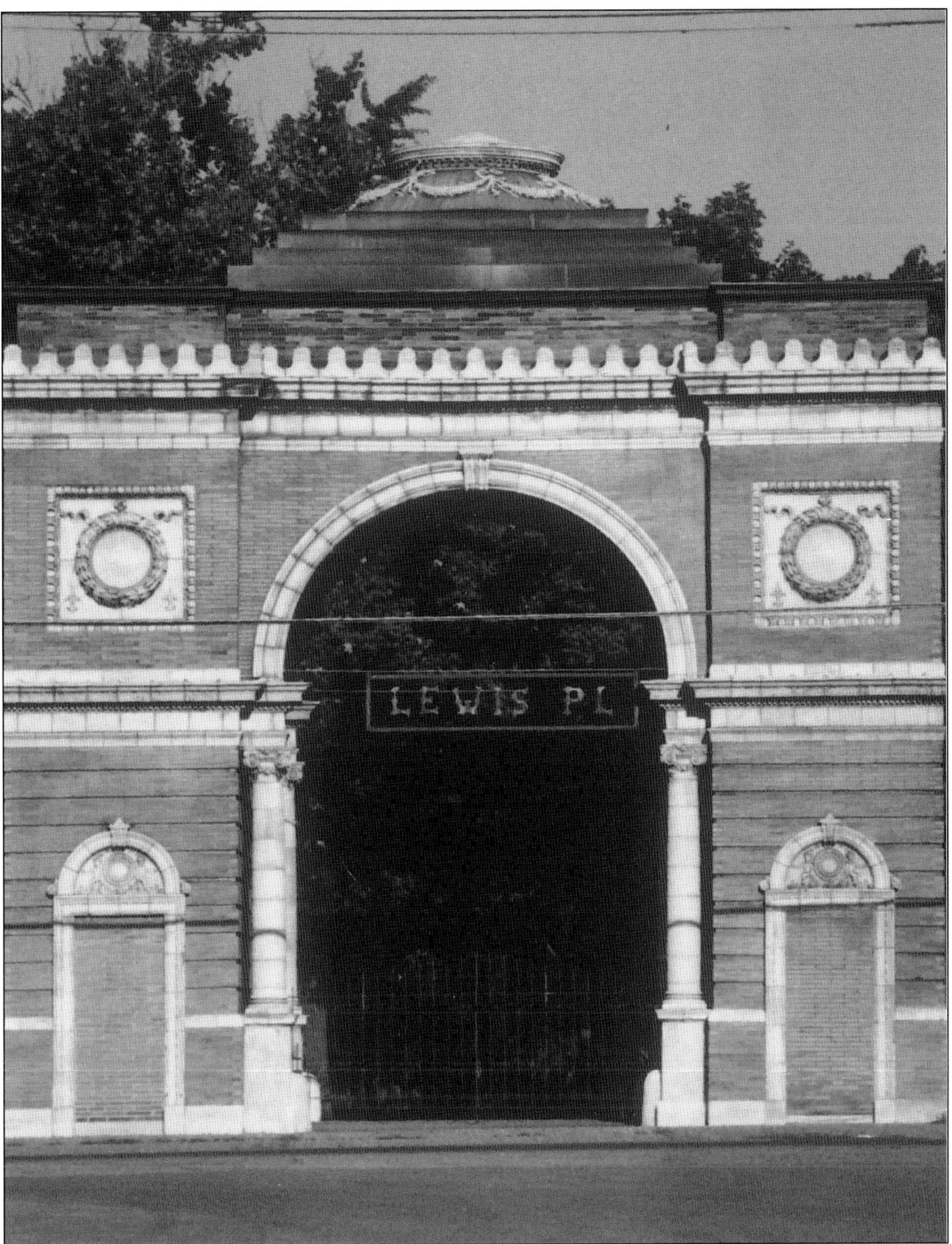

The integration of Lewis Place was one of the preludes to the attack on racial restrictions on housing. In the 1940s Attorney Robert Witherspoon and others persuaded fair-skinned blacks to "pass for white" in order to purchase several homes on Lewis Place, pictured here. They later transferred the deeds to the actual owners of the property. When the association met at its block meeting, the owners showed up with their deeds in their hands and voted down the restrictive covenant on the street. (Photo by John A. Wright.)

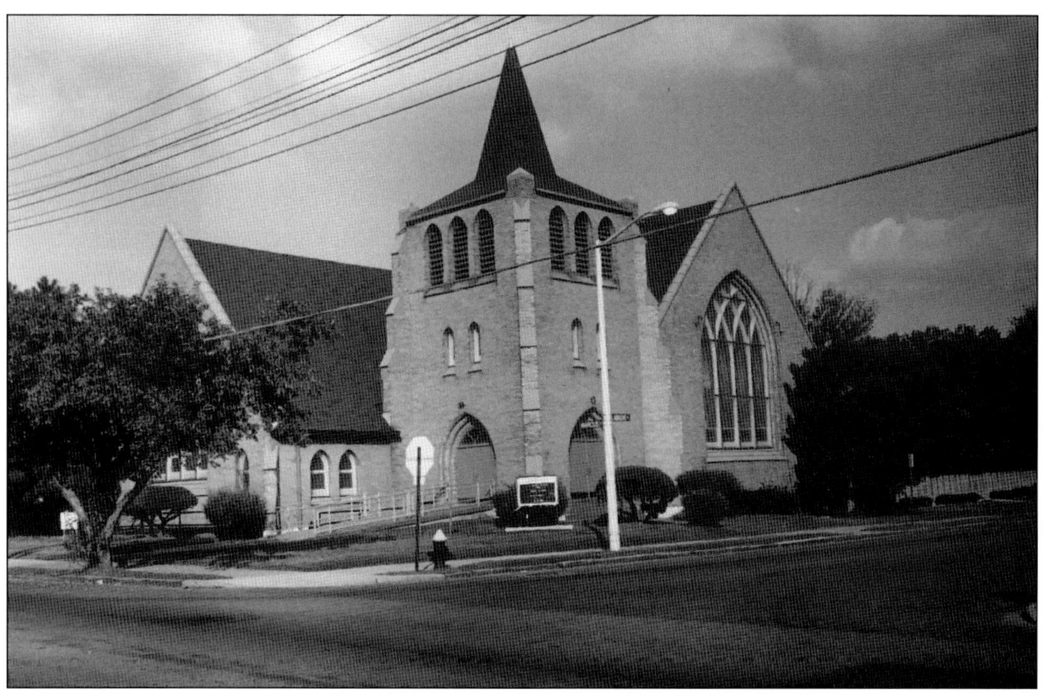

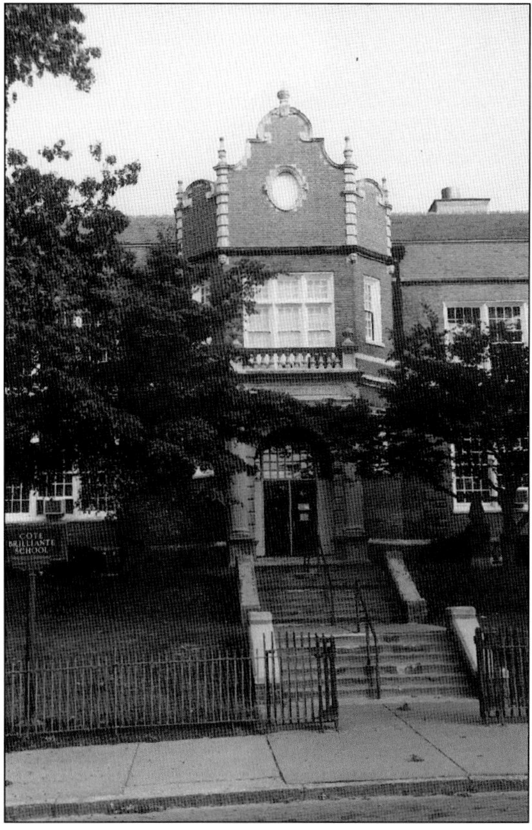

The Marcus Avenue Improvement Association was organized in 1910 to prevent the purchase of homes by Negroes from the south side of Natural Bridge to the north to Easton Avenue on the south, and Newstead Avenue on the east to Kingshighway Blvd. on the west. The Association used Cote Brilliante Presbyterian Church, pictured here, as its meeting place. When the neighborhood became integrated, rather than integrating the church, the congregation moved. (Photo by John A. Wright.)

The Marcus Avenue Improvement Association marshaled its forces to support real estate companies in keeping blacks out of the community. They also petitioned the St. Louis Board of Education to keep Cote Brilliante Elementary School, pictured here, white. Because of the petition, Cote Brilliante Elementary was closed from September 12, 1944, to September 1, 1945. It only opened to blacks because of community pressure to relieve the over-crowded schools in The Ville community. (Photo courtesy of John A. Wright.)

This home at 4600 Labadie was purchased by J.D. Shelley and his wife in 1939. Shortly after they moved in, a suit was filed against them by their white neighbors on behalf of the Marcus Avenue Improvement Association, claiming their home was under a restrictive covenant based on race. This suit (***Shelly v. Kramer***) went all the way to the Supreme Court which ruled in favor of the Shelleys, and thus ending the use of restrictive covenants based on race all across America. (Photo by John A. Wright.)

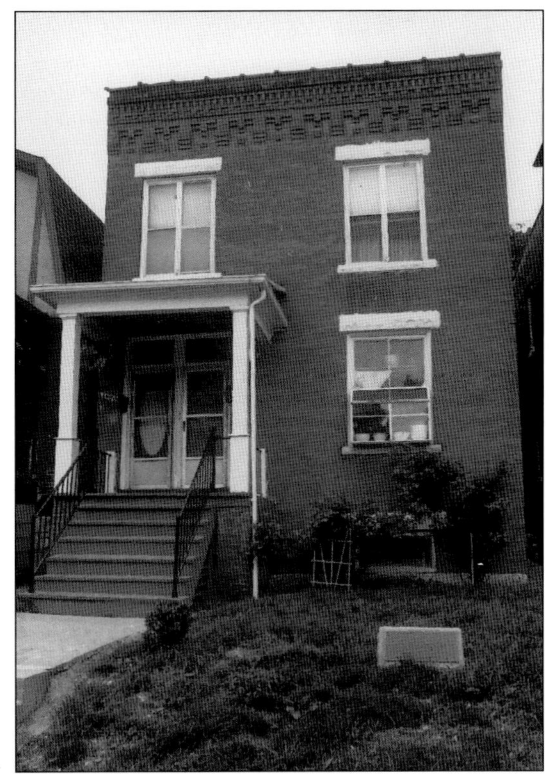

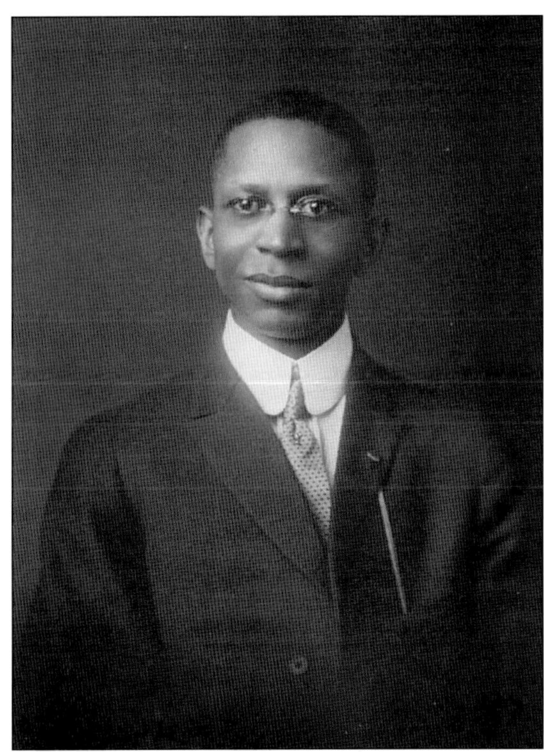

James T. Bush Sr., pictured here, was the real estate broker who sold the property above to the Shelleys. He assumed responsibility for their defense and formed the Real Estate Brokers' Association of St. Louis which financed the Shelleys' case. In 1987, the University of Missouri at St. Louis announced a new Center for Law, Social Change, and Conflict Resolution, which was to be named in his honor. (Photo courtesy of Margaret Bush Wilson.)

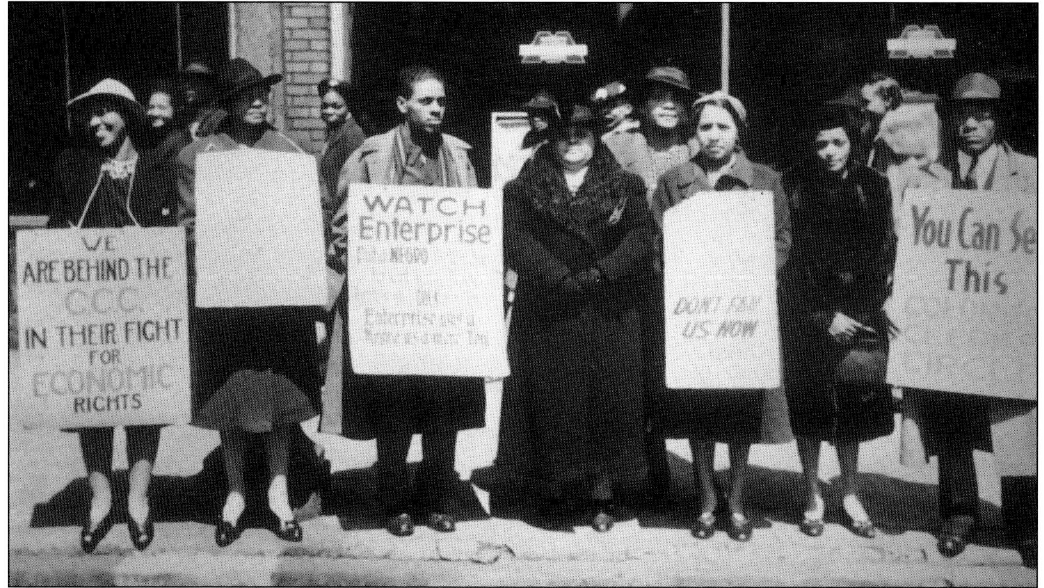

While efforts were taking place for open housing, the Colored Clerks Circle, pictured here, were waging a fight for equal employment. With the assistance of the Urban League they pressured Woolworth on Sarah and Easton Avenue (now Dr. Martin Luther King Dr.) to employ more African-American clerks. (Photo courtesy of the University of Missouri-St. Louis, Western Manuscript Collection.)

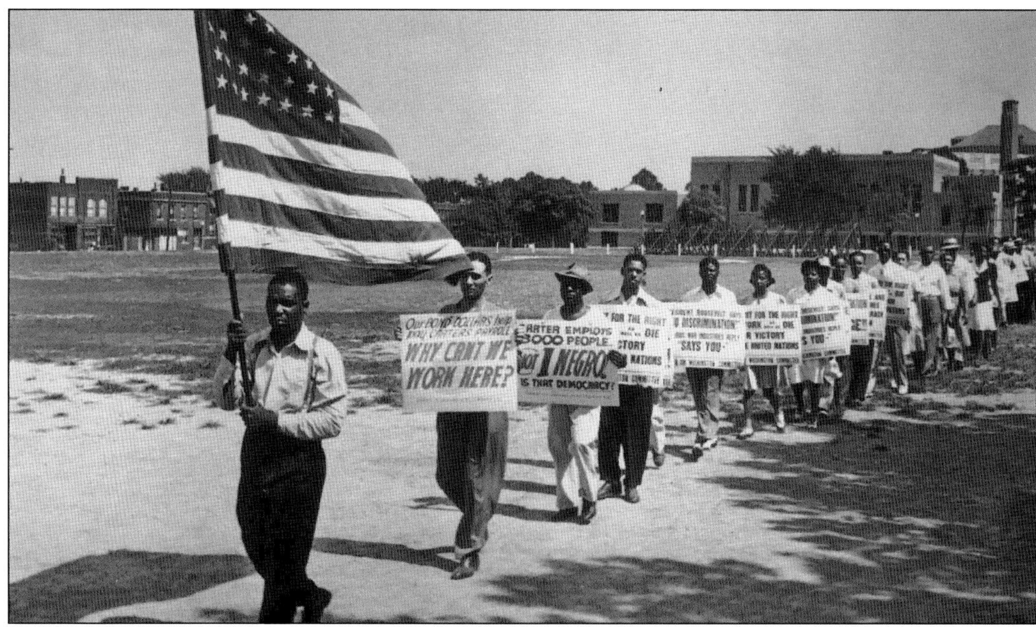

In August 1942, several hundred men and women marched from Tandy Park in The Ville to the Carter plant at 2800 N. Spring Avenue to protest the company's reluctance to hire African-American employees. During World War II, when automobile production was curtailed, Carter partially converted to the manufacture of shell fuses for the War Department. (Photo courtesy of the University of Missouri-St. Louis, Western Manuscript Collection.)

In spite of segregation, The Ville provided its residents with a thriving business district. Pictured here are two examples of some of the businesses that existed along Easton Avenue (now Dr. Martin Luther King Dr.). (Photo by Nathan Young. Courtesy of the University of Missouri-St. Louis, Western Manuscript Collection.)

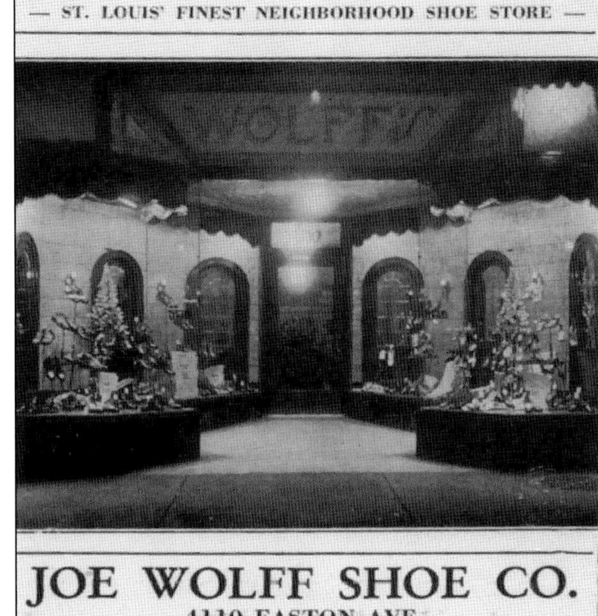

IF YOU DO NOT KNOW HOW TO SEW—

SINGER will teach you in its Sewing Class

IF YOU WANT TO KNOW MORE ABOUT

Dressmaking — Cutting and Fitting — Home Decoration — Draperies and Fabrics —

THE MODERN SINGER INSTRUCTIONS ARE OPEN TO YOU

Each WEDNESDAY you may enroll FREE for a Special Three Lesson Course in Dressmaking or Home Decorating.

Are You Getting the Modern Singer Sewing Machine Services?

● CALL at the SINGER STORE

4257w EASTON AVENUE

Telephone: NE-0276

"The Singer Vacuum Cleaner Is a Miracle Worker in a Home."

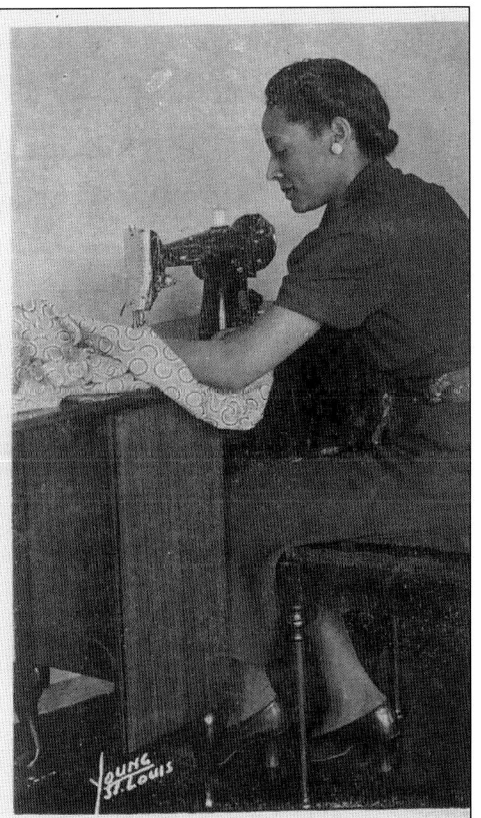

Compliments

BILLY BURK'S CAFE

2419 Pendleton Ave.

FRanklin 8286

Compliments of

WHITE'S SHOE REPAIR AND DRESSMAKING SHOP

All Work Guaranteed

2426 NORTH TAYLOR AVENUE

FRanklin 9803

Compliments of

Schryer Confectionery

4350 Kennerly Ave.

EVergreen 8846

PASTE THIS NEAR YOUR TELEPHONE

FOrest 3720

For DRUGS

SPECIAL DELIVERY SERVICE

The Drug Mart

Cut Rate Drugs - Prescription Specialist

2601 NORTH TAYLOR AVENUE

(Taylor and Cottage)

WOOD'S TAILORING CO.

Makers of Clothes That Fit

4261 West Easton

NEwstead 6300

Res., 4334 Ashland Res. Phone, EV. 3002

Love & Chapman

CENTRAL CLEANERS

4301 EASTON AVE., St. Louis, Mo.

Phone, FRanklin 8117

Compliments of

SKLAR'S MARKET

SERVICE and QUALITY

4300 NORTH MARKET STREET

FRanklin 7886

Phone: FRanklin 9118 A. A. Greene, Prop.

EASTON-TAYLOR NEWSTAND

Candies - Cigarettes - Cigars - Ice Cream

Newspapers, Magazines, Greeting Cards and Books

Shoes Shined and Dyed

4467 EASTON AVE., St. Louis, Mo.

Seen here is an advertisement by The Ville businesses from an unknown publication. (Advertisement courtesy of John A. Wright.)

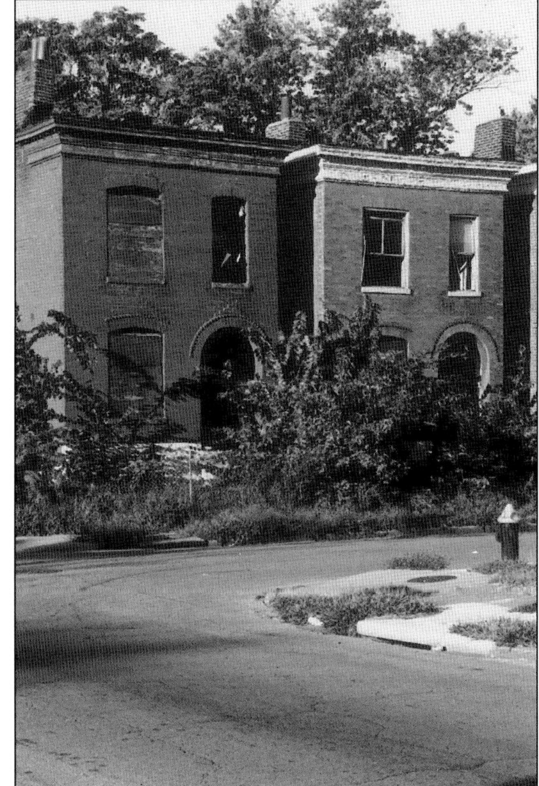

As more and more individuals began to leave The Ville during the 1960s and 70s, home ownership declined and deterioration set in. Many homes that were once very desirable began to fall into disrepair, such as these pictured in the 4400 block of Cote Brilliante Avenue. The demolition of the Mill Creek area in 1959 also had an impact on The Ville community when thousands who were displaced were forced to crowd into the community. (Photo by John A. Wright.)

With the end of restrictive covenants denying property on the basis of race, many African-Americans who could afford larger homes began to move from The Ville. Homes like this one on Northland Place, three blocks west of The Ville, were attractive to some professionals. (Photo by John A. Wright.)

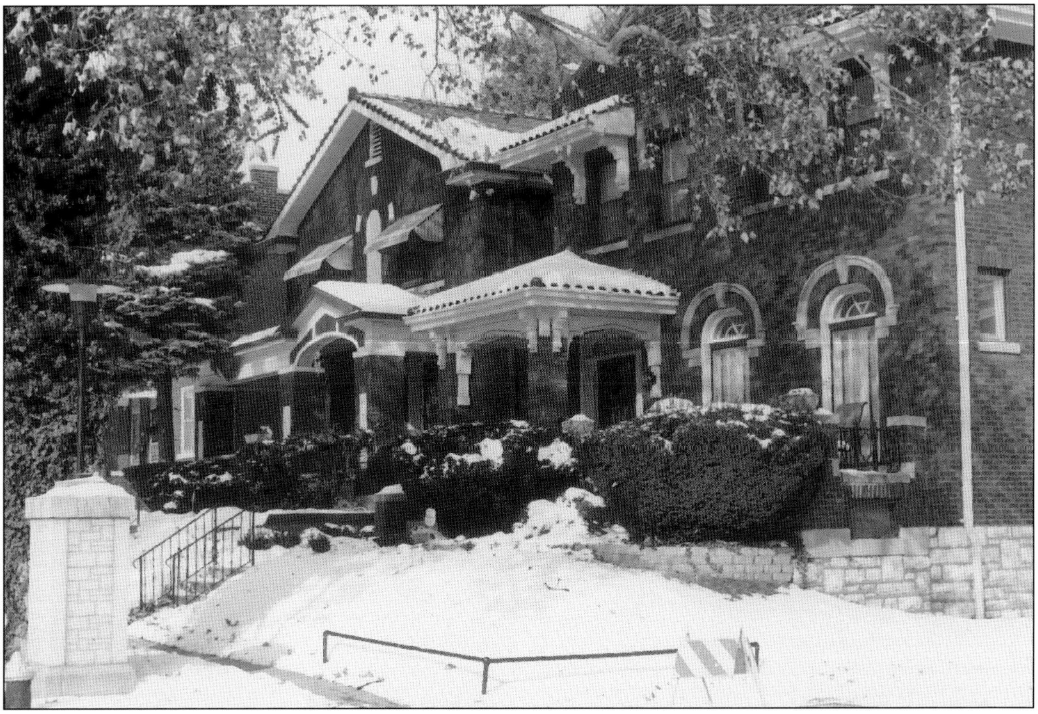

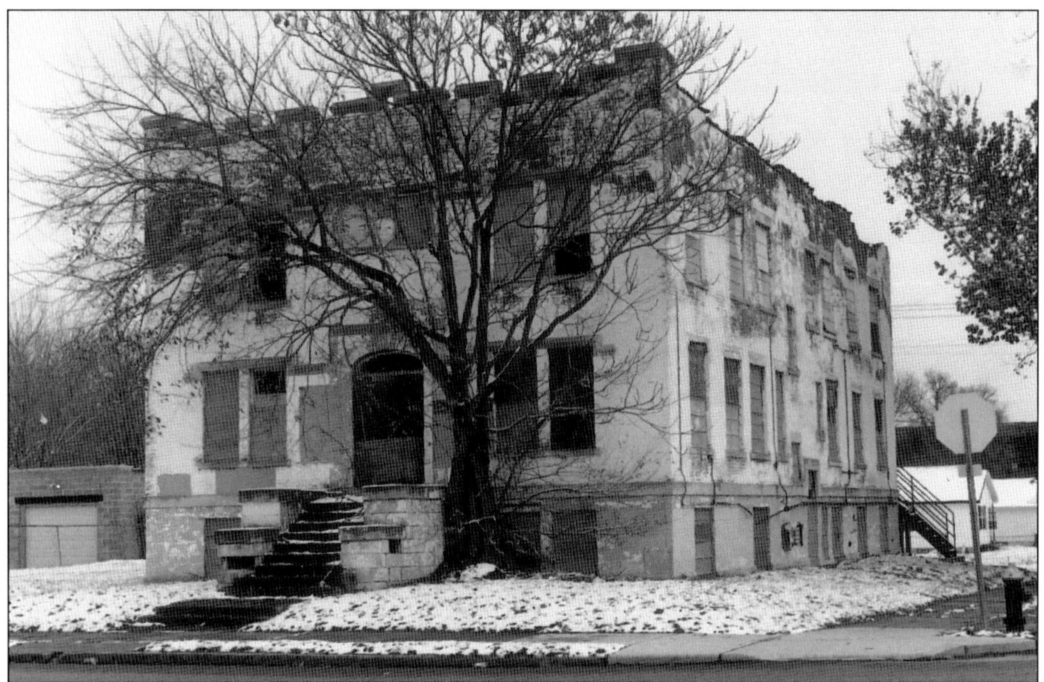

With the desegregation of public hospitals, Community Hospital, in this picture, at Maffitt and Taylor Avenues, was no longer able to compete. This 30-bed hospital was operated by the Signorelli family for years, at first as a hospital for whites. It opened to African-Americans in the late 1950s and served them until it closed in the mid 1960s. During the hospitals years under black administration, Dr. Walter Young served as the Chief of Staff. Since the hospital had no elevators all operations were performed on the first floor. (Photo by John A. Wright.)

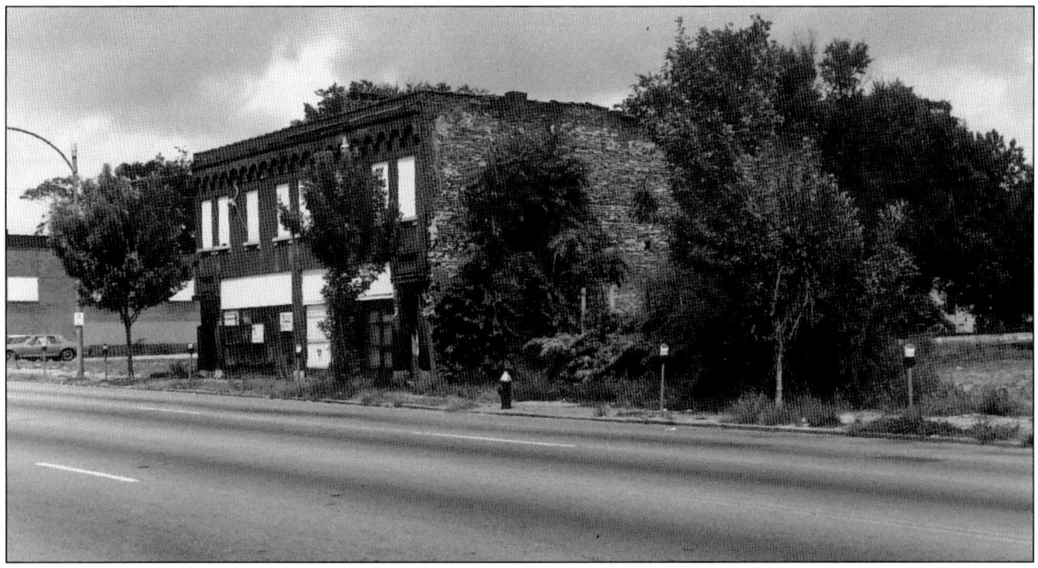

As African-Americans began to abandon the The Ville, the once thriving business district began to look like this section in the 4400 block of Dr. Martin Luther King Dr. (Photo by John A. Wright.)

Five

The Ville
A New Day Dawning

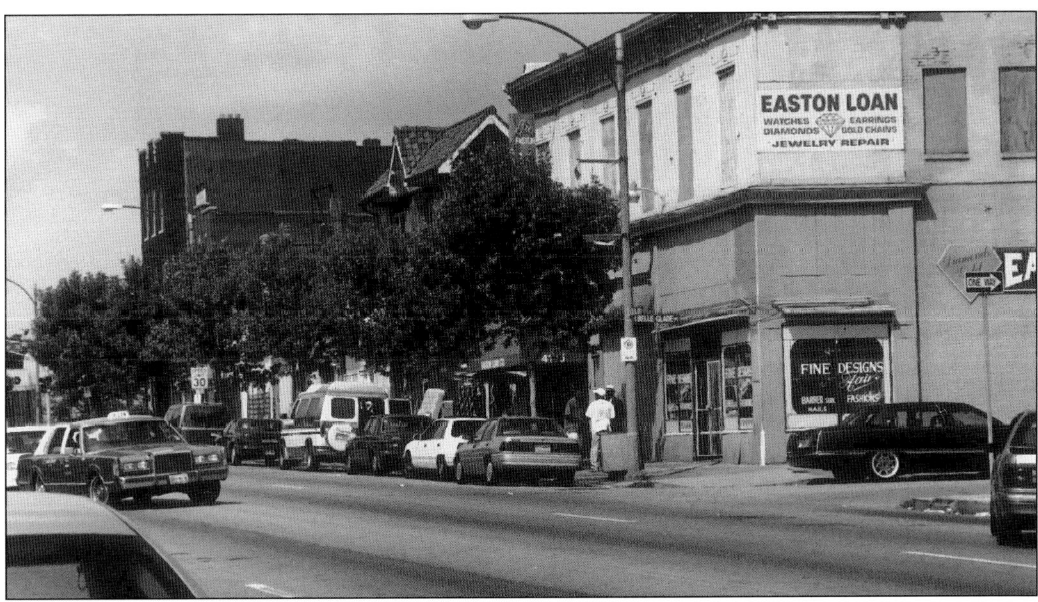

The once thriving Easton Avenue (now Dr. Martin Luther King Dr.) is beginning to show signs of revitalization. This short section of the boulevard has regained several successful businesses along with street improvements. (Photo courtesy of John A. Wright.)

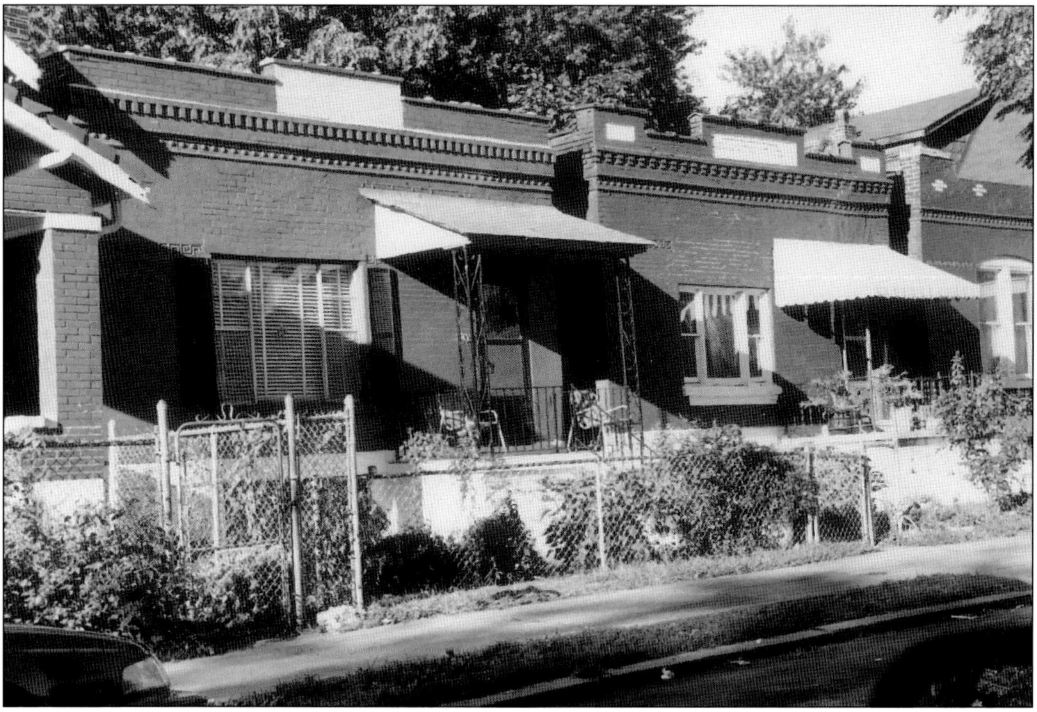

Through the years, many home owners have remained in The Ville and maintained their property like these on Sarah Avenue. (Photo by John A. Wright.)

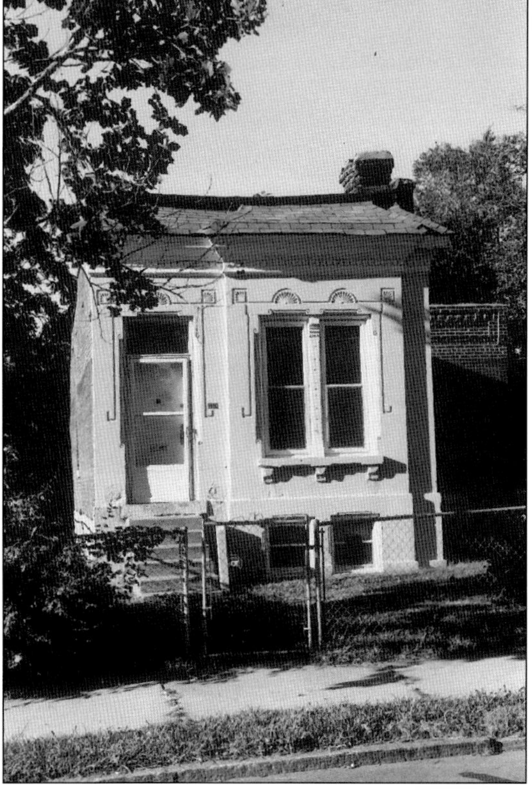

This small single family home at 4418 St. Ferdinand Ave. has maintained its charm throughout the years, and shows a commitment of the owner for the community. (Photo by John A. Wright.)

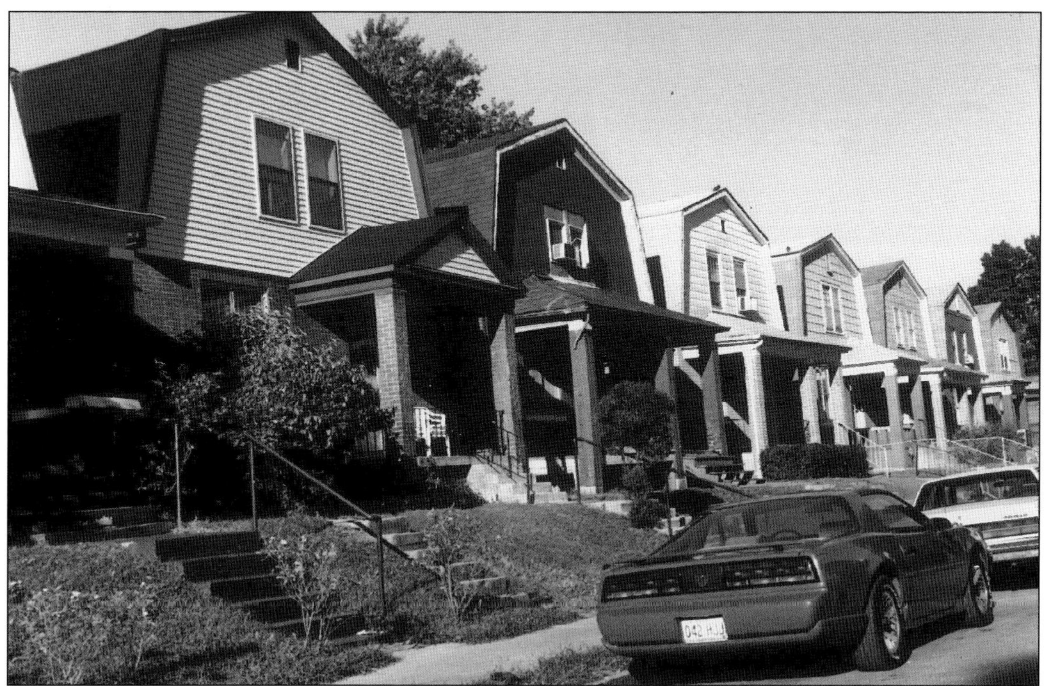

This area of well kept homes in the 4300 block of Cote Brilliante Ave. demonstrates what can be done when neighbors work together to stabilize an area. (Photo by John A. Wright.)

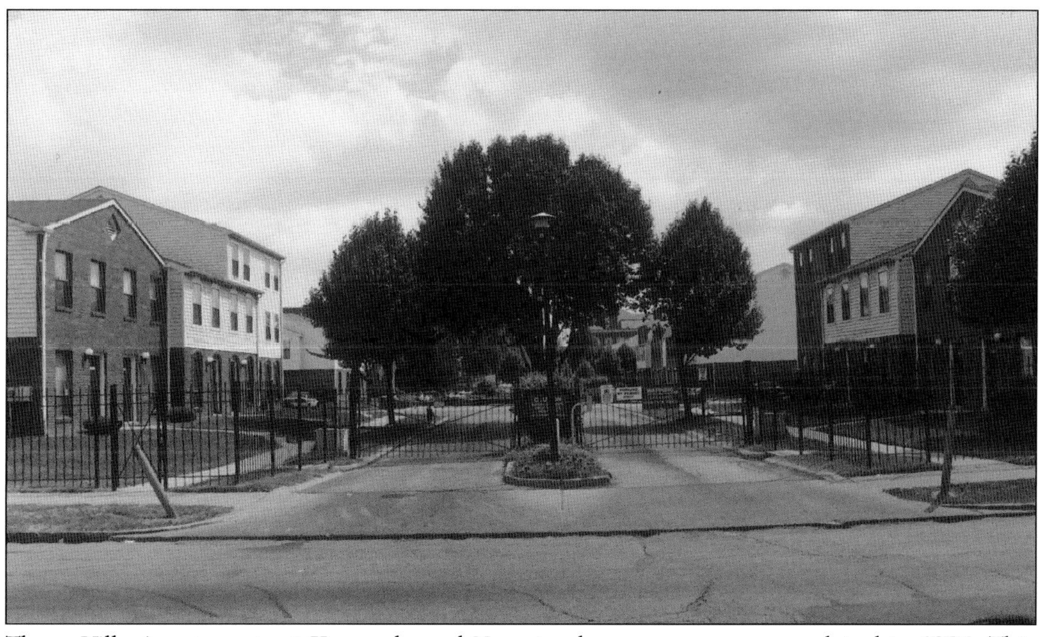

These Ville Apartments at Kennerly and Newstead avenues were completed in 1985. This 110 unit complex represented an important step in the redevelopment of the inner core of The Ville community and a boost towards its revitalization. (Photo by John A. Wright.)

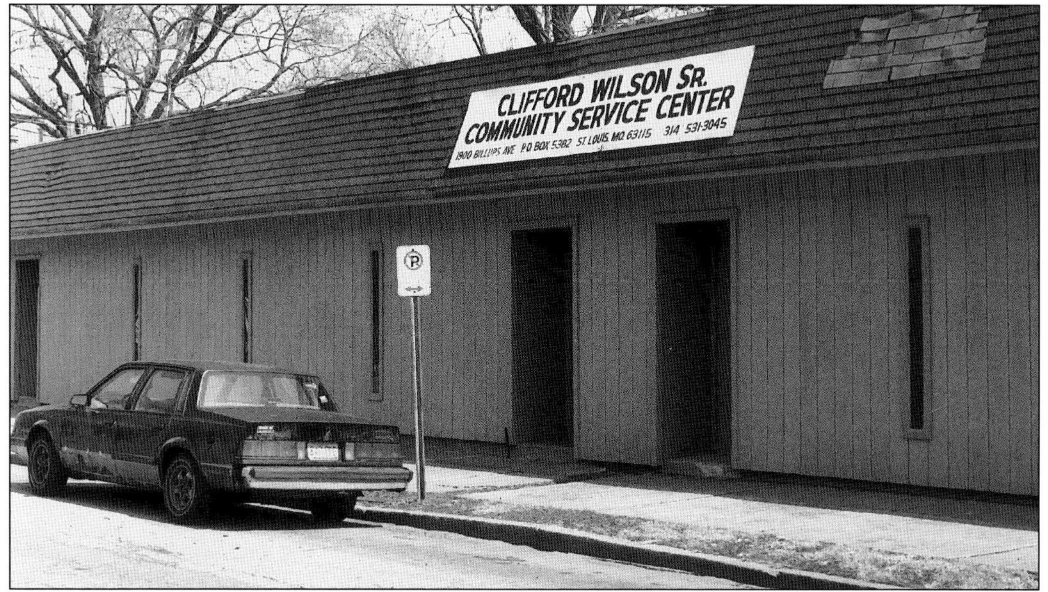

To help meet the needs of a revitalized community, the Clifford Wilson Sr. Community Center, pictured here, has opened at 1900 Billups Avenue. The center is named for Wilson, former alderman of the 4th Ward. It operates a food pantry, serves hot meals, provides free notary service for seniors, conducts educational forums, and assists families with some of the tools they need for every day survival. (Photo by John A. Wright.)

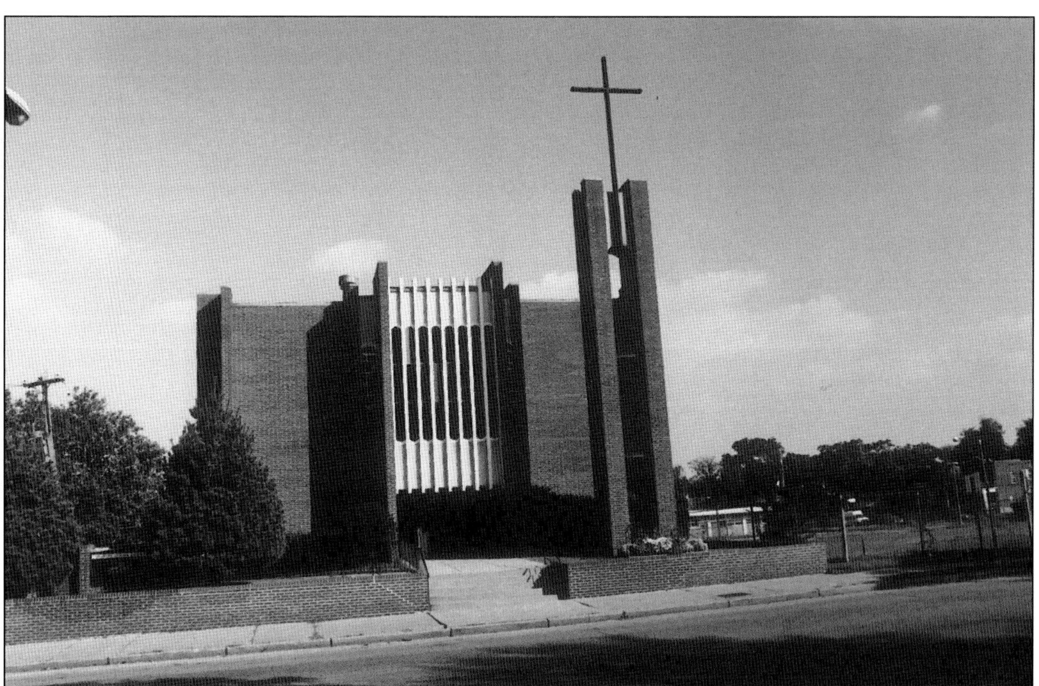

In 1966, the members of St. Phillip's Lutheran Church at 2424 Annie Malone Dr. discussed leaving the area, but chose instead to reaffirm their commitment to The Ville by constructing this new church building on the same site as their old church. (Photo by John A. Wright.)

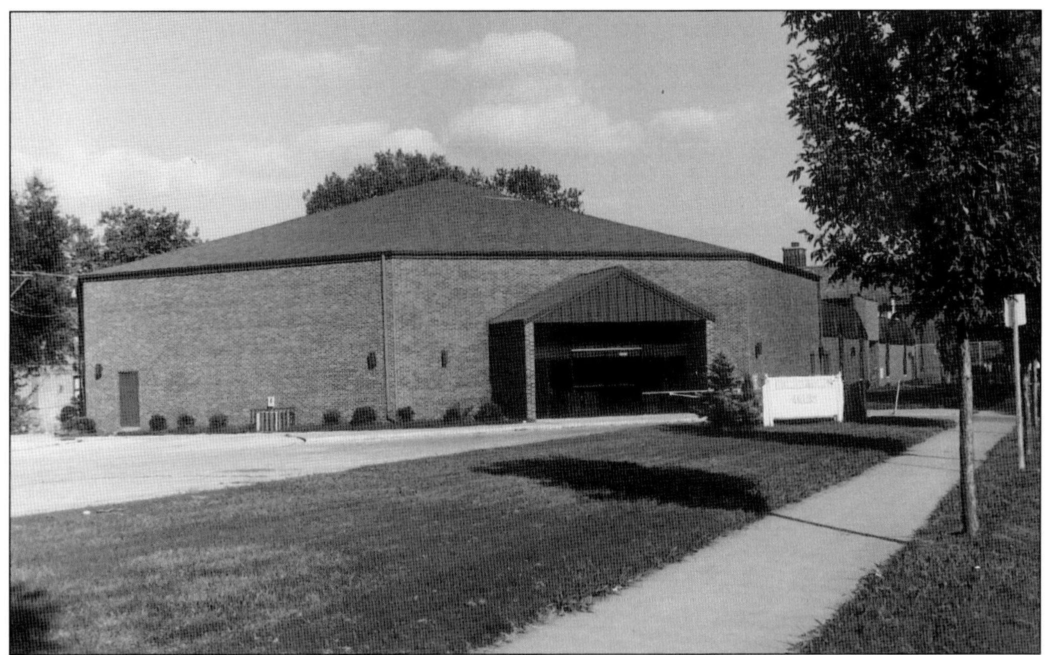

In the 1990s, Kennerly Temple Church of God in Christ at 4259 Kennerly Avenue reaffirmed its commitment to the community by building this new building. (Photo by John A. Wright.)

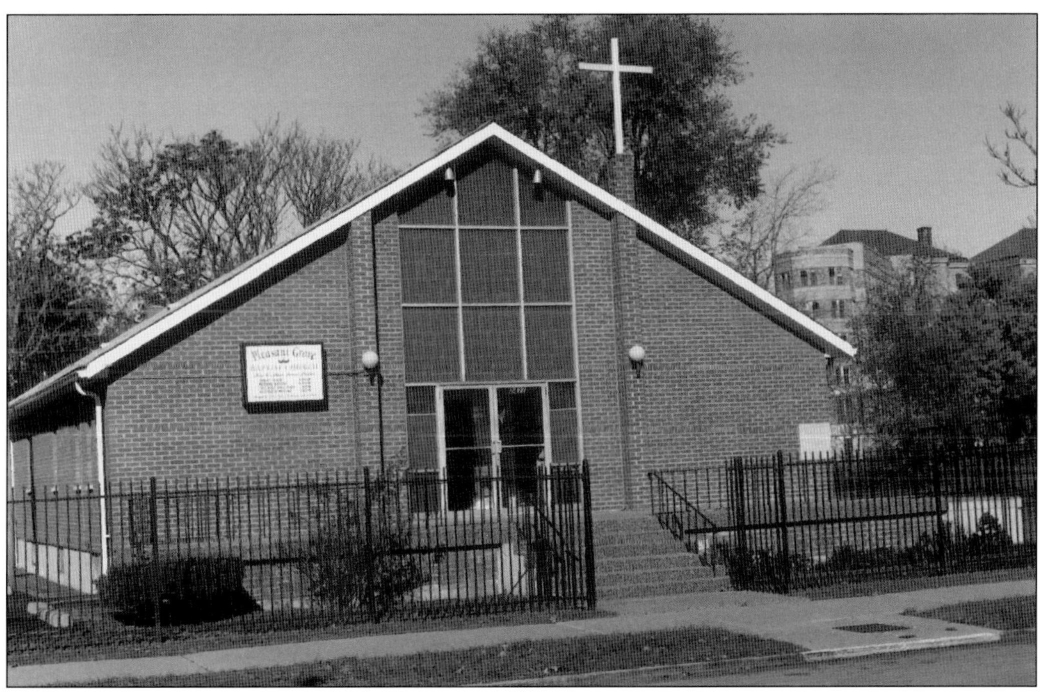

Pleasant Grove Missionary Baptist Church organized in 1914 and built this church in 1974 at 2411 Bell Glade Ave. under the leadership of Minister Daniel Cornell Davis. It is now in the process of expanding by building a larger facility on the lot next door. (Photo by John A. Wright.)

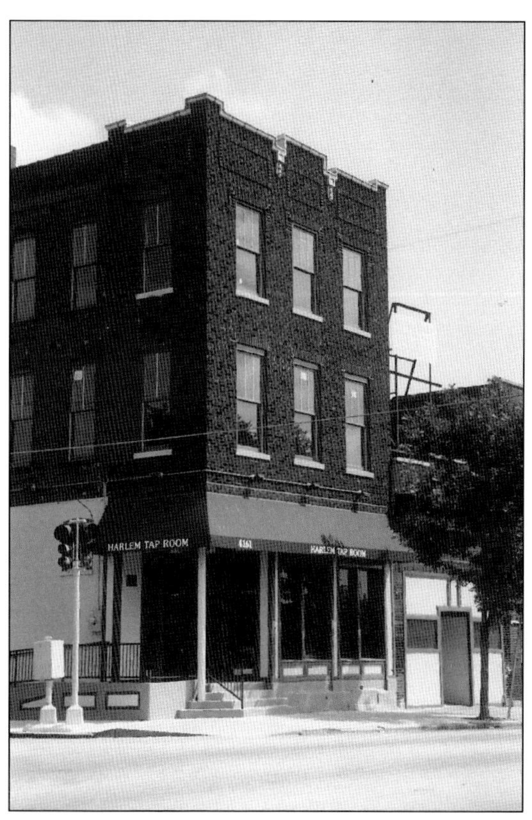

The Harlem Taproom can still be found at 4131 Dr. Martin Luther King Dr. This familiar entertainment spot opened in 1946, and was once part of the "Chitterlings Circuit." During its early years it attracted a number of top entertainers. The owner has shown commitment to the community by investing in this facility. (Photo by John A. Wright.)

An old favorite for over 50 years for young and old has been Billy Burkes' Restaurant at 1915 Millups Avenue. No matter how far former residents travel many often return to reflect on old times and reward their taste buds with pleasant culinary memories. (Photo by John A. Wright.)

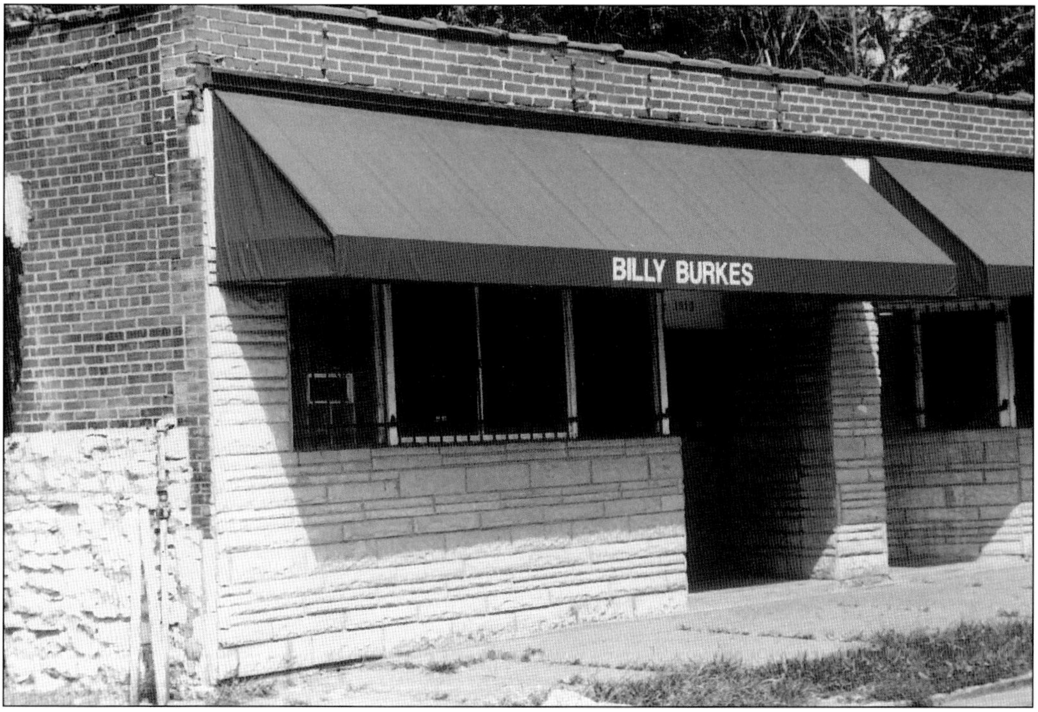

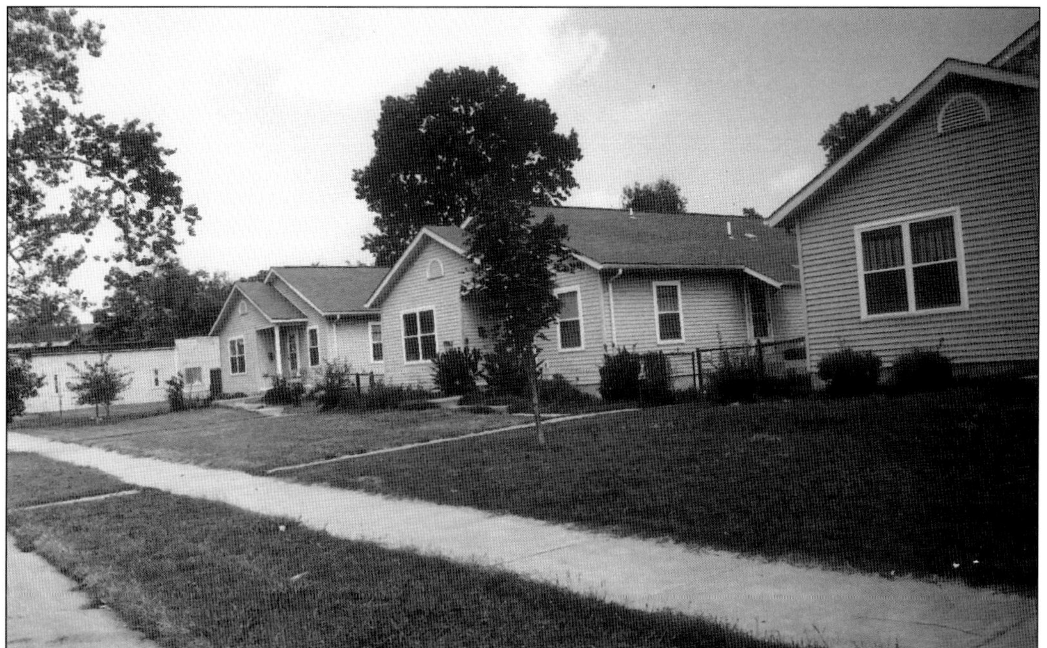

Lack of housing maintenance in the 4300 and 4400 blocks of Maffitt Ave. had deteriorated the area. However, thanks to the efforts of Delta Sigma Theta Sorority and Habitat for Humanity, these new homes have replaced blighted housing. (Photo by John A. Wright.)

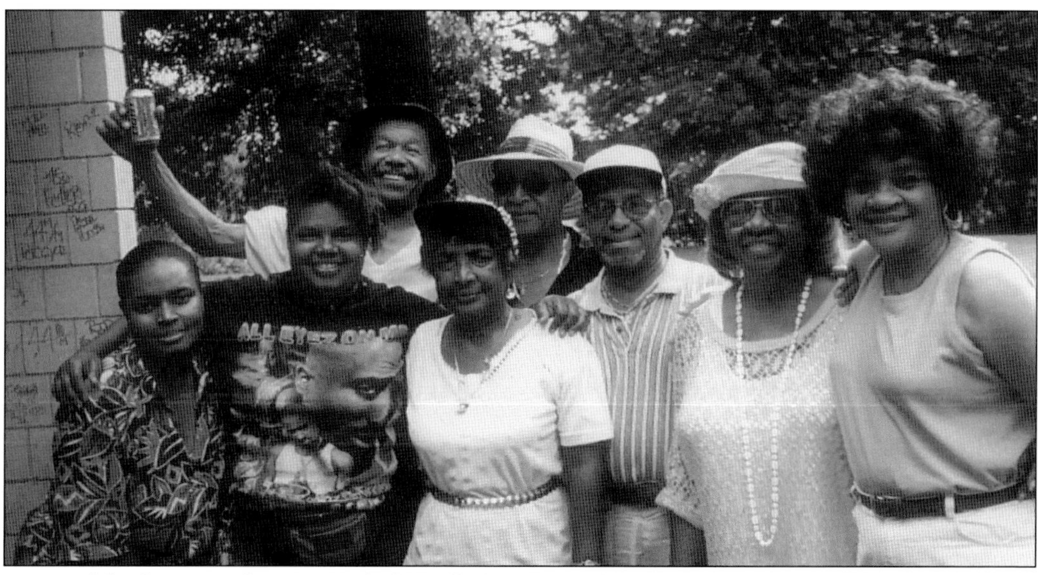

Many of the barriers that created The Ville have long been removed. However, many former residents who look back on their lives in the area and are reminded that they enjoyed a special place in time that may never happen again. Pictured here are some of the Maffitt Avenue and Friends group at their 1996 picnic in O'Fallon Park. This group comes together each year to reminisce about old times. They are, from left to right: Ronda Clemmons, Sharon Cody, Sam Harris, Doris Rowan, Melvin Turner, Ronald Palmer, Mable George, and Gloria Graham. (Photo courtesy of Mable George.)

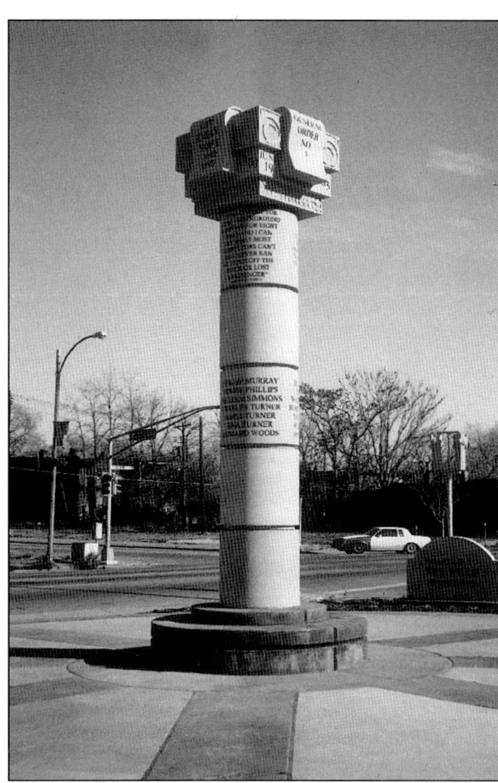

This monument marks the beginning of a new day for The Ville as a community. While it celebrates the past it symbolizes the future. (Photo by John A. Wright.)

THE VILLE FOUNDATION

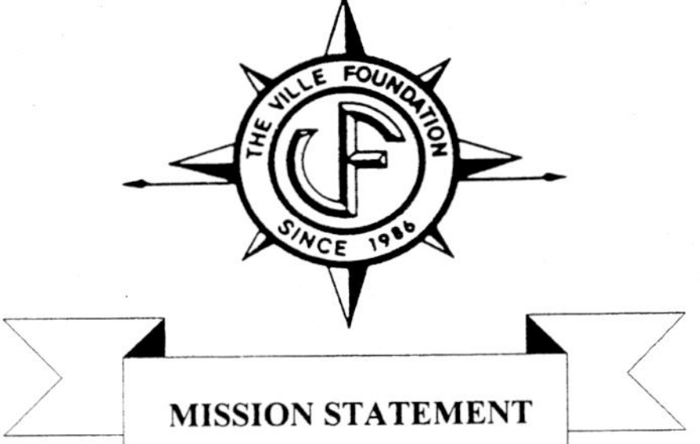

To increase the awareness of the historic "Ville" neighborhood while encouraging preservation and continuous comprehensive development with a principal focus on tourism.

To promote and market the historic "Ville" neighborhood on a local, state, national and global basis with intense efforts to secure National Historic District designation.

To annually recognize, through in-kind services and monetary awards a selected business, organization, institution and or private group involved in the preservation and/or development (socially, culturally, economically or physically) of the historic "Ville" neighborhood.

Pictured here is The Ville Foundation's Mission Statement. The goal of the foundation is to preserve the past while building the future. Maybe through the efforts of The Ville Foundation, community institutions, and past and present residents, this special place in time called "The Ville" will be remembered and preserved for all time. (Courtesy of John and Odester Saunders.)